The Speedy Gourmet Library

THE COMPLETE START-YOUR-MEAL COOKBOOK

by Johna Blinn

Edited by Tom Dorsey

Published by Playmore Inc., Publishers and Waldman Publishing Corp., New York, New York

Printed in Canada/Cover Printed in the United States of America

Edited by Malvina G. Vogel

Cover photo: Copyright © 1986 Peter J. Kaplan

Acknowledgments:

This writer is especially indebted to the expert advice, encouragement and cooperation of many. I am particularly indebted to Ruth Lundgren, Olive Dempsey, Chris Pines, Caryl Saunders, Claire Boasi, Anita Fial, Pat Mason, A.C. Collins, Marilyn Kaytor, Ed Justin, The Fresh Garlic Association, Lea & Perrins Worcestershire Sauce, American Mushroom Association, Tuna Research Foundation, McIlhenny Co., Anita Mizner, Howard Helmer, Prince Foods Light Pasta, Barbara Robinson, Sunkist Growers, Inc., California Milk Advisory Board, American Egg Board, Florida Celery Committee, California Iceberg Lettuce Commission, American Dairy Association, American Spice Trade Association, Virginia Schroeder, Alice Gautsch, Eileen Edwards Denne, Borden's Lite-Line Pasteurized Process Cheese Product, Quaker Oats Co., Carolyn Coughlin, California Fresh Market Tomato Advisory Board, Margaret Spader, Fleischmann's (unsalted margarine and 100% corn oil margarine), Florida Citrus Commission, National Broiler Council, Idaho Potato Commission, California Table Grape Commission, Campbell Soup Co., Angostura International Limited, Rice Council, Rae Hartfield, Betsy Slinkard, Argo and Kingsford's Corn Starch, United Fresh Fruit and Vegetable Association, Gloria Marshall, Marilyn Dompe, National Fisheries Institute, Inc., Patricia O'Keefe, California Artichoke Advisory Board, Mazola Corn Oil, Castle & Cooke Foods (Dole/Bumble Bee), Virginia Pinegreen, Donna Higgins, Del Monte Kitchens, Dot Tringali, Kay Murphy O'Flynn, Washington State Apple Commission, Dee Munson, Lois Westlund, Egg Beaters Cholesterol-free Egg Substitute, California Avocado Commission, Charcoal Briquet Institute, Alaska Seafood Marketing Institute, Washington State Potato Commission, Hellmann's and Best Foods Mayonnaise, Roxie Howlett, Diamond Walnut Kitchen, Skippy Peanut Butter, Karo Corn Syrup, Planter's Peanut Oil Test Kitchen, Standard Brands, Inc., National Turkey Federation, Christine Dozel, Jan Kerman, South African Rock Lobster Service Corporation, Nucoa Margarine, Diane Cline, Frances Fleming, Virginia Schroeder, Lawry's Ltd., California Milk Advisory Board, Ray Clark, National Duckling Council, California Bartlett Growers, Inc., O'Neal F. Caliendo, Yvonne Martin, National Capon Council, National Goose Council, National Livestock and Meat Board, American Lamb Council, Olive Administrative Committee, Fleischmann's Active Dry Yeast, Blue Bonnet Margarine, California Dried Fig Advisory Board, Beef Industry Council, Peanut Advisory Board, National Pork Producers Council, Kikkoman International Inc., New Zealand Lamb Co., Jan Works, Schiling Division McCormick and Co., National Cherry Growers & Industries Foundation, Susan Martinson, Jan Sirochman, Golden Grain Macaroni Co., Sweet Potato Council of California, Donna Hamilton, B.J. McCabe, Leafy Greens Council, Marcia L. Watts, California Turkey Industry Board, Frani Lauda, Italian Wine Center, National Macaroni Institute, J. Marsiglia, California Almond Growers Exchange, Bertolli's (olive oil, red-Italian wine vinegar, spaghetti sauce and wines), North American Blueberry Council, Fenella Pearson, Florio (dry and sweet Marsala wines), Ken Bray, 21 Brands (Liquore Galliano), Sherrie Newman, Wyler's Beef-Flavored Instant Bouillon, Jamaica Resort Hotels, Borden Company, Los Angeles Smoking and Curing Company, Mrs. Cubbison's Foods, Inc., Catherine Stratemeyer, Southern Belle English Walnuts, Denmark Cheese Association, Shirley Mack, Beans of the West, International Multifoods (Kretschmer Wheat Germ) and Imported Winter Grapes Association.

J.B.

BARONET
B·O·O·K·S

BARONET BOOKS is a trademark of Playmore Inc., Publishers and Waldman Publishing Corp., New York, N.Y.

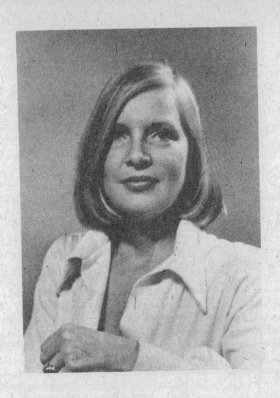

The Author

To many of the top movie and television stars, Johna Blinn is a celebrity. For almost 20 years they have welcomed her into their homes, onto sets, just about anywhere to talk about food, entertaining and lifestyles. Her column, "Celebrity Cookbook," is syndicated throughout the world and appears weekly in more than 140 newspapers and periodicals. A collection of hundreds of these conversations and recipes appears in *Celebrity Cookbook*, published by Waldman Publishing Corporation. Currently, Johna Blinn is writing a series on Celebrity Food-styles for *FAMILY CIRCLE*, America's largest supermarket magazine (circulation, 20 million), where she has already profiled Tom Brokaw, Angela Lansbury, John Madden, Michael Landon, Robert Urich, Raymond Burr, Steve Garvey, Diane Sawyer and others.

Blinn is a former assistant food editor of LOOK magazine and is the author of a number of books, including *The Shangri-la Cookbook, Fabulous Appetizers, Fabulous Soups, Fabulous Salads, Fabulous Vegetarian Recipes, Fabulous Poultry & Game, Fabulous Meats, Fabulous Fish & Seafood, Fabulous Desserts, Fabulous Low Calorie Recipes, Fabulous Oriental Recipes, Fabulous Oven & Stovetop Recipes*, and *Fabulous Italian Recipes*, all published by Waldman Publishing Corporation. In addition, Blinn is a frequent contributor of up close and personal interviews, profiles and entertainment features to *USA TODAY* and other American and foreign newspapers and magazines.

A graduate of the State University of Iowa, Blinn took graduate work in Home Economics at the University of Wisconsin and taught home economics in Iowa, Virginia and New York. Now based in Los Angeles, she is married to a nationally known newspaper syndicate editor, writer and management consultant, and they have two grown children.

CONTENTS

APPETIZERS
SOME LIKE IT HOT

Introduction 10

Cheese

Cheese & Green Chilies Squares 12
Cheese Straws 12
Chili Cheddar Prunes 12
Mini Cheese Pizzas, Microwaved 13
Swiss Cheese Fondue 13
Olive Cheese Nuggets 14

Spinach Merry-Go-Rounds 14
Mexican Potato Skins with Cheese
  & Other Fillings 15
Popeye's Tidbits 16
Sizzling Cheese Pinwheels 16

Eggs

Egg Canapés, Microwaved 17
Quiche 17

Peanut Quiche 18
Swiss Cheese Pie (Quiche) 18

Fish & Seafood

Clam Fritters 19
Dilly Calamari 19
Hot Crab Meat Appetizer 19
Deviled Crab, California Style 20
King Crab Appetizer Puffs 20
Beer Batter Halibut Appetizers 21
Rock Lobster Egg Rolls 21
Broiled Shrimp Deluxe 22
Halibut Tempura 22
Salmon Appetizer Rolls 22

Down-East Oyster Appetizers 23
Hot Salmon Balls with Curry Dip 23
Broiled Shrimp 24
Shrimp on Fire 24
California Shrimp Appetizer 25
Chinese Shrimp Toast 25
Tuna Bites with Szechuan Sauce 26
Tuna Chili con Queso 26
Tuna Empanaditas 27
Tuna Turnovers 27

Meat

Barbecued "Surprise" Meatballs 28
Rosey Beef Balls 28
Chinese Egg Rolls 29
Cocktail Nachos 30
Meatballs in Creamy Tomato Sauce 30
Beef-Stuffed Zucchini 31
Mexican Meatballs 31
Zesty Almond Chipped Beef Dip 32
Russian Turnovers 32
Canapés Monte Cristo 33
Deviled Ham Biscuits 33
So-Simple London Broil 33
Drunk Weiners 34

Ham en Croute (Ham in Pastry) 34
Frankfurter Turnovers 35
Stuffed Pumpernickel Loaf 35
Kraut Pizzas 36
Nutted Party Rounds 36
Brewed Cocktail Franks 37
Porky Picks 37
Smoky Frank Bites 37
Crab-Bacon Roll-Ups 38
Meat-Stuffed Mushrooms 38
Mexican Pork Tacos 39
Scotch Bananas 39

Poultry

Barbecued Chicken Wings 40
Chicken-Potato Balls 40
Chicken Tacos 40
Chinatown Chicken Puffs 41
Ginger Teriyaki Skewers 41
Golden Chicken Nuggets with
  Sweet-Sour Sauce 42

Savory-Sauced Turkey Franks 42
Hot 'n' Spicy Chicken Wings 43
Nectarine-Chicken Cream Puffs 43
Lemon-Yogurt - Chicken Stuffed Potatoes,
  Microwaved 44
Sweet & Spicy Chicken Wings 44

Vegetarian

Aquacate Azteca (French Fried
  Avocado Ring) 45
Artichoke Appetizer 45

Asparagus with Vinaigrette 46
Stuffed Eggplant Dip 46
Corn-on-a-Stick 47

Vegetarian (cont.)

Spiced Fruit Cocktail 47
Asparagus-Bread Rolls 48
Eggplant Squares 48
Minted Mushrooms 48
Tasty Stuffed Mushroom Appetizers 49
Toasted Mushroom Rolls 49

Onion Puffs 50
Onion Wedgies 50
Washington Chips 50
Fried Zucchini Sticks 51
Spinach Turnovers 51
Vegetable Empanaditas (Turnovers) 52

SOME LIKE IT COLD

Cheese

California Walnut Cheese Logs 53
Chutney-Cheese Spread 53
Crab Ball Appetizers 53
Cheese Ball 54
Curried Papaya 54
Danish Cheese Dunk 54
Edam Cheese Spread 55
Golden Party Cheese Ball 55

Fresh Pears with Curried Cheese Ball 56
Green Balls 56
Melon & Cheese Appetizers 56
Savory Cheese Snacks 57
Walnut Cheese Bowl 57
Roquefort-Brie & Walnut Spread 58
Wheat Germ Herb Balls 58
Winter Pears with Camembert Cheese Ball 58

Dips & Spreads

Roquefort-Sour Cream Dip 59
Super-Duper Dips 59
Alaska Snow Crab Louis Dip 60
Avocado Herb Butter 60
Green Goddess Dip 60
Avocado Parsley Dip 61
Guacamole 61
Shrimp Dip à la Rose 61
Banana Curry Dip 62
Garbanzo Bean Dip 62
Vegetable-Cottage Cheese Dip 62
Alaska Snow Crab with Snappy Red Dip 63
Hummus 63

Zesty Red Dip for Snow Crab 63
Cocktail Sauce for Crudité 64
Cranberry-Pineapple Dunk 64
Fruit Dip 64
Eggplant Party Dip 65
Helen's Shrimp Spread 65
International Spread 65
Curried Tuna Dipping Sauce 66
Smoky Salmon Cheese Spread for Bagels 66
Food To Serve on Picks: Cold & Quick 67
Tabbouli Appetizers 68
Tuna Dip 68

Eggs

Confetti Egg Salad Spread 69
Tasty Deviled Eggs 69

Wheat Germ Pâté 69

Poultry

Chicken Liver Paste 70

Chicken Veronique Appetizers 70

Fish & Seafood

Crab & Water Chestnut Appetizer 71
Seviche 71
Seviche Supreme 71
Alaska King Crab with Sauce Verte 72
Crab Louie 72
King Crab Split Legs with Horseradish Dip 73
New Orleans Crab Spread 73
Smoked Oysters 73
Shrimp Avocado Cocktail in Artichokes 74

Shrimp Pâté 74
Shrimp & Stuffed Celery Canapés 75
Tower of Shrimp 75
Spicy Gefilte Fish 76
Smoked Fish Pâté 76
Tuna Bites Superb 77
Tuna Mosaic Pâté 77
Happy Shrimps 78
Salmon Pâté 78

Meat

Beef Steak Tartare 79
Cherry Ham Canapés 79
Yogurt Beef Ball Appetizers 79
Ground Ham Spread 80

Oahu Appetizer 80
Salami Cornucopia 80
Easy Liverwurst Pâté 81
Make-Ahead Assorted Canned Meat Platter . . . 81

Sandwiches

Frosted Tuna Party Loaf 82
Open-Face Sandwiches 83
Ribbon Sandwiches 83

Assorted Fillings for Cream Puffs
& Stacked Sandwiches 84
Chicken Stacks 85
Stuffed French Bread 85

Vegetarian

Avocado Mousse 86
Stuffed Celery with Variations 86
British Glazed Nuts 87
Cucumber Sherbet 87
Duchesses (Small Cocktail Cream Puffs) 88
Melon on Skewers 88
Cool Italian Mushroom Dip 89
Munch-Crunch 89

Elegant Mushroom Pâté 90
Marinated Mushroom Hor d'Oeuvres 90
Mushroom Tidbits 91
Walnut Mushroom Pâté 91
Potato Chips 92
Snack Mix 92
Walnuts Parmisano 92

SOUPS

Introduction 93

Soup Stocks

Homemade Beef Stock 95
Homemade Chicken Stock 95

Chilled Soups

Crab-Lettuce Soup 96
Cream of Avocado Soup 96
Frosted Crab Soup 96
Curried Apple Onion Soup 97
Health Soup 97
Chilled Blueberry Bisque 98
Gazpacho 98
Consommé Madrilene 99
Herbed Buttermilk Soup 99

Sengalese Soup 99
August Soup 100
Iced Pea & Potato Soup 100
Russian Yogurt Soup 100
Avocado & Ginger Vichyssoise 101
Chilled Tomato-Carrot Soup 101
Banana Vichyssoise 102
Vichyssoise 102

Cream Soups & Bisques

Crab Bisque 103
Elegante Cream of Asparagus Soup 103
Spanish Cream of Almond Soup 103
Artichoke-Shrimp Bisque 104
Cream of Artichoke Soup 104
Chicken Asparagus Soup 105
German Beef & Corn Soup 105
Cream of Chicken Bisque 106
Cream of Pheasant Soup 106
Baked Garlic Soup 107
Hearty Lentil-Pumpkin Soup 107
Clam Coriander Tomato Bisque 108

Cream of Tomato-Dill Soup 108
Mussels & Mushroom Soup 109
Sherried Seafood Bisque 109
Creamy Spinach Curried Soup 110
Harvest Potato Soup 110
Winter Potage 110
Onion Veloute 111
Potage Printanier 111
Fresh Tomato Seafood Soup 112
Old-Fashioned Tomato Bisque 112
Creamy Sweet Potato Soup 113
Rock Lobster Corn Soup Stew 113

Chowder

Chili Corn Chowder 114
Classic French Onion Soup 114
Frankfurter Creole Chowder 114
Boston Clam Chowder 115
Nor'easter Fish Chowder 115
Jiffy Tuna-Potato Chowder 116
Mom's Turkey Chowder 116

Fisherman's Chowder 117
Pennsylvania Dutch Ham & Apple Soup
    with Dumplings 117
Vegetable Chowder 118
Vegetable Clam Chowder 118
Cheese-Shrimp Chowder 119
Indonesian Fish Chowder with Pineapple 119

Dumpling, Pasta, Rice & Bread Soups

Baked Portuguese Egg Soup 120
Chicken-Corn Soup with Egg Dumplings 120
Beef Savory Soup with Spaetzle 121
Country-Style Chicken Noodle Soup 121
Chicken Soup with Kreplach 122
Danish Beer & Bread Soup 123
Greek Liver Soup 123
Greek Chicken Soup with Avgolemono
    (Lemon Egg Sauce) 124

Zucchini Soup with Rice 124
Hungarian Goulash Soup with
    Pinched Noodles 125
Italian Bread Soup 126
Tuna Won-Ton Soup 126
Mona's Chicken Soup with
    Meatballs & Dumplings 127

Hearty Soups

African Bean & Peanut Soup 128
Golden Cauliflower Soup 128
Barley Vegetable Soup 129
Beef Barley Vegetable Soup 129
Black Bean Soup I 130
Black Bean Soup II 130
Camper's Corn Chowder 131
Cheese Vegetable Soup 131
Chicken & Ham Gumbo 131
Chicken & Snow Pea Soup 132
Chicken Zucchini Soup 132
Corned Beef & Cabbage Chowder 133
Crockpot Inflation-Fighter Five-Bean Soup 133
Creole Gumbo 134
Creole Shrimp Gumbo 134
Chili Bean Soup 135
Garbanzo Chili Pot 135
Curry-Pumpkin Soup 136
Esau's Pottage 136
Georgia Peanut Soup 136
Flaming Onion Soup 137
Halloween Witches' Brew 137
Ham & Garbanzo Bean Soup 138
Ham & Three-Bean Soup 138
Hearty Ham & Bean Soup 139
Hearty Meatball & Vegetable Soup 139
Herbed Vegetable Soup 140
Irish Cockaleekie Soup 140
Irish Haddock Soup 140

Hot Borscht 141
Luscious Lentil Soup 141
Lamb Mulligatawny Soup 142
Lamb Vegetable Soup 142
Lentil-Spinach Soup 143
Senate Bean Soup I 143
Senate Bean Soup II 143
Jamaican Pumpkin Soup 144
Mom's Split Pea Soup with Croutons 144
Philadelphia Pepper Pot Soup 145
Pork Soup-Stew, Polish Style 145
Dilled Split Pea Soup 146
Polish Mushroom Soup 146
Russian Vegetable & Fish Soup 146
Sauerkraut Soup 147
Seafood Soup 147
South American Black Bean Soup 148
Split Pea Soup Supreme 148
Hearty Turkey Soup 149
Turkey Vegetable Soup 149
Sopa de Legumbres (Mexican Vegetable Soup) . 150
Worcestered Beef & Vegetable Soup 150
Hearty Vegetable Soup 151
Steak Soup, Kansas Style 151
Lamb Barley Soup 152
Mom's Hearty Vegetable Soup 152
French-Canadian Pea Soup 153
Southern Corn-Okra Soup 153
Wheat Germ Pork Ball Soup 154

Soups Pronto

Borscht 155
Lima Bean Cheese Soup Pronto 155
Quick Beef-Vegetable Soup 155
Bloody Mary Soup 156
Cheesy Soup 156
Consommé Burgundy 156
Chinese Hot & Sour Soup 157
Gourmet Cheese Soup 157
Ham & Rice Soup, Microwaved 158
Quick Manhattan Clam Chowder 158
Quick 'n' Hearty Corn & Fish Soup 158
Creamed Corn Soup 159
Spanish Garlic Soup 159
Chinese Beef & Cabbage Soup 160
Seafood Bisque Pronto 160
Lettie's Liver Soup 161
Pork Vegetable Soup, Southern Style 161

Minestrone Pronto 162
Summer Squash Soup 162
Tangy Appetizer Soup 162
Clear Mushroom Soup & Cheese Brambles 163
Spinach-Lime Soup 163
Chicken Cup Oriental 164
Dieter's Egg Drop Soup 164
Japanese Bean Curd Soup 164
Okra Soup Supreme 165
Sour Cream Mushroom Soup 165
Sunny Black Magic Sipper 165
Quick Clam Tomato Soup 166
Tomato Beef Bouillon 166
Tomato Bouillon 166
Cary's Sausage Vegetable Soup 167
Food Processor Fresh Tomato Soup 167

Dessert Soups

Blackberry Soup 168
Gooseberry Soup 168
Grape Dessert Soup 168
Cold Raspberry Soup 169

Huckleberry Soup 169
Orange Fruit Soup 169
Apple Curry Soup 170
Swedish Fruit Soup (fruktsoppa) 170

Soup Accompaniments

Soup Service & Garnishes 171
Curry Cheese Muffins 171
Helen's Pepper Cornbread 171
Biscuit Salt Sticks 172
California Wheat Germ Buns 172

Fancy Bread Fingers 173
Knaidlach 173
Poppy Seed Biscuit Twists 173
Kasha Kreplach 174
Potato Knishes 174

SALADS

Introduction 175

MAINLY GREENS

Caesar Salad 177
Little Caesar Salad 177
Dutch Hot Cabbage Salad 178
Orange & Red Onion Salad
  with Vinaigrette Dressing 178
Buffet Garden Salad 179
Deviled Red Cabbage Salad 179
Escarole Salad 179

Ever-Green Salad with
  Herbed French Dressing 180
Garden Chicory & Onion Salad 180
Chinese Spinach Salad 181
Garden Salad with Blue Cheese Vinaigrette . . . 181
Spinach & Mushroom Salad 182
Tossed Greens Salad 182
Salad de Castel Novel 183
Western Way Salad 183

FRUIT SALADS

California Walking Salad 184
Cherry Ambrosia Salad with
  Honey-Orange Dressing 184
Fresh Fruit Salad 185
Fresh Orange Waldorf Salad 185
Fruit & Celery Salad 185
Fruit Peanut Salad 186
Orange & Avocado Salad 186
Orange Fall Fruit Combo 186
Parsley-Pear Bowl 187
Picture-Pretty Waldorfs 187

Polynesian Fruit Platter 187
Pear Salad Mozambique with Spicy Dressing . . . 188
Pineapple Banana Peanut Salad 188
Walnut Fruit Salad Plate 189
Winter Fruit Compote 189
Apple Salad à la Moutarde 190
Fresh Fruit Elegance 190
Pineapple Tuna Slaw 190
Sun Island Mold 191
Waldorf Salad with Pineapple 191

VEGETABLE SALADS

Celeriac & Carrot Salad 192
Corn Patch Salad, Microwaved 192
Dilled Sour Cream-Cucumber Salad 192
Fall Salad Platter 193
Fatoush (Mixed Vegetable Salad) 193
Fennel, Tomato & Chicory Salad 193
Italian Salad with Croutons 194
Marinated Brussels Sprouts Salad 194
Marinated Greek Salad 194
Minted Mixed Vegetable Salad 195

Pepper & Onions Vinaigrette 195
Picnic Cole Slaw 195
Sliced Cucumbers & Onions
  with Yogurt Dressing 196
Sweet Potato Salad with
  Honey Vinaigrette Dressing 196
Four-Bean Salad 197
Zucchini-Carrot Salad with
  Blue Cheese Dressing 197

COMBINATION SALADS

Fowl

Chicken-Walnut Sandwich Salads 198
Hawaiian Fresh Pineapple Chicken Salad
  with Ginger Dressing 198
Cobb Salad Supreme
  with French Dressing 199
California Summer Turkey & Fruit Salad 200
Festive Chicken Salad 200

Oriental Cherry Chicken Salad 200
Pineapple-Turkey Salad with
  Lime Dressing 201
Turkey Salad Continental 201
Hot Turkey-Broccoli Salad 202
Turkey 'n' Spaghetti Summer Salad 202

Fish & Seafood

Crab-Noodle Salad 203
Rock Lobster Green Noodle Salad 203
Crab-Corn Vinaigrette Salad 204
Surfers' Salad 204
Rock Lobster & Bean Salad 205
Rock Lobster Salad, Hot or Cold 205
Canned Salmon, Tuna & Pea Salad 206
Marinated Oyster Salad 206
Salmon Flower Salad 207
Shrimp Avocado Boats 207
Salmon-Macaroni Salad 208
Salmon Pasta Salad 208

Mushroom-Shrimp & Dill Salad 209
Seafood Salad with Avocado
  Hollandaise Dressing 209
Avocado Half-Shells with Seafood 210
Walnut-Shrimp Salad 210
Avocado Salad Niçoise 211
Seafood-Stuffed Tomatoes 211
Ripe Olive Tuna Salad Sandwich 212
Tuna Tabboulch 212
Walnut-Stuffed Tomato 213
Zesty Seafood Vegetable Salad 213

COMBINATION SALADS (cont.)

Meats

Artichoke Chef's Salad with Curry Dressing 214
Avocado, Spinach & Bacon Salad. 214
Artichokes with Hot Corn Salad 215
Italian-Style Antipasto Spaghetti Salad 215
Buffet Green Bean Salad. 216
Dig Deep Salad 216
Picnic Bean Salad 216
Mediterranean Meatball Salad 217
Layered Chef Salad 218
Ripe Olive Pizza Salad. 218
Hot Dutch Potato Salad 219
Monterey Baked Salad 219

California Salami Salad 220
Tostada Salad 220
Tropical Pork Salad with Tarragon Dressing 221
Yam 'n' Ham Salad 221
Frying Pan Salad of Spinach & Nectarines 222
Oriental Pepper Steak Salad Cups. 222
Golden West Platter 223
Pineapple Rice Salad 223
American Macaroni Salad 224
Italian Macaroni Salad. 224
Patio Macaroni Salad 224

Vegetarian

Autumn Salad 225
Avocado Accordion Salad with
   Pineapple-Honey Dressing 225
Avocado Salad Mexicano 226
California Avocado-Mushroom Salad 226
Beans 'n' Rice Salad 227
Cabbage Slaw. 227
Carousel Rice Salad 227
Bean Sprout-Sunflower Salad 228
Bulgur Salad. 228
Celestial Carrot Salad 229
Chilean Grape Salad with Herbed Dressing 229
Cold Pasta Salad for 25. 230
French Brie Salad 230
Golden Apple-Spinach Salad 230
Feta Greek Salad 231
Fresh Fruit Salad with
   Poppy Seed Dressing 231

Macaroni Olive Salad 232
Piña Frijole Salad 232
"Dilled" Potato Salad 233
Tossed Taco Salad with Spicy Dressing 233
Tomato Rice Supper Salad 234
Vegetable Salad Surprise 234
Creamy Italian Bean Salad 235
Macaroni Ambrosia Salad 235
Wilted Spinach Salad 235
Macaroni Slaw 236
Summer Garden Salad 236
Waldorf Macaroni Salad 236
Fresh Supper Salad with
   Tangy Lemon Dressing 237
Florida Fiesta Salad. 237
Fresh Citrus Pasta Salad 238
Tossed Orange Salad 238
Winter Haven Salad 238

MOLDED SALADS

Aspic & Vegetable

Dilled Clam & Tomato Aspic 239
Thanksgiving Cranberry Salad with
   Sour Cream Dressing 239
Corn Relish Salad Mold. 240
Cottage Cheese-Pecan Ball Salad 240
Molded Cranberry Waldorf Salad 240
Chicken Mousse 241
Salmon Luncheon Mold 241

Chicken Perfection Salad 242
Easy Tomato Aspic 242
Dilled Halibut & Cucumber Salad 243
Potato Salad Pie 243
Molded Seafood Salad 244
Turkey Salad Mold 244
Grape & Asparagus Aspic 245
Tuna-Tomato Mousse. 245

Buffet & Dessert

Buffet Jellied Cantaloupe Salad. 246
Molded Fruit Medley. 246
Frosty Citrus Mold. 247
Lei Day Salad 247
Supreme Molded Fruit Salad 247
Creamy Peach Salad Mold 248
Pineapple Glow Salad. 248

Sparkling Cherry Fruit Mold 248
Fresh Pear-Mint Salad. 249
Lemony Walnut-Vegetable Mold. 249
Fresh Strawberry Mold 250
In-the-Pink Strawberry Salad Mold 250
Fruit Fluff Dessert Salad, Microwaved 251
Ginger Pear Salad Mold 251

SALAD DRESSINGS

Basic French Dressing. 252
Basic Mayonnaise Plus Variations 252
Slender Blender Dressing Plus Variations. 253
Spicy French Dressing. 253
Garlic Mayonnaise Dressing 254
Ripe Olive French Dressing 254
Tarragon Salad Dressing 254

Garlic Vinaigrette 255
Golden Nugget Dressing 255
South of the Border Salad Dressing 255
San Francisco Dressing 256
Summer Salad Dressing 256
Wonderful Ranch Salad Dressing 256

Appetizers

Introduction

The cocktail party is making a comeback as many find it the best way to entertain a host of people elegantly and still keep the cost down. More and more people are cost-cutting by capitalizing on the growing trend *away* from hard liquor by limiting beverage service to fine wines, rum punches and soda water. The cocktail hour is a great way to present a beautiful spread of good things to eat for a fraction of what a full-fledged buffet or sit-down dinner would cost. It provides a bountiful amount of food for those who have big appetites, while not calling attention to non-drinkers or calorie-counters, as they drink and eat lightly.

All it takes is a little time and imagination. You can turn raw vegetables and/or fruits into beautiful, edible centerpieces. What used to be thought of as "food stretchers" become tasty tidbits on silver or foil-covered hors d'oeuvre trays. For example, hostesses are having their butchers trim back the once-lowly chicken wings, turning them into the popular conversation piece, "drummettes."

Cocktail "nibbles" can be varied, from munch-crunch (assorted mixed herbed cereals) to British glazed nuts, from the ubiquitous cheese or onion dip or more

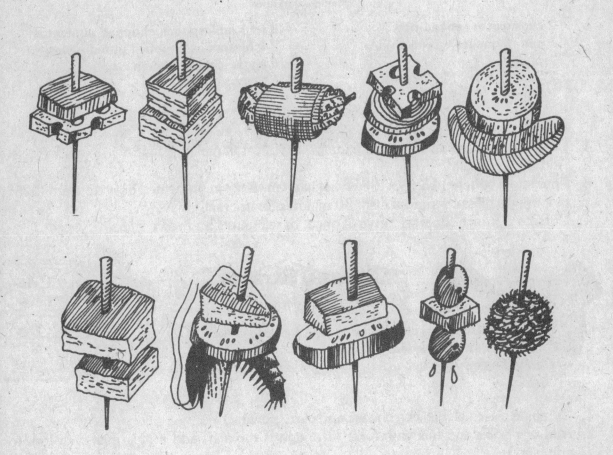

traditional fare like foods-on-a-toothpick, pâté, quiche and open face sandwiches to international favorites such as Chinese lobster rolls or Scandinavian sardine spread. All of these can be created to meet weight watchers' demands, often using leftover hunks of meat, fish or poultry and fresh vegetables, served with tangy sauces and dips. Hot trays or chafing dishes make it easy for the cook-host or hostess to serve such heated dishes as meatballs, turnovers or hot canapés. Include an appetizing array of crackers, biscuits, breads and Melba rounds.

With emphasis today on eating healthly and staying slim, raw and natural foods star at cocktail parties in *crudité* (French for what Americans call "rabbit food"), often including such colorful fare as tiny cherry tomatoes, black olives, parsnips, broccoli, celery and carrots — all the crunchy good things.

The main point in planning hors d'oeuvres is to combine things that are tasty and satisfying, while providing interesting contrast in flavor, color and texture. The relaxed atmosphere of this kind of entertaining, combined with the knowledge that you have not blown the family's weekly paycheck on a single party, makes it a happy way to go!

J.B.

11

Cheese & Green Chilies Squares

Makes 70 squares

2 cups warm cooked rice
1 can (4 ounces) green chilies, chopped
2½ cups grated Monterey Jack cheese (10 ounces)

3 to 4 tablespoons chopped pimientos
2 tablespoons chopped pitted olives
6 eggs, slightly beaten
1 teaspoon salt

1. Combine rice, chilies, cheese, pimientos and olives in mixing bowl.
2. Add eggs and salt.
3. Pour into a buttered 13 x 9 x 2-inch baking pan. Bake in preheated 350° F. oven (325° F. if using a glass ovenproof dish) 30 minutes, or until set.
4. Cut into 1¼-inch squares. Serve at once, or refrigerate and serve later.

Cheese Straws

Makes about 6 dozen

1 package (10 ounces) pie-crust mix
1 cup grated sharp Cheddar cheese
¼ teaspoon curry powder

2 egg yolks
milk
paprika or sesame seeds

1. Combine pie-crust mix with cheese and curry powder.
2. Add egg yolks and mix with fork. (If dough is too stiff, add a little milk with fork to combine.)
3. Roll out on floured board to ⅛-inch thickness.
4. Sprinkle lightly with paprika, or brush with milk and sprinkle with sesame seeds.
5. Cut into 3 x ½-inch strips.
6. Bake on greased cookie sheet in preheated 425° F. oven 8 to 10 minutes.
7. Cool on a rack. Serve hot or cold.

Chili Cheddar Prunes

Makes 3 dozen hors d'oeuvres

1 cup shredded Cheddar cheese
3 tablespoons canned diced green chilies

2 tablespoons chopped pecans
2 tablespoons dairy sour cream or unflavored yogurt

12 ounces (about 2 cups) pitted prunes

1. Combine cheese, chilies, nuts and sour cream in bowl; mix to blend thoroughly. Set aside.
2. Slit prunes and form into cups; fill generously with cheese mixture.
3. Place on oiled baking sheet; heat 3 inches below broiler about 2 minutes, or until cheese begins to melt.

Mini Cheese Pizzas, Microwaved

Serves 6

1 can (8 ounces) tomato sauce
¼ teaspoon basil
¼ teaspoon oregano
¼ pound sliced pepperoni

6 English muffins, split and toasted
1 green pepper, halved and thinly sliced
6 mushrooms, thinly sliced
12 slices Cheddar cheese or mozzarella

1. Mix tomato sauce, basil and oregano in 1-cup glass measuring cup; microcook on HIGH 1 minute.
2. Heat browning dish in microwave on HIGH 5 minutes.
3. Meanwhile, divide pepperoni slices among muffin halves.
4. Spoon 1 tablespoon sauce over pepperoni; top with green pepper, mushroom slices, and one slice of cheese on each muffin half.
5. Put 4 muffins at a time on browning dish. Microcook on HIGH 1½ to 2 minutes, or until cheese is almost melted.
6. Remove from oven; let stand 2 minutes (cheese will finish melting).
7. Repeat with remaining muffins.

NOTE: Pizzas can be made in oven without the browning dish; but bottom crust will not crisp.

Swiss Cheese Fondue

Makes 1 quart

1 pound Swiss cheese, grated
3 tablespoons flour
1½ teaspoons salt
1 clove garlic, halved

2 cups Sauterne
¼ cup Cognac
dash paprika
1 loaf French bread

1. Mix cheese with flour and salt.
2. Rub bottom and sides of heavy skillet with cut garlic.
3. Add Sauterne to skillet and heat over low heat until wine begins to bubble. (Do not boil.)
4. Place cheese by spoonfuls into wine, stirring constantly until each spoonful is melted before adding next one. Keep heat low.
5. After all cheese is melted, bring mixture to a boil.
6. Remove from heat; stir in Cognac; sprinkle paprika over top.
7. Serve over a warmer, or in a chafing dish to keep hot.
8. Cut bread into fork-size pieces.

NOTE: To eat, spear bread on fondue fork or long toothpick and into hot cheese mixture. This is a real conversation piece!

Olive Cheese Nuggets

Makes about 2½ dozen

¼ pound sharp cracker barrel
  Cheddar cheese, shredded
¼ cup soft butter
¾ cup sifted all-purpose flour

⅛ teaspoon salt
½ teaspoon paprika
24 to 30 pimiento-stuffed
  green olives

1. Blend together cheese and butter.
2. Sift flour, salt and paprika into cheese-butter mixture. Mix to form dough.
3. Shape around olives, using about 1 teaspoon dough per olive.
4. Place on ungreased baking sheet. Bake in preheated 400° F. oven 12 to 15 minutes, or until light and golden brown.
5. Serve hot. Great with martinis!

Spinach Merry-Go-Rounds

Makes about 2½ dozen slices

2 packages (10 ounces each) frozen
  chopped spinach, thawed and
  squeezed dry
2 cups cottage cheese, drained
½ cup grated Parmesan cheese
½ cup minced green onions
2 tablespoons chopped fresh dill, or
  2 teaspoons dried dill weed

2 tablespoons processed blue cheese spread
1 teaspoon Tabasco sauce
1 teaspoon salt
1 pre-rolled sheet frozen puff pastry,
  thawed
packaged dry bread crumbs

1. Combine spinach, cottage cheese, Parmesan cheese, green onions, dill, blue cheese, Tabasco sauce and salt in medium bowl; mix well.
2. Cut folded pastry sheet in half. Roll each half to an 8 x 18-inch rectangle.
3. Sprinkle pastry lightly with bread crumbs to within 1-inch of all edges.
4. Divide spinach mixture in half and spread lengthwise down the center of each rectangle.
5. Fold edges over filling; seal seams and ends with water.
6. Place on ungreased cookie sheet seam side down; prick surface with fork.
7. Bake in a preheated 400° F. oven 25 minutes, or until golden. Slice spinach rolls 1-inch thick on diagonal; serve at once.

NOTE: Rolls may be wrapped in foil and refrigerated or frozen for future use. To reheat, place uncovered, in a preheated 350° F. oven until warmed through; slice.

Mexican Potato Skins with Cheese Filling

Serves 6

6 large potatoes
¼ cup corn oil
½ cup sharp Cheddar cheese,
    shredded

½ cup Monterey Jack cheese,
    shredded
1 quart corn oil for frying
½ cup dairy sour cream

2 scallions, chopped

1. Rub potatoes with oil.
2. Wrap in foil; bake in preheated 400° F. oven 1 hour.
3. Mix grated cheeses together.
4. Cool potatoes 30 minutes after baking, then cut in half. Scrape out inside of each potato half, leaving ⅛-inch of potato attached to skin.
5. Deep-fry potato skin in hot oil until crispy.
6. Sprinkle cheeses over and on top of potato. Make certain to cover edges of potato with cheese.
7. Run under broiler, or bake at high heat in oven, to melt cheese.
8. Garnish with combination of sour cream and scallions.

Other Fillings
Zesty Ground Beef

2 pounds lean ground beef
1 teaspoon oregano leaves
2 tablespoons beef fat
¾ cup minced onion

2 tablespoons chili powder
2 teaspoons salt
1 teaspoon ground cumin
1 teaspoon ground garlic

3 cups canned green chili salsa

1. Brown ground beef in heavy skillet. Drain fat and reserve. Put meat aside.
2. Use reserved beef fat to sauté oregano and garlic for 30 seconds.
3. Add onion; sauté until transparent.
4. Add beef and remaining ingredients; simmer 20 minutes.
5. Spoon into potato skins.

Shredded Chicken

1 pound chicken breasts, boned
    and skinned
3 cups water
1 small onion, quartered
1 bay leaf
¼ teaspoon black pepper

2 chicken bouillon cubes
½ teaspoon cumin seed
½ teaspoon garlic, ground
1 tablespoon chopped onion
1 teaspoon chili powder
1 tablespoon grated Parmesan cheese

1. Put chicken, water, onion, bay leaf, pepper, bouillon, cumin seed and garlic in saucepan. Bring to a boil.
2. Reduce heat; simmer 15 minutes, or until tender.
3. Let chicken cool in its broth, then shred it finely with your hands.
4. Add chopped onion, chili powder and cheese. Mix well and spoon into potato skins.

Sizzling Cheese Pinwheels

Makes about 5 dozen

20 to 30 slices white bread
1 package (3 ounces) cream cheese, softened to room temperature
2 tablespoons prepared yellow mustard

½ cup shredded sharp Cheddar cheese
½ cup finely diced salami
20 to 30 slices lean bacon

1. Trim crusts from bread. Flatten each slice by rolling with rolling pin or bottle.
2. Beat together cream cheese and mustard. Stir in Cheddar cheese and salami.
3. Spread mixture evenly on each slice of bread.
4. Roll up slice, diagonally, starting with one of the corners. Cut in half.
5. Roll a half-slice bacon around each pinwheel and fasten with wooden toothpick.
6. Place on broiler pan and bake in preheated 425° F. oven 20 to 25 minutes, or until bacon is crisp and browned. Serve piping hot.

Popeye's Tidbits

Makes 70

½ cup water
1 package (10 ounces) frozen chopped spinach
3 cups cooked rice
1 cup (8 ounces) dry-curd cottage cheese

1 cup grated Parmesan cheese
1 teaspoon salt
1 teaspoon seasoned pepper
¼ teaspoon garlic powder
5 eggs
corn oil

1 cup fine dry bread crumbs

1. Bring water to a boil in small saucepan. Add spinach and cook just until it is thawed. Drain and squeeze dry.
2. Combine spinach, rice, cheeses and seasonings in mixing bowl.
3. Beat 3 eggs just enough to blend yolks. Add to rice mixture and mix well.
4. Grease a 13 x 9 x 2-inch baking pan with corn oil. Coat with ⅔ cup bread crumbs.
5. Spoon rice mixture over crumbs.
6. Beat remaining eggs until frothy. Brush over rice mixture.
7. Sprinkle with remaining crumbs.
8. Bake in preheated 350° F. oven (325° F., if using glass dish) 30 minutes, or until firm. Cut into 1¼-inch squares. Serve warm or cold.

NOTE: Easy to make and inexpensive for a crowd!

Egg Canapés, Microwaved

Makes 48 canapés

¼ cup butter or margarine
⅔ cup minced green onions
¼ cup chopped fresh parsley
1 teaspoon tarragon
10 hard-cooked eggs, sliced

¼ teaspoon salt
½ teaspoon white pepper
2 to 4 tablespoons dry white wine
12 to 14 slices cracked wheat
  bread, toasted

1. Melt butter on HIGH 1 minute.
2. Add onions, parsley and tarragon to butter. Cook, uncovered, on HIGH 3 minutes.
3. Cool slightly.
4. Place eggs in blender or food processor container and chop.
5. Add butter mixture, salt, pepper and wine; blend to form a spreadable mixture.
6. Cut toast into triangles; spread with mixture. Serve piping hot.

Quiche

Makes 12 tarts

1 cup flour
¼ teaspoon salt

⅓ cup 100% corn oil margarine
3 to 4 tablespoons cold water

1. Place flour and salt in a medium bowl. Cut in margarine until mixture is the texture of coarse meal.
2. Add water and mix thoroughly to form a smooth ball.
3. Roll out on floured surface to ⅛-inch thickness.
4. Cut dough with a 3¼-inch round cookie cutter. Press circles into 2½-inch tart shells.
5. Place on baking sheet and bake in preheated 400° F. oven 10 minutes.
6. Fill shells with "egg" filling. Reduce oven to 325° F. and bake 15 minutes more.
7. Remove from tins and serve.

"Egg" Filling

3 tablespoons 100% corn oil
  margarine
3 tablespoons chopped mushrooms
3 tablespoons chopped onions

½ cup frozen cholesterol-free egg substitute
½ cup skim milk
1 teaspoon grated Parmesan cheese
pinch of nutmeg

1. Melt margarine over medium heat in medium skillet.
2. Sauté mushrooms and onions; drain and set aside.
3. Combine egg substitute, milk, cheese, nutmeg and sautéed vegetables in a small bowl. Mix well.

Swiss Cheese Pie
(Quiche)

Serves 6

1 prepared 9-inch pie shell
12 slices lean bacon
1 tablespoon minced onion
½ tablespoon butter or margarine
4 eggs

2 cups heavy cream
¼ teaspoon ground nutmeg
dash cayenne
⅛ teaspoon white pepper
1 cup grated Swiss cheese

1. Partially bake pie shell in preheated 425° F. oven 8 minutes. Cool.
2. Fry bacon until crisp, but not too brown. Dry thoroughly on paper towels; crumble and set aside.
3. Sauté onion in butter until limp; set aside.
4. Combine eggs, cream, nutmeg, cayenne and pepper; pour into partially baked pie shell.
5. Sprinkle bacon, cheese and cooked onion into pie shell.
6. Bake in preheated 425° F. oven 15 minutes. Reduce oven temperature to 300° F. and bake 30 to 35 minutes longer, or until a silver knife inserted in center comes out clean.
7. Cut to serve in wedges, hot or at room temperature.

NOTE: Makes a very popular appetizer offering or main course dish.

Peanut Quiche

Serves 8

1 cup flour
¾ teaspoon salt
½ cup margarine
2 tablespoons cold water
1½ cups shredded Swiss cheese
¼ teaspoon dry mustard

⅓ cup minced onion
¼ cup chopped cocktail peanuts
1 tablespoon flour
3 eggs
1 cup light cream

1. Combine flour and ½ teaspoon salt in a bowl. Cut in margarine until mixture resembles coarse meal.
2. Add water and mix thoroughly. Form into a smooth ball.
3. Cover and refrigerate 15 minutes.
4. Roll out on a lightly floured board.
5. Transfer to a 9-inch pie plate and shape edge. Set aside.
6. Combine Swiss cheese, onion, peanuts and 1 tablespoon flour in a bowl. Toss gently to mix; sprinkle evenly into pie shell.
7. Combine eggs, light cream, remaining salt and mustard in a bowl; beat until smooth. Pour evenly over cheese mixture.
8. Bake in preheated 425° F. oven 15 minutes. Reduce heat to 300° F. and bake 30 minutes longer, or until a knife inserted 1-inch from edge comes out clean. Serve hot or cold.

Dilly Calamari

Serves 6

3 to 4 pounds whole squid,
    fresh or frozen
water
1 tablespoon butter or margarine
1 teaspoon flour

½ cup dairy sour cream
1 tablespoon fresh lemon juice
1 tablespoon dill weed
dash salt
dash sugar

dash black pepper

1. Thaw frozen squid; clean.
2. Cook mantles (body parts of squid) in boiling salted water until tender; drain.
3. Cut into squares; set aside.
4. Melt butter, stir in flour.
5. Combine sour cream and ½ cup water; gradually add to flour mixture, stirring constantly until smooth and thickened.
6. Add squid, lemon juice, dill weed, salt, sugar and pepper. Serve hot.

Clam Fritters

Makes 10

3 cans (6½ ounces each)
    minced clams
½ cup reserved clam broth
1 egg, beaten
1 teaspoon grated onion

½ teaspoon salt
few grains ground black pepper
about ½ cup flour
1 teaspoon baking powder
peanut oil

1. Drain clams; reserve ½ cup broth.
2. Mix together broth, egg, onion, salt and pepper.
3. Combine flour and baking powder; stir into egg mixture. Mix in clams.
4. Pour 1-inch depth peanut oil into a large skillet. Heat to 375° F.
5. Spoon rounded tablespoonfuls of batter into hot peanut oil; cook until lightly browned on both sides. Drain on paper towels.

Hot Crab Meat Appetizer

Makes about 2 cups

1 package (8 ounces) cream
    cheese, softened
1½ cups (7½ ounces) crab meat,
    drained and flaked
2 tablespoons minced onion

2 tablespoons milk
½ teaspoon cream-style prepared
    horseradish
¼ teaspoon salt
dash pepper

⅓ cup sliced almonds, toasted

1. Combine softened cream cheese, crab meat, onion, milk, horseradish and seasonings. Mix until well blended.
2. Spoon into 9-inch pie plate or ovenproof dish; sprinkle with nuts.
3. Bake in preheated 375° F. oven 15 minutes. Serve as dip or spread, with crackers, chips or raw vegetables.

Deviled Crab, California Style

Serves 8

2 pounds dungeness crab meat, or shredded cooked chicken
2 cups cracker crumbs, broken into large pieces
1 cup minced celery
¾ cup chopped onion
¾ cup melted butter

¾ cup heavy cream
1½ teaspoons dry mustard
¼ to ½ teaspoon salt
dash cayenne
2 tablespoons minced parsley
1 tablespoon chopped green pepper
10 drops Tabasco sauce

1. Rinse crab meat in cold water; drain.
2. Combine crab with crumbs, celery and onion.
3. Add butter and cream.
4. Season with mustard, salt, cayenne, parsley, green pepper and Tabasco; mix thoroughly.
5. Place mixture in buttered casserole dish; cover and bake in preheated 350° F. oven 30 minutes.

NOTE: Can be baked in individual buttered ramekins.

King Crab Appetizer Puffs

Makes about 3 dozen appetizers

1 package (6 to 8 ounces) frozen crab meat, thawed
6 tablespoons butter or margarine
¼ cup sliced green onions
1 cup chopped mushrooms

1 cup shredded Monterey Jack cheese
1 package (3 ounces) cream cheese
⅓ cup real mayonnaise
2 tablespoons minced fresh parsley
¼ pound filo pastry sheets

1. Drain and slice crab. Set aside.
2. Melt 2 tablespoons butter in skillet. Add onions; sauté 1 minute.
3. Add mushrooms, sauté 1 minute longer.
4. Combine sautéed mixture with crab, cheeses, mayonnaise and parsley.
5. Spread filo sheets out in layers, two at a time. Cut each group of two into 10 x 2-inch strips.
6. Melt remaining butter; brush each strip with it.
7. Spoon a scant tablespoon filling onto end of each row. Fold pastry over filling to form a triangle; continue folding in triangles, as you would a flag, for the length of the strip.
8. Brush seam with melted butter.
9. Place seam-side down on greased baking sheet. Bake in preheated 350° F. oven 30 minutes, or until crisp and golden. Serve piping hot.

NOTE: Filo sheets are available frozen in the gourmet section of many supermarkets or Middle-Eastern food shops.

Beer Batter Halibut Appetizers

Makes about 3 dozen appetizers

1½ pounds North Pacific halibut
1⅓ cups buttermilk pancake mix
2 tablespoons corn meal
½ teaspoon salt
¼ teaspoon onion powder

¼ teaspoon garlic powder
¼ teaspoon dry mustard
⅛ teaspoon pepper
¾ cup beer
oil for deep frying

1. Cut halibut into 1-inch pieces.
2. Combine ⅓ cup pancake mix, corn meal, salt, onion powder, garlic powder, mustard and pepper. Set aside.
3. Gradually add beer to remaining pancake mix; stir to blend.
4. Dip halibut pieces into dry ingredients to coat, then into beer batter.
5. Heat oil to 375° F. Fry halibut, a few pieces at a time, until crisp and golden, about 2 minutes.
6. Drain on paper towels; keep warm in oven while frying remaining fish. Serve hot.

Rock Lobster Egg Rolls

Makes 1½ dozen

½ cup milk
½ cup water
2 tablespoons cornstarch
1 cup flour
2 eggs
16 frozen rock lobster tails
 boiling salted water

1 can (10¾ ounces) condensed cream of
 mushroom soup
1 can (1 pound) bean sprouts, well drained
1 cup grated sharp Cheddar cheese
¼ teaspoon garlic powder
½ teaspoon crumbled dill weed
 peanut oil for deep fat frying

1. Combine milk, water, cornstarch, flour and eggs; beat until smooth.
2. Spoon 2 tablespoons batter into hot, lightly buttered 6-inch skillet. Rotate pan to spread batter evenly.
3. When top of pancake is dry, remove from pan and place on waxed paper.
4. Repeat, using remaining batter and stacking pancakes. Set aside.
5. Drop frozen rock lobster tails into boiling salted water. When water reboils, boil 2 to 3 minutes.
6. Drain immediately and drench with cold water.
7. With scissors, cut away underside membrane and pull out meat.
8. Chop meat finely and mix with remaining ingredients into a thick paste.
9. Divide mixture equally among pancakes. Fold in edges and roll up. Chill.
10. At serving time, drop rolls into oil heated to 360° F. Fry 4 to 5 minutes, or until deep brown. Drain on absorbent paper.

Halibut Tempura

Makes about 7 dozen appetizers

⅔ cup flour
⅔ cup cornstarch
½ teaspoon salt
⅛ teaspoon white pepper
1 egg

¼ cup corn oil
1 cup ice water
2 pounds halibut
soy sauce (optional)
lemon (optional)

1. Cut halibut into 1 x 1 x ½-inch pieces. Set aside.
2. Combine flour, cornstarch, salt and pepper.
3. Beat together egg, oil and ice water.
4. Add egg mixture all at once to dry ingredients; beat with rotary beater until mixed. (Do not over-mix; batter will be lumpy.)
5. Set bowl of batter inside larger bowl filled with ice water.
6. Dip halibut into batter; deep-fry in oil heated to 375° F. 3 minutes, or until golden.
7. Drain on paper towels; serve immediately. If desired, serve Tempura with soy sauce or lemon and salt.

Broiled Shrimp Deluxe

Serves 10 to 12

2 cloves garlic, pressed
½ cup peanut oil
¼ cup soy sauce
¼ cup chili sauce

1 tablespoon fresh lemon juice
3 tablespoons chopped parsley
2 pounds green shrimp, shelled and deveined

1. Combine all ingredients except shrimp.
2. Marinate shrimp in this mixture for 2 hours.
3. Broil in marinade 4 to 5 minutes.
4. Serve on toothpicks.

Salmon Appetizer Rolls

Makes 28 to 30 rolls

1 can (7¾ ounces) salmon, drained and flaked
½ cup real mayonnaise
2 tablespoons lemon juice
1 teaspoon horseradish

1 teaspoon grated onion
½ cup water
2 cups all-purpose butter-milk biscuit mix
paprika

1. Mix together salmon, mayonnaise, lemon juice, horseradish and onion.
2. Sprinkle water over biscuit mix while tossing with fork to blend well.
3. Flatten dough slightly and roll out to 14-inch circle on lightly floured surface.
4. Spread with salmon mixture.
5. Cut into wedge-shaped pieces, making round edge about 1 to 1½ inches wide. Roll up, beginning at the wide end.
6. Sprinkle with paprika.
7. Bake in preheated 425° F. oven 12 to 15 minutes, or until lightly browned.

Down-East Oyster Appetizers

Makes 1 dozen appetizers

⅓ cup chopped onion
1 clove garlic, minced
¼ cup butter
½ pound fresh spinach
½ cup wheat germ

1 can (8 ounces) oysters,
   drained and chopped
3 tablespoons dry vermouth
2 teaspoons fresh lemon juice
¼ teaspoon oregano leaves, crushed

¾ cup grated Monterey Jack cheese

1. Sauté onion and garlic in butter 2 minutes over medium-high heat.
2. Wash and drain spinach. Cook over medium heat, stirring often, until spinach is wilted. Drain, squeeze dry and chop.
3. Combine spinach, wheat germ, oysters, vermouth, lemon juice, oregano and ¼ cup cheese with sautéed onions.
4. Spoon 2 tablespoons mixture into each of 12 small buttered scallop shells. Sprinkle with remaining ½ cup cheese.
5. Place on baking sheet. Bake in preheated 425° F. oven 5 to 8 minutes, or until heated through and cheese melts.

Hot Salmon Balls with Curry Dip

Makes 5 dozen

1 can (15½ ounces) salmon
water
1½ cups buttermilk baking mix
½ cup grated Parmesan cheese
1 egg, beaten

1 tablespoon fresh lemon juice
¼ teaspoon Tabasco sauce
⅓ cup minced onion
corn oil
Curry Dip

1. Drain and flake salmon, reserving liquid.
2. Add water to reserved liquid to equal ¼ cup, if necessary.
3. Stir together baking mix and cheese.
4. Combine egg, lemon juice and Tabasco; mix well.
5. Add egg mixture to dry ingredients; stir to blend. Stir in salmon and onion.
6. Drop by teaspoonsful into 1½ inches of oil heated to 375° F. Fry until golden brown; turn once.
7. Drain on paper towels. Serve piping hot with Curry Dip.

Curry Dip

Makes about 1 cup

¾ cup mayonnaise
¼ cup plain yogurt

1 teaspoon curry powder
2 tablespoons minced parsley

1. Combine mayonnaise and yogurt.
2. Stir in curry powder and parsley.
3. Cover and chill for several hours.

Broiled Shrimp

Serves 8 to 10

2 cloves fresh garlic,
 finely minced
½ cup peanut oil
¼ cup soy sauce
¼ cup chili sauce

1 tablespoon fresh lemon juice
3 tablespoons chopped parsley
2 pounds raw shrimp, shelled
 and deveined

1. Mix together all ingredients.
2. Let shrimp marinate at least 2 hours.
3. Broil in the sauce for 4 to 5 minutes. (Do not overcook.)
4. Serve piping hot on toothpicks for easier handling. Delicious with white wine or cocktails!

Shrimp on Fire

Makes 16 to 18 servings

1 egg white, lightly beaten
2 tablespoons dry white wine
1 teaspoon cornstarch
¾ teaspoon salt
1½ pounds medium shrimp,
 peeled and deveined
corn oil for frying

½ cup plus 2 tablespoons
 minced green onions
1 tablespoon chopped fresh ginger
½ cup chicken broth
2 tablespoons catsup
¾ teaspoon Tabasco sauce
½ teaspoon sugar

½ teaspoon sesame oil

1. Combine egg white, wine, cornstarch and ¼ teaspoon salt in medium bowl; mix well.
2. Add shrimp. Cover and refrigerate 1 hour.
3. Drain shrimp; reserve egg white mixture.
4. Pour oil into heavy saucepan to depth of 3 inches; heat to 320° F. Fry shrimp, a few at a time, until shrimp turn pink.
5. Drain all but 2 tablespoons oil from pan. Add 2 tablespoons green onions and ginger; stir-fry 1 minute.
6. Stir in broth, catsup, Tabasco sauce, remaining ½ teaspoon salt and sugar. Bring to a boil.
7. Add reserved egg white mixture, shrimp and remaining green onions. Stir.
8. Sprinkle with sesame oil. Serve in chafing dish.

Chinese Shrimp Toast

Makes 3 dozen appetizers

9 slices day-old sandwich bread
4 ounces cooked shrimp, minced
⅔ cup wheat germ
¼ cup cilantro or parsley, minced
¼ cup minced green onions

2 eggs, lightly beaten
1 tablespoon fresh lemon juice
2 teaspoons soy sauce
½ teaspoon ginger
corn oil for deep frying
minced parsley

1. Trim crusts from bread and cut slices diagonally into 4 triangles.
2. Place on baking sheet in single layer. Bake in preheated 250° F. oven 10 to 15 minutes, or until crisp. Cool on rack.
3. Combine shrimp, wheat germ, cilantro, green onions, eggs, lemon juice, soy sauce and ginger.
4. Spread about 2 teaspoons filling on each triangle.
5. Heat oil, 1-inch deep, to 400° F. in saucepan or deep-fat fryer. Fry a few triangles at a time, shrimp-side down, 20 to 30 seconds until golden.
6. Drain on paper towels. Sprinkle shrimp side lightly with parsley. Serve hot.

NOTE: If desired, bake appetizers in preheated 375° F. oven 8 to 10 minutes.

California Shrimp Appetizer

Serves 4 to 6

¼ pound butter
2 tablespoons minced parsley
4 teaspoons minced shallots
4 cloves minced fresh garlic
¼ teaspoon paprika
⅛ teaspoon cayenne
⅛ teaspoon salt

2 teaspoons Pernod
½ teaspoon fresh lemon juice
flour
1½ pounds shrimp, shelled and deveined
⅓ cup olive oil
juice of ½ lemon
¾ cup dry white wine

1. Cream butter several minutes with a wooden spoon.
2. Add parsley, shallot, garlic, paprika, cayenne, salt, Pernod and lemon juice; blend well.
3. Flour shrimp. Heat olive oil in large skillet, shake excess flour from shrimp; add shrimp to skillet. Quickly cook shrimp 3 minutes.
4. When shrimp turn pink, start to cook them on other side.
5. Drain oil from shrimp, squeeze on lemon, add wine, and shake pan briefly over heat 1 minute.
6. Add garlic butter; toss shrimp quickly with aid of a wooden spoon.
7. When butter is melted, serve shrimp immediately, sprinkled with additional chopped parsley.

Tuna Bites with Szechuan Sauce

Makes 4 dozen

2 cans (7 ounces each) tuna
2 eggs
1 tablespoon cornstarch
1 teaspoon sugar
¼ teaspoon ground ginger

1 can (8 ounces) water chestnuts,
  drained and minced
¼ cup minced scallions
1 teaspoon Tabasco sauce
corn oil for frying or deep frying
Szechuan Sauce

1. Drain tuna. Combine tuna, eggs, cornstarch, sugar and ginger in small bowl of electric mixer; beat at high speed until mixture is smooth.
2. Stir in water chestnuts, scallions and Tabasco sauce.
3. Roll mixture into ¾-inch balls.
4. Heat oil in large skillet over medium heat; brown balls on all sides, about 3 or 4 minutes.
5. Drain on paper towels. Serve with Szechuan Sauce.

Szechuan Sauce

Makes 1 cup

½ cup catsup
½ cup soy sauce

2 teaspoons sugar
¼ teaspoon ground ginger

¼ teaspoon Tabasco sauce

1. Combine all ingredients in small saucepan.
2. Stir over low heat until heated through.

Tuna Chili con Queso

Makes 2½ cups

1 tablespoon butter or margarine
¼ cup chopped onion
1 can (1 pound) tomatoes,
  drained and cut up
1 bay leaf
2 tablespoons flour
¼ cup milk

1 can (4 ounces) green chilies,
  drained, seeded and chopped
1 cup (4 ounces) shredded Monterey
  Jack or mild Cheddar cheese
1 can (7 ounces) tuna, drained
¼ teaspoon salt
corn chips

1. Melt butter in a saucepan; sauté onion until tender.
2. Add tomatoes and bay leaf. Simmer 5 minutes, stirring occasionally.
3. Mix flour and milk to make a paste; add to saucepan. Simmer 5 minutes.
4. Remove bay leaf. Add green chilies and cheese. Stir until cheese melts.
5. Stir in tuna and salt. Keep warm and serve with chips.

Tuna Empanaditas

Makes about 30

½ cup chopped onion
butter
1 can (6½ or 7 ounces) tuna, drained
1 can (8 ounces) whole tomatoes, undrained

¼ cup chopped pimiento-stuffed olives
¼ cup chopped seedless raisins
2 tablespoons plain bread crumbs
2 packages (10 or 11 ounces each) pie-crust mix

1. Sauté onion in butter until soft.
2. Flake tuna, add to skillet with tomatoes, olives, raisins and bread crumbs; mix well. Set aside.
3. Prepare pie-crust mix according to package directions; divide into 4 equal parts.
4. Roll out on lightly floured board to ⅛-inch thickness. Cut into 4-inch rounds.
5. Place rounded tablespoon filling on each round. Moisten edges of pastry with water; fold one side over and press edges together with fork tines.
6. Repeat with remaining dough and tuna filling.
7. Place empanaditas on ungreased cookie sheet. Bake in preheated 400° F. oven 25 minutes, until golden.

Tuna Turnovers

Makes about 2 dozen

1 tablespoon butter
1 tablespoon flour
¼ cup milk
¼ teaspoon salt
1 teaspoon grated onion
dash Tabasco sauce

1 can (7 ounces) chunk-style tuna, water-packed, drained
½ cup chopped ripe olives
2 tablespoons diced pimiento
1 package prepared pie crust mix
2 tablespoons cream

1. Melt butter; blend in flour; stir in milk and salt. Cook, stirring, until thick.
2. Remove from heat and blend in onion and Tabasco.
3. Stir tuna into butter sauce with olives and pimiento; cool.
4. Following package instructions, roll out pastry very thin on lightly floured board; cut into 2½-inch squares.
5. Place 1 rounded teaspoon of filling on center of each square; bring opposite corners together over filling and fasten with toothpick.
6. Arrange on cookie sheet; chill.
7. When ready to serve, brush turnovers lightly with cream; bake in preheated 450° F. oven 10 minutes, or until crisp and golden.
8. Serve piping hot for an inexpensive and terrific-tasting turnover!

Rosey Beef Balls

Makes 48 balls

water
1 envelope beef-flavored
  mushroom soup mix
2 pounds lean ground beef or
  veal
1 egg, beaten
2 beef bouillon cubes

¼ cup flour
¼ cup butter or margarine
1 cup rosé wine
2 sprigs parsley
2 tablespoons catsup
¼ teaspoon thyme
1 clove garlic, minced

2 tablespoons snipped fresh parsley

1. Add ¼ cup hot water to soup.
2. Mix with beef and egg.
3. Shape into balls using 1 tablespoon beef-soup mixture.
4. Bake in lightly greased roasting pan in preheated 325° F. oven 20 minutes, or until done.
5. Meanwhile, add ½ cup boiling water to bouillon cubes in saucepan.
6. Blend flour with melted butter; add bouillon and wine gradually, stirring well after each addition.
7. Add parsley sprigs, catsup, thyme and garlic; cook, stirring constantly, until thickened and smooth.
8. Reduce heat, cover, and continue cooking 15 minutes.
9. Remove and discard parsley sprigs.
10. Remove meatballs from sauce with slotted spoon to serving dish. Sprinkle with snipped parsley. If desired, pass hot sauce for dunking.

NOTE: A tasty bite for the cocktail buffet table.

Barbecued "Surprise" Meatballs

Makes 24 meatballs

1 egg, beaten slightly
1 pound ground chuck
¼ cup minced onions
¼ cup bread crumbs
dash pepper

surprise centers: (all well drained)
red maraschino cherries, cut in half;
small pimiento-stuffed olives;
dill pickles, cut in ½-inch cubes;
sweet gherkins, cut in ½-inch cubes

1. Add beaten egg to meat, onions, bread crumbs and pepper; mix thoroughly.
2. Shape into 1¼-inch meatballs, pressing cherry half, olive, pickle or gherkin cube into center of each meatball.
3. Chill 30 minutes.
4. Thread meatballs on skewers, piercing through the "center" and leaving about ½ inch between each meatball.
5. Grill over medium coals for about 10 minutes, turning occasionally. When brown, remove from skewers.

Chinese Egg Rolls

Makes about 12 rolls

For the Filling

1 pound lean ground beef
¼ cup butter
4 cups finely shredded cabbage,
  partially cooked
½ cup minced green onion

1½ cups minced celery
2 cups canned bean sprouts,
  well drained
1 teaspoon salt
freshly ground black pepper to taste

pinch of sugar (optional)

1. Brown beef lightly in butter.
2. Add vegetables and seasonings; cook 5 minutes.
3. Drain and cool.

For the Batter

2 cups plus 1 tablespoon sifted
  all-purpose flour
2 tablespoons cornstarch
1 teaspoon salt

1 egg, beaten
1 teaspoon sugar
water
peanut oil

1. Sift dry ingredients; add egg and sugar.
2. Gradually beat in water until a smooth, thin batter is formed.
3. Grease a 6-inch skillet lightly with peanut oil.
4. Pour about 4 tablespoons of batter into center of pan; tilt pan to spread batter over entire surface.
5. Cook over low heat until edges pull away from sides; gently turn pancake with fingers and cook other side.
6. Remove from pan and cool.
7. Place a heaping tablespoon of filling in center of each pancake. Spread to within ½-inch of edge.
8. Roll, folding in sides, and seal with a mixture of 1 tablespoon flour and 2 tablespoons water.
9. Fry egg rolls in deep hot fat, 360° F., until golden brown. Serve with Chinese mustard sauce (available in Oriental food stores).

Cocktail Nachos

Serves 12

1 pound lean ground beef
1 cup minced onion
1 teaspoon corn oil
1 teaspoon seasoned salt
½ teaspoon ground cumin
2 cans (1 pound each) refried beans
1 package (1¼ ounces) taco
  seasoning mix
2 cups grated Monterey Jack cheese

1 can (4 ounces) chopped green chilies
1 cup grated Cheddar cheese
¾ cup chunky taco sauce
fried tortilla chips
garnish: use any or all of the following:
  1 cup guacamole (see page 61)
  ½ cup dairy sour cream
  ¼ cup chopped green onion
  1 cup sliced ripe olives

1. Brown meat and onion in corn oil; drain off excess fat.
2. Season with seasoned salt and cumin.
3. Combine beans and seasoning mix; blend well.
4. Mix in Monterey Jack cheese.
5. Spread beans in a shallow, oval 10 x 15-inch baking dish. Cover with meat mixture; top with chilies, then Cheddar cheese. Pour taco sauce over cheese.
6. Bake, uncovered, in preheated 400° F. oven 20 to 25 minutes, or until heated.
7. Arrange tortilla chips around edge of platter. Garnish as desired.

Meatballs in Creamy Tomato Sauce

Serves 6

1½ cups bread cubes
½ cup milk
1½ pounds ground beef
½ cup minced onion
1 teaspoon salt
¼ teaspoon pepper
2 tablespoons corn oil

2 cups beef bouillon
¼ cup real mayonnaise
¼ cup flour
1 can (16 ounces) whole
  tomatoes
1 bay leaf
4 cups hot cooked rice

1. Mix together bread cubes and milk; let stand 5 minutes.
2. Mix together bread mixture, meat, onion, salt and pepper. Shape into 18 meatballs.
3. Heat corn oil in 10-inch deep skillet over medium heat; add meatballs.
4. Cook, stirring occasionally, 15 minutes, or until browned.
5. Remove meatballs from skillet and pour off fat.
6. Return skillet to heat and stir in bouillon.
7. Stir together mayonnaise, flour and additional salt and pepper until smooth; mix in tomatoes.
8. Gradually add tomato mixture to bouillon, stirring to break up tomatoes.
9. Add meatballs and bay leaf. Cover and cook over medium heat 30 minutes.
10. Remove bay leaf. Serve over hot cooked rice.

Mexican Meatballs

Makes about 90 (¾-inch) meatballs

1½ pounds ground beef
2 eggs, slightly beaten
1 medium onion, minced
½ cup fine dry bread
   crumbs
1½ teaspoons salt
1⅓ tablespoons chili powder
½ teaspoon garlic salt
½ teaspoon ground pepper

2 tablespoons corn oil
1 bottle (12 ounces) chili sauce
1 cup tomato juice
1 cup water
½ cup dark corn syrup
2 tablespoons lemon juice
1 teaspoon oregano
¼ teaspoon garlic salt
¼ teaspoon Tabasco sauce

1. Mix together beef, eggs, onion, bread crumbs, salt, 1 teaspoon chili powder, garlic salt and pepper. Shape into ¾-inch balls.
2. Heat corn oil in 12-inch electric fry pan or large skillet over medium heat.
3. Add about one-half meatballs. Brown on all sides, shaking pan to keep balls round.
4. Remove first batch from skillet; repeat. Drain any fat from skillet.
5. Combine chili sauce, tomato juice, water, corn syrup, lemon juice, remaining chili powder, oregano, garlic salt and Tabasco in skillet.
6. Bring to a boil; reduce heat and simmer, stirring occasionally, about 15 minutes, or until flavors have blended and sauce has reached desired consistency.
7. Add meatballs; cover and simmer 10 minutes. (If sauce becomes too thick add additional tomato juice as needed.)
8. Serve warm from serving dish or chafing dish with picks.

NOTE: *If skillet is smaller than 12 inches, make sauce in 3-quart saucepan. Add meatballs and simmer 10 minutes. Serve in skillet or serving dish, replenishing as needed.*

Beef-Stuffed Zucchini

Serves 6

2 pounds zucchini
½ pound ground beef
¼ cup real mayonnaise
1 teaspoon lemon juice
2 teaspoons dehydrated
   onion flakes

2 teaspoons dried parsley flakes
1 teaspoon dried oregano flakes
1 teaspoon salt
¼ teaspoon pepper
⅔ cup spaghetti sauce
   (homemade or canned)

1. Wash zucchini and cut in half lengthwise. Scoop out inside, leaving about ¼-inch shell.
2. Coarsely chop scooped-out zucchini and mix together with ground beef, mayonnaise, lemon juice, onion flakes, parsley, oregano, salt and pepper. Spoon mixture into shells.
3. Place in shallow baking dish and pour spaghetti sauce over each shell.
4. Bake in preheated 350° F. oven 30 minutes, or until zucchini is tender when pierced with a fork.

Russian Turnovers

Makes about 16

1 cup chopped onion
2 tablespoons butter
1 pound lean ground beef
salt to taste
pepper to taste

2 hard-cooked eggs, chopped
¼ cup cooked rice
pastry for double-crust pie
    (homemade or prepared)
melted butter or margarine

1. Sauté onion in butter until golden. Add meat, cooking over low heat, stirring to break up meat. Season to taste with salt and pepper.
2. Add eggs and rice; stir over low heat 2 to 3 minutes, or until mixture is heated through.
3. Roll pastry very thin (thinner than pie crust). Cut into 2½ or 3-inch rounds.
4. Place 1 heaping tablespoon meat mixture on half of each circle. Fold over each half, pinching edges together to seal.
5. Place on greased baking sheets. Brush lightly with melted butter. Bake in preheated 325° F. oven 20 minutes, or until golden brown. Serve hot.

NOTE: Russian turnovers, or piroschki, can be made with various fillings, using leftover chicken, turkey, pork or fish. A delicious morsel to serve with cocktails, but also a wonderful snack for hungry teenagers.

Zesty Almond Chipped Beef Dip

Makes 2 cups

8 ounces cream cheese, softened
2 tablespoons milk
¾ cup snipped dried or chipped
    beef, or 2½ to 3 ounces smoked
    sliced beef
2 tablespoons dried onion flakes

2 tablespoons chopped green pepper
¼ teaspoon seasoned pepper
½ cup dairy sour cream
¼ cup chopped almonds
seasoned pepper or paprika (for garnish)
cocktail crackers

1. Blend together cream cheese and milk.
2. Mix in beef, onion flakes, green pepper, seasoned pepper, sour cream and almonds.
3. Spoon mixture into small ungreased casserole. Bake in preheated 350° F. oven 15 minutes, or until hot.
4. Place on table warmer or candle warmer. Garnish with seasoned pepper or paprika.
5. Serve with cocktail crackers.

So-Simple London Broil

Serves 12

2-pound flank steak
⅓ cup original Wor-
    cestershire sauce
salt to taste

bread rounds
horseradish-flavored mustard
    (optional)

1. Score one side of the steak diagonally, 1½ inches apart. Lay flat in a tight-fitting glass or enamel pan, or doubled plastic bag.
2. Pour Worcestershire over meat. Cover or seal. Marinate 5 hours.
3. Remove meat from marinade, reserving marinade.
4. Place meat on a rack in a broiler pan; sprinkle lightly with salt. Broil under a preheated hot broiler, 7 to 8 minutes on each side, basting frequently with reserved marinade.
5. Cut into thin slices on the diagonal. Serve on bread rounds spread lightly with horse-radish-flavored mustard, if desired.

NOTE: A real man pleaser!

Canapés Monte Cristo

Makes 18 to 20 canapés

5 slices bread
2 tablespoons butter or margarine
2 cups ground cooked ham
1 tablespoon prepared yellow mustard
dash of cayenne

salt to taste
2 tablespoons heavy cream
5 thin slices processed cheese,
    (about ½ pound)
paprika

1. Cut bread with fancy cutters. Sauté bread on one side in melted butter in hot skillet until lightly browned.
2. Mix ham, mustard, cayenne, salt and cream together; roll into small balls and place on untoasted side of bread. Top with cheese cut into same shape.
3. Just before serving, broil until cheese is melted. For added color, sprinkle each canapé with paprika.

Deviled Ham Biscuits

Makes 2 dozen

1 cup milk, or ½ cup evaporated
    milk and ½ cup water

2 cups packaged biscuit mix
1 can (2¼ ounces) deviled ham

1. Stir milk into biscuit mix and beat dough until thoroughly combined.
2. Fill each 2½-inch greased muffin pan ¼ full of biscuit mixture; place a small amount of deviled ham in each; top with additional mixture until pans are half full.
3. Bake in preheated 475° F. oven 10 to 12 minutes, or until browned.
4. If desired, each biscuit may be glazed by brushing tops with milk or slightly beaten egg white to which 2 tablespoons water have been added, about 3 minutes before removing from oven. Complete baking and serve hot.

Ham en Croute
(Ham in Pastry)

Serves 10 to 12

2 tablespoons prepared
yellow mustard
1 tablespoon sherry
dash ground cloves

1 can (3 pounds) ham
1 Double-Crust Mayonnaise
Pastry
1 egg yolk

1 tablespoon water

1. Mix together mustard, sherry and cloves. Spread evenly over ham.
2. Roll out half the dough to ⅛-inch thickness. Place on ungreased cookie sheet.
3. Place ham on crust. Trim dough to about 2 inches around ham.
4. Roll out remaining dough as large as possible. Drape loosely over ham, press edges together, trim off excess, and flute around base of ham.
5. Roll out trimmed dough and cut small (2 x 1½-inch) triangles.
6. Mix egg yolk with water; brush crust with mixture.
7. Place triangles around upper edge of ham overlapping each. Brush with egg yolk mixture.
8. Prick crust with fork and bake in preheated 400° F. oven 30 minutes, or until nicely browned.

Double-Crust Mayonnaise Pastry

2 cups sifted all-purpose flour
1 teaspoon salt

½ cup real mayonnaise
3 tablespoons cold water

1. Mix flour and salt in bowl.
2. Stir in mayonnaise thoroughly with fork.
3. Sprinkle with water; mix well.
4. Press firmly into ball with hands.

Drunk Weiners

Serves about 20

½ cup bourbon
¾ cup catsup
2 teaspoons sugar

2 teaspoons chopped onion
1 pound weiners, cut in
bite-size pieces

1. Combine bourbon, catsup, sugar and onion in small saucepan.
2. Add weiner bits and simmer 45 minutes.
3. Transfer to chafing dish and serve with tiny forks or wooden picks for a crowd.

NOTE: Inexpensive and tasty!

Stuffed Pumpernickel Loaf

Serves 10 to 12

1 pound fresh mushrooms, minced
1 cup minced onion
½ cup finely chopped green
   pepper
1 teaspoon thyme, crushed
1 small clove garlic, pressed
¼ cup butter or margarine

1½ pounds liverwurst, mashed
¼ cup chopped parsley
1 teaspoon dry mustard (more if desired)
1 round loaf pumpernickel bread
   (14 inches in diameter)
prepared mustard
pickles

1. Sauté mushrooms, onion, pepper, thyme and garlic in butter until mushrooms are tender, stirring often. Set aside and cool.
2. Stir mushroom mixture into liverwurst until well blended.
3. Add parsley and mustard. Blend well.
4. Cut off 1-inch top of bread; set aside. Scoop out bread, leaving about 1-inch bread around edges. (Reserve scooped-out bread for bread crumbs.)
5. Fill shell with mushroom mixture. Replace top on bread.
6. Heat in preheated 250° F. oven 20 minutes.
7. Serve with mustard and pickles.

NOTE: This works well with other favorite fillings, using leftover cooked meat or poultry. Bear in mind that fillings should not be too gooey, or they will soak the crust. Same idea can be used on hard rolls.

Frankfurter Turnovers

Makes 8 to 10

8 to 10 slices sandwich bread
butter or margarine
1 pound (8 to 10) frankfurters

prepared yellow mustard
¾ cup corn relish, drained
8 to 10 wooden picks

radish roses, pickles and olives

1. Roll each slice of bread with a rolling pin until half its original thickness.
2. Spread one side of each slice with butter.
3. Cut each frankfurter lengthwise, almost through.
4. Place 1 frankfurter, cut-side up, diagonally on unbuttered side of each bread slice.
5. Spread each frankfurter with ½ teaspoon mustard; fill with 1 tablespoon corn relish.
6. Fold 2 opposite corners of bread over frankfurter; secure with a pick.
7. Bake on a greased baking sheet in preheated 450° F. oven 8 to 10 minutes, or until lightly toasted.
8. Before serving, place a radish rose, pickle or olive on pick closing each foldover.

Nutted Party Rounds

Makes 48 canapés

1 can (7 ounces) luncheon meat,
  minced
¾ cup dairy sour cream
1 tablespoon real mayonnaise
2 teaspoons horseradish
1½ teaspoons prepared yellow
  mustard

¼ teaspoon salt
¼ teaspoon onion powder
¾ cup finely chopped cocktail peanuts
48 two-inch bread rounds, toasted on
  one side

1. Combine meat, sour cream, mayonnaise, horseradish, mustard, salt and onion powder. Chill at least 1 hour.
2. Just before serving, stir in peanuts.
3. Spread untoasted side of each bread round with 2 teaspoons of ham-peanut mixture.
4. Run under broiler until lightly browned. Serve immediately.

Kraut Pizzas

Serves 6

1 package (15⅝ ounces) complete
  pizza mix (flour mix, pizza sauce,
  Parmesan cheese)
½ pound frankfurters, thinly sliced
¼ cup minced onion
1 garlic clove, crushed

1 tablespoon butter or margarine
2½ cups drained, loosely packed
  sauerkraut, about 1 can (16 ounces)
¼ teaspoon basil leaves
1 package (8 ounces) mozzarella
  cheese, grated

1 small green pepper, cut into 6 rings

1. Prepare pizza flour mix according to package directions.
2. On a floured board, divide dough into 6 equal pieces. Form each piece into a ball and roll each ball into a 7-inch circle.
3. Place circles on large greased baking sheet. Fold in edge of each circle enough to form a 6-inch circle. Using folded portion, form an edge, about ½-inch high, around each circle.
4. Sauté frankfurters, onion and garlic in butter over medium heat, stirring occasionally, until onion is tender.
5. Stir in pizza sauce, sauerkraut and basil; heat until hot.
6. Evenly fill pizza shells with mixture; sprinkle with grated Parmesan cheese, then with mozzarella cheese; top with a pepper ring.
7. Bake in preheated 425° F. oven 15 to 17 minutes, or until cheese is melted and crust is lightly browned. Serve immediately.

NOTE: Great for childrens' parties too!

Smoky Frank Bites

Makes about 40 pieces

1 pound skinless frankfurters
2 tablespoons butter or margarine
1½ teaspoons Angostura aromatic
    bitters

¼ teaspoon onion salt
¼ teaspoon garlic salt
¼ teaspoon celery salt

1. Cut frankfurters into 1-inch pieces. Set aside.
2. Heat butter in a skillet and stir in remaining ingredients.
3. Add frankfurter pieces and stir to coat.
4. Cook over medium heat, stirring occasionally, until pieces are dark brown and crusty.
5. Spear on toothpicks and serve piping hot.

Brewed Cocktail Franks

Makes about 2 dozen

2 cups beer
2 onions, sliced
2 carrots, sliced

1 celery stalk, sliced
1 teaspoon original Worcestershire
    sauce
1 pound cocktail franks

1. Put beer, vegetables and Worcestershire in large saucepan. Bring to a boil.
2. When foam subsides, simmer 10 to 15 minutes to blend flavors.
3. Add franks; bring back to a boil.
4. Turn off heat; cover and let stand for 5 to 10 minutes.
5. Remove franks and serve hot.

Porky Picks

Serves 10 to 15

2 packages (8 to 10 ounces each)
    brown 'n' serve sausage links
2 tablespoons cornstarch
¼ cup cold water
1 can (13½ ounces) pineapple
    chunks, drained, with ½ cup
    syrup reserved

¾ cup dark corn syrup
¼ cup white vinegar
½ teaspoon salt
½ cup green pepper, cut in
    ½-inch squares
½ cup maraschino cherries,
    drained

1. Cut each sausage link crosswise into thirds. Brown lightly in skillet.
2. Blend cornstarch and water.
3. Combine cornstarch mixture, pineapple syrup, corn syrup, vinegar and salt in chafing dish or skillet.
4. Bring to a boil; simmer 5 minutes.
5. Add sausage, pineapple chunks, green pepper and cherries. Heat. Serve speared on toothpicks.

Meat-Stuffed Mushrooms

Makes 1½ dozen appetizers

18 large cleaned mushrooms
1 small ripe tomato, peeled
1 pound lean ground beef or lamb
2 tablespoons minced fresh parsley or fresh dill
1 small clove garlic, pressed
scant teaspoon salt

¼ teaspoon freshly ground black pepper
¼ teaspoon basil
2 tablespoons corn oil
3 tablespoons water
2 tablespoons grated Parmesan or Romano cheese

1. Break off mushroom caps; set aside.
2. Cut off stem ends, and mince remaining portion of stems.
3. Chop tomato; combine with minced mushrooms.
4. Combine beef, mushroom-tomato mixture, parsley, garlic, salt, pepper and basil; mix well.
5. Fill each mushroom cap with meat mixture.
6. Arrange mushroom caps, stuffed-side up, in shallow baking dish; sprinkle with oil, then with cheese.
7. Bake in preheated 350° F. oven about 25 minutes. Serve hot.

Crab-Bacon Roll-Ups

Makes about 2 dozen appetizers

12 slices lean bacon
½ cup tomato juice
1 large egg, well beaten
¾ cup fine dry bread crumbs
¼ teaspoon salt
⅛ teaspoon white pepper

¼ teaspoon original Worcestershire sauce
1 teaspoon chopped fresh parsley
1 teaspoon chopped celery or watercress leaves
1 can (6½ ounces) crab meat, drained and flaked

1. Select bacon that is about 1½ inches in width; cut in halves and set aside.
2. Mix together tomato juice and egg.
3. Add bread crumbs, seasonings, chopped vegetables and crab meat; mix well.
4. Divide into 24 portions, shaping into finger-size rolls.
5. Wrap in pieces of bacon and fasten with wooden picks; broil under very hot broiler 10 to 12 minutes, turning often to brown bacon evenly.
6. Drain quickly on paper towels; serve hot.

Mexican Pork Tacos

Serves 12

1 pound boneless pork shoulder
1 tablespoon shortening
1 cup chopped onion
1 clove garlic
1 tablespoon flour
2 teaspoons chili powder
1 teaspoon salt
1 teaspoon oregano

1 can (8 ounces) tomato sauce
½ cup water
1 tablespoon cider vinegar
¼ cup sliced pitted black olives
12 taco shells
3 cups shredded lettuce
1½ cups coarsely chopped tomato
dairy sour cream

shredded Monterey Jack cheese

1. Cut pork in thin strips; brown in shortening.
2. Add onion, garlic, flour, and seasonings; stir and heat well.
3. Add tomato sauce, water and vinegar; heat until thickened, stirring.
4. Cover and simmer 30 minutes.
5. Stir in olives.
6. Heat taco shells. Fill each with ¼ cup shredded lettuce, 2 tablespoons chopped tomato and 3 to 4 tablespoons pork filling.
7. Top with sour cream or shredded cheese.

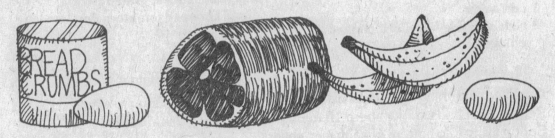

Scotch Bananas

Makes 12 pieces

1 pound bulk pork sausage
¼ teaspoon salt
2 medium bananas, cut in 1-inch
 crosswise pieces

2 eggs, slightly beaten
unseasoned fine dry bread crumbs
fat for frying

1. Sprinkle sausage with salt; mix well.
2. Allowing 2 tablespoons sausage per chunk of banana, mold sausage around banana to completely cover the surface and form a ball.
3. Dip sausage balls into beaten egg and then into bread crumbs. Shake off excess crumbs.
4. Heat fat to 350° F. in a large, deep pan.
5. Add 6 banana-sausage pieces to the fat at one time; fry 10 to 12 minutes. The Scotch Bananas will be dark and crusty.
6. Drain. Serve hot.

Barbecued Chicken Wings

Makes 20 to 30 pieces

2½ to 3 pounds chicken wings
½ cup vinegar
½ cup sugar
½ cup catsup

1 tablespoon flour
1 teaspoon celery salt
½ teaspoon cloves
½ teaspoon dry mustard

1. Cut off tips of chicken wings and discard. Disjoint remaining wing parts.
2. Place in a single layer in baking pan.
3. Combine remaining ingredients in saucepan and bring to a simmer. Pour over wings.
4. Bake in preheated 350° F. oven 1 hour. (Cover pan during first 20 minutes; remove for last 40 minutes.)

Chicken Tacos

Makes 10 tacos

1 package (1¼ ounces) chicken taco
  seasoning mix
1 cup water
3 cups shredded or diced cooked
  chicken

10 taco shells
shredded lettuce, grated cheese
  and chopped tomatoes (for
  topping)

1. Combine seasoning mix, water and chicken in large skillet. Bring to a boil.
2. Reduce heat and simmer about 10 minutes, or until liquid is absorbed.
3. Spoon filling into bottom of each taco shell.
4. Top with lettuce, cheese and tomato.

Chicken-Potato Balls

Makes 40 balls

1 cup ground cooked chicken
1 cup mashed cooked potatoes
2 tablespoons skim milk
1 cup bread crumbs

½ cup 100% corn oil margarine, melted
¼ teaspoon onion salt
⅛ teaspoon pepper
1 teaspoon rosemary, crushed

1. Mix together chicken, potatoes, milk, ⅓ cup bread crumbs, ¼ cup margarine, onion salt, pepper and rosemary.
2. Roll mixture by teaspoonfuls into balls.
3. Dip balls in remaining margarine; coat with remaining bread crumbs.
4. Place balls on baking sheet. Bake in preheated 350° F. oven 15 minutes, or until hot.

Chinatown Chicken Puffs

Makes 25

½ pound white chicken meat, minced
3 tablespoons dry sherry
3 tablespoons soy sauce
2 tablespoons Chinese oyster sauce
½ tablespoon minced fresh ginger root
1 clove garlic, crushed

½ cup finely chopped scallions
  (including green tips)
½ of a 17¼-ounce package (1 sheet)
  frozen puff pastry
1 egg white
1 tablespoon water

1. Combine chicken, sherry, soy sauce, oyster sauce, ginger and garlic in a skillet; cook over medium heat for 10 minutes.
2. Add scallions; continue cooking until sauce coats chicken.
3. Remove from heat; cool.
4. Thaw 1 folded puff pastry sheet 20 to 30 minutes; unfold gently.
5. On a lightly floured board roll pastry sheet into a 12½ x 12½-inch square. Cut into 2½-inch squares (25).
6. Brush squares with egg wash made by combining egg white with water.
7. Place 1 teaspoon chicken mixture into center of each square. Pull 4 corners of dough to top center of square, pinch together, and twist slightly.
8. Bake on ungreased baking sheet in preheated 400° F. oven 10 to 15 minutes, or until puffed and golden.
9. Serve warm or at room temperature.

Ginger Teriyaki Skewers

Makes 32

4 chicken breasts, skinned and boned
¼ cup bottled teriyaki sauce
2 teaspoons grated orange peel
½ teaspoon ground ginger

1 can (1 pound 4 ounces) pineapple
  chunks in juice
½ large green pepper, chunked
16 cherry tomatoes

1. Cut boned chicken into 1-inch pieces; place in shallow dish.
2. Blend teriyaki sauce, orange peel and ginger. Set aside.
3. Drain pineapple, reserving ¼ cup juice.
4. Add pineapple juice to teriyaki sauce; pour over chicken, cover, and marinate 1 hour.
5. Skewer chicken, pineapple chunks and a green pepper chunk or cherry tomato on each of 32 small skewers.
6. Broil 4 inches from heat 10 to 12 minutes.

Golden Chicken Nuggets with Sweet-Sour Sauce

Makes 5 dozen

1¾ pounds boned and skinned
  chicken breasts
1 packet (4.2 ounces) crispy crumb
  coating for chicken
  (available at supermarkets)

½ cup corn oil
1 egg
1 tablespoon water
Sweet-Sour Sauce

1. Pound chicken until ½-inch thick. Cut into 1-inch pieces.
2. Empty coating mix evenly onto sheet of waxed paper.
3. Spread half the oil in each of two 15 x 10-inch jellyroll pans.
4. Beat egg with fork in large bowl. Blend in water.
5. Add chicken pieces; toss gently to moisten.
6. Place chicken in crumb coating, a few pieces at a time, sprinkling coating over chicken. Press firmly on all sides until evenly coated.
7. Arrange chicken in single layer in pans. Bake in preheated 400° F. oven 10 minutes.
8. Turn chicken pieces; bake 5 minutes longer, or until tender and crisp.
9. Remove from pan immediately. Serve with Sweet-Sour Sauce.

Sweet-Sour Sauce

Makes ¾ cup

5 tablespoons chopped chutney
¼ cup currant jelly
2 teaspoons dry mustard

1½ teaspoons sugar
½ teaspoon ground ginger
1 teaspoon vinegar

1. Combine chutney, jelly, mustard, sugar, ginger and vinegar.
2. Heat until jelly melts.

NOTE: Great for make-ahead cocktail parties! Coated chicken pieces can be frozen and baked without thawing. Bake in preheated 400° F. oven 7 minutes; turn and bake 3 minutes longer.

Savory-Sauced Turkey Franks

Makes about 4 dozen appetizers

1 package (10 to 12 ounces)
  turkey franks

⅓ cup Dijon-style mustard
½ cup red currant jelly

1. Cut franks diagonally in about ¾-inch pieces.
2. Combine mustard and jelly in small saucepan. Cook over low heat, stirring frequently, until jelly is melted.
3. Add franks to mustard mixture and stir until heated.
4. Serve hot in chafing dish; provide cocktail picks.

Nectarine-Chicken Cream Puffs

Makes 2 dozen

¼ cup butter
½ cup water
⅓ cup whole wheat flour
⅓ cup all-purpose flour
3 eggs
Nectarine-Chicken Filling
1 fresh nectarine, thinly sliced (for garnish)

1. Combine butter with water in saucepan. Place over medium heat until butter is melted and mixture comes to a boil.
2. Add flours, stirring until mixture forms a ball and leaves sides of pan. Remove from heat.
3. Beat in eggs with spoon, one at a time, until smooth.
4. Drop by tablespoons onto lightly greased baking sheet, 1½ inches apart.
5. Bake in preheated 400° F. oven 10 minutes. Reduce oven temperature to 350° F.; bake 15 minutes longer, or until golden.
6. Cool on rack.
7. Split puffs open and fill with Nectarine-Chicken Filling.
8. Pile puffs on serving plate. Garnish with nectarine slices.

Nectarine-Chicken Filling

Makes about 1½ cups

1 cup diced, cooked chicken
1 cup finely chopped (1 medium) fresh nectarine
¼ cup minced celery
¼ cup plain yogurt
2 tablespoons chopped green onion
1 tablespoon fresh lemon juice
¼ teaspoon salt
¼ teaspoon dried tarragon, crumbled

Combine ingredients and fill puffs.

Hot 'n' Spicy Chicken Wings

Serves 8

12 chicken wings
corn oil for frying
¼ cup butter or margarine, melted
1 tablespoon catsup
1 teaspoon Tabasco sauce
½ teaspoon garlic powder

1. Remove tips from wings, discard.
2. Separate first and second joints of wings with a sharp knife. Pat wings dry with a paper towel.
3. Heat about 2 inches of oil in a heavy saucepot heated to 350° F.
4. Fry wings, a few at a time, about 6 minutes until golden; drain on paper towels.
5. Combine butter, catsup, Tabasco sauce and garlic powder in small bowl; mix well.
6. Toss wing pieces in butter mixture to coat thoroughly. Serve hot or at room temperature.

Sweet & Spicy Chicken Wings

Serves 4

3 pounds chicken wings	¼ cup brown sugar, packed
flour	1 envelope Italian dressing mix
salt	1 teaspoon celery salt
black pepper	½ cup catsup
red pepper	¼ cup vinegar
ground ginger	¼ cup water
oil for deep frying	Tabasco sauce

1. With poultry scissors, cut wings in halves at joints, trimming and discarding wing tips.
2. Combine in a bag flour and a dash each of salt, black pepper, red pepper and ginger.
3. Add wings; shake to coat.
4. Fry wings in deep, hot oil until golden and crispy, about 20 minutes.
5. Make sauce by combining brown sugar, dressing mix, celery salt, a dash of ginger, catsup, vinegar, water and Tabasco sauce to taste.
6. Dip wings in sauce and place in baking dish. Bake in preheated 400° F. oven 10 to 15 minutes. Serve hot.

Lemon-Yogurt-Chicken Stuffed Potatoes, Microwaved

Serves 24

24 new potatoes, 1½ inches in diameter	½ cup lemon yogurt
	salt to taste
1 whole chicken breast, skinned and boned	white pepper to taste
	¼ teaspoon nutmeg
¼ cup butter or margarine (at room temperature)	⅛ teaspoon finely grated lemon rind

¼ cup chopped pine nuts (for garnish)

1. Pierce each potato and arrange on microwave baking sheet; cook on HIGH 16 to 18 minutes, or until soft, rearranging once after first 8 minutes cooking time. Let stand 10 minutes.
2. Place chicken on small plate; cook on HIGH 6 to 8 minutes. Drain and mince chicken.
3. Combine minced chicken, butter, yogurt, salt, pepper, nutmeg and lemon peel.
4. Carefully slice off top from each potato; scoop out pulp, leaving ⅛-inch shell.
5. Add potato pulp to chicken mixture; mash to blend well.
6. Fill each shell with potato-chicken mixture; garnish with pine nuts.
7. Arrange filled potatoes on microwave-safe platter; cook on HIGH 3 to 4 minutes, or until piping hot. Serve at once.

NOTE: This delightfully different hot canapé can be made with left-over turkey too.

Artichoke Appetizer

Serves 4

3 tablespoons olive oil
1 small onion, finely chopped
3 cloves garlic, mashed or grated
6 to 7 medium-size raw artichoke
    hearts, or canned and drained
    hearts
4 small tomatoes, cored and chopped

3 tablespoons minced parsley
8 pimiento-stuffed olives, sliced
2 to 3 tablespoons red wine vinegar
salt to taste
pepper to taste
lettuce leaves
wheat crackers

1. Heat oil in skillet and cook onion and garlic until softened.
2. Add artichoke hearts; sauté 6 to 8 minutes longer, or until artichokes are tender.
3. Add tomatoes, parsley and olives; add vinegar and salt and pepper to taste.
4. Cover and simmer 10 minutes.
5. Serve on lettuce leaves with wheat crackers.

Aguacate Azteca
(French Fried Avocado Ring)

Serves 8

½ cup sifted all-purpose flour
2 teaspoons sugar
½ teaspoon baking powder
½ teaspoon salt
¼ teaspoon nutmeg
½ cup milk

1½ teaspoons corn oil
2 teaspoons grated lemon rind
2 California avocados
salad oil for deep frying
Crema

1. Sift together flour, sugar, baking powder, salt and nutmeg.
2. Add milk, oil and lemon rind. Beat until smooth.
3. Cut avocados crosswise into halves; remove seeds.
4. Slice avocados into ¼-inch rings and strip off skin.
5. Dip rings in batter.
6. Fry rings in deep oil heated to 350° F. until golden.
7. Drain on paper towels. Serve with Crema.

Crema

1 cup dairy sour cream
1 teaspoon cinnamon

2 tablespoons sugar

Combine all ingredients; chill.

Asparagus with Vinaigrette

Serves 4 to 6

2 pounds fresh asparagus
ice water
3 tablespoons boiling water
¼ cup Dijon-style mustard
⅓ to ½ cup olive oil

2 tablespoons wine vinegar
salt to taste
pepper to taste
1 teaspoon dried tarragon or 1 tablespoon
 fresh tarragon

1. Snap off white ends of asparagus spears and peel.
2. Parboil 3 to 5 minutes, or until tender.
3. Drain; plunge immediately into ice water. Drain; set aside.
4. Slowly beat boiling water into mustard with a wire whisk. Gradually add oil.
5. Beat constantly with whisk until sauce is thick and creamy.
6. Add vinegar, a little at a time, until sauce is tart.
7. Season to taste with salt and pepper; add tarragon. Serve the sauce alongside the asparagus, dipping each spear.

NOTE: If asparagus are out of season, use 1 pound fresh green beans.

Stuffed Eggplant Dip

Makes 3½ cups

1 large eggplant
1 tablespoon fresh lemon juice
water
¼ cup corn oil
1 green pepper, seeded
 and diced
2 celery stalks, diced
1 onion, diced
1 carrot, finely chopped

1 garlic clove, crushed
1 tablespoon red wine vinegar
2 tomatoes, peeled, seeded,
 and chopped
2 tablespoons chopped cilantro
 leaves
¼ teaspoon dried basil leaves
1 teaspoon salt
⅛ teaspoon cayenne pepper

pita bread or sourdough bread, cut in wedges

1. Cut eggplant in half lengthwise. Scoop out pulp, leaving a ½-inch shell; reserve pulp.
2. Brush inside of shells with lemon juice to prevent browning; set aside.
3. Steam or cook reserved pulp in boiling water until tender, about 8 minutes; set aside.
4. Heat oil in skillet. Add green pepper, celery, onion and carrot. Sauté until vegetables are tender, 3 to 4 minutes.
5. Stir in garlic, vinegar, tomatoes, cilantro, basil, salt, cayenne pepper and cooked eggplant pulp.
6. Cook, stirring occasionally, over medium heat 10 to 15 minutes, or until vegetables are very tender.
7. Spoon cooked vegetable mixture into eggplant shells. Serve warm, or refrigerate 1 hour and serve as a dip with pita or sourdough bread wedges.

Spiced Fruit Cocktail

Makes 3 quarts

1 fresh pineapple
2 pounds fresh peaches
2 pounds fresh pears
1 pound Thompson seedless green
  grapes
1 quart water
2 cups sugar

thin peelings from 1 lemon
¼ cup lemon juice
3 cinnamon sticks
6 whole allspice
1 ginger root, broken into
  pieces

1. Remove crown from pineapple and discard. Peel and cut pineapple into wedges, discarding center core. Cut pineapple into tidbits (makes about 5 cups); set aside.
2. Drop peaches into boiling water for up to 1 minute; slip off skins; set aside.
3. Peel and cut pears into slices; set aside.
4. Remove stems from grapes; set aside.
5. Bring water with remaining ingredients to boiling point in a large heavy saucepot; simmer 5 minutes.
6. Add fruits. Return to boiling point, stirring occasionally. Boil 1 minute.
7. Pack hot fruits into hot sterilized preserving jars, leaving ½-inch headspace.
8. Place 1 additional cinnamon stick in each jar.
9. Cover fruit with boiling syrup, leaving same ½-inch headspace. Seal with lids and screw bands.
10. Stand on a rack in a large kettle of boiling water with enough water to come ½-inch above jars. Return water to boiling; reduce heat; cover and simmer 30 minutes. Remove jars from water and complete the seal, if necessary.

NOTE: If desired, substitute pitted sweet cherries or dark grapes for seedless grapes.

Corn-on-a-Stick

Makes 16 appetizers

4 ears fresh corn
16 wooden skewers
2 cups corn oil
½ pound butter
¼ teaspoon oregano
¼ teaspoon marjoram

¼ teaspoon basil
2 cloves fresh garlic, minced
¼ teaspoon savory
2 tablespoons chopped fresh parsley
salt
white pepper

1. Cut corn into 2-inch chunks and stick a skewer into each chunk.
2. Place chunks in fry basket, sticks up; deep-fry in corn oil 2 minutes. Drain.
3. Melt butter with remaining ingredients except salt and pepper; dunk corn into the bubbling mixture. Sprinkle ears with salt and white pepper.

NOTE: This herbed butter dip is also good for dunking cooked shrimp, rock lobster chunks, plain broiled chicken livers, Vienna sausages and scallops.

Eggplant Squares

Makes about 25 appetizers

1 small eggplant, peeled and cut in
   1-inch cubes
½ cup frozen cholesterol-free egg
   substitute

⅓ cup cornmeal
⅓ cup seasoned bread crumbs
⅓ cup 100% corn oil margarine,
   melted

1. Dip eggplant cubes in egg substitute.
2. Combine cornmeal and bread crumbs; coat cubes evenly with mixture.
3. Dip cubes in margarine and set on baking sheet.
4. Bake in preheated 350° F. oven 15 minutes, or until golden. Serve hot on toothpicks.

Minted Mushrooms

Serves 8 to 10

1 pound small mushrooms,
   quartered, or 2 cans (6 to 8
   ounces each) button mushrooms,
   drained
3 tablespoons olive or salad oil

3 anchovy fillets, minced
2 tablespoons tomato sauce
¾ teaspoon mint flakes, crumbled
¼ teaspoon instant garlic powder
⅛ teaspoon ground black pepper

toast (optional)

1. Sauté mushrooms in hot oil.
2. Add remaining ingredients; cook over medium heat about 5 minutes, stirring frequently.
3. Serve on toast, if desired, as first course, or on picks as appetizer.

Asparagus-Bread Rolls

Makes 16 rolls

1 loaf fresh white bread, unsliced
prepared mustard or mayonnaise

1 can (16 ounces) asparagus,
   drained

1. Cut bread into very thin slices; remove crusts.
2. Spread each slice with mustard or mayonnaise.
3. Roll each slice around an asparagus; fasten with toothpick.
4. Place in shallow pan, cover with damp cloth, and chill thoroughly. Remove picks just before serving.

NOTE: Yield on this depends upon size and number of spears per can.

Tasty Stuffed Mushroom Appetizers

Makes about 2 dozen

5 small, ripe, firm tomatoes
  (1½ pounds)
3 tablespoons butter or margarine
⅓ cup chopped mild onion
1 clove fresh garlic, crushed

½ teaspoon salt
¼ teaspoon oregano, crushed
pinch white pepper
1½ tablespoons minced fresh parsley
1 pound medium-size mushrooms

parsley sprigs (optional garnish)

1. Blanch tomatoes quickly in boiling water, then rinse quickly in cold water. Peel immediately.
2. Cut tomatoes into quarters and remove seeds.
3. Chop coarsely to measure 1½ cups; set aside.
4. Melt 1 tablespoon butter in saucepan. Sauté onion until limp.
5. Add garlic, cook 1 minute longer, stirring over low heat.
6. Stir in salt, oregano, pepper and reserved tomatoes. Simmer, uncovered, until mixture thickens, about 20 to 25 minutes, stirring occasionally.
7. Stir in parsley; set aside.
8. Rinse and pat-dry mushrooms. Remove stems (reserve for soup, stews or sauces).
9. Place mushrooms, cap-side down, in a shallow baking pan.
10. Melt remaining butter; brush each mushroom cap lightly with butter.
11. Place under a preheated hot broiler, 5 inches from heat source; broil 2 minutes.
12. Remove from broiler. Turn mushrooms over; fill with tomato mixture.
13. Bake in preheated 350° F. oven 10 minutes, or until filling is hot.
14. Garnish with parsley sprigs, if desired. Serve piping hot.

NOTE: Fussy, but worth the effort. These are delicious morsels that taste like more!

Toasted Mushroom Rolls

Serves 8 to 10

1 cup chopped mushrooms
1 tablespoon sweet butter
1 tablespoon flour

salt to taste
pepper to taste
⅓ cup milk

bread slices, crusts trimmed

1. Cook mushrooms in butter.
2. Add flour, salt, pepper and milk. Cook until thickened, stirring.
3. Cool. Spread on thin slices of crustless bread; roll up and fasten with toothpicks.
4. Toast in oven until delicately brown on all sides. Serve hot.

Onion Puffs

Makes 120 puffs

1 package (10 ounces) patty shells,
   thawed
real mayonnaise

onion slices
paprika

1. On floured board or pastry cloth, roll out one of the patty shells, forming a 6-inch circle
2. Cut into smaller circles, using 1½-inch cutter. (Makes about 20 puffs.)
3. Place on ungreased baking sheet.
4. Top each circle with a small dab of mayonnaise, an onion slice and another dab o mayonnaise. Sprinkle with paprika. Chill 10 minutes.
5. Repeat with remaining shells.
6. Bake in preheated 400° F. oven 12 to 15 minutes, or until golden. Serve hot.

Onion Wedgies

Serves 6 to 8

2 cups sliced onion
2 tablespoons shortening
1 recipe baking powder biscuits,
   using 1 cup flour
½ teaspoon salt

⅛ teaspoon white pepper
1 egg
¼ teaspoon evaporated milk
   or light cream

1. Sauté onion in shortening until golden and almost tender.
2. Roll dough out on lightly floured board in a circle to fit a 9-inch cake pan. Push dough up sides a bit.
3. Season onion with salt and white pepper; spread on top of dough.
4. Beat egg slightly and mix with evaporated milk; pour over onion.
5. Bake in preheated 450° F. oven 25 minutes.
6. Cut in wedges to serve. Should be nice and hot!

Washington Chips

Makes about 100 chips

3 large (about 1¾ pounds)
   Washington russet potatoes
cold water

oil
salt

1. Scrub potatoes thoroughly; do not pare. Slice crosswise into very thin slices.
2. Soak potatoes 30 minutes in cold water; drain thoroughly.
3. Fry potatoes, a few at a time, in deep, hot oil heated to 375° F. until golden brown.
4. Drain on paper towels; sprinkle with salt. Serve piping hot.

NOTE: Potatoes can be sliced in the food processor. Select potatoes to fit the shape of food processor feed tube.

Spinach Turnovers

Makes 18 turnovers

2 cups all-purpose flour
1¼ teaspoons salt
¾ cup plus 2 tablespoons 100%
   corn oil margarine, divided

4 tablespoons ice water
½ cup chopped onion
1 packages (10 ounces) frozen chopped
   spinach, cooked and drained

1 teaspoon fresh lemon juice

1. Combine flour and 1 teaspoon salt in a large bowl.
2. Cut in ¾ cup margarine until mixture resembles coarse meal.
3. Mix in water and toss lightly.
4. Form dough into a ball; refrigerate at least 15 minutes.
5. Meanwhile, sauté onion in remaining margarine until transparent.
6. Mix in spinach, lemon juice and remaining salt. Set aside.
7. Roll out pastry to ⅛-inch thickness on a lightly floured surface. Cut into 3-inch circles with a floured biscuit cutter.
8. Center 1 teaspoon spinach filling on each pastry circle. Fold in half; seal edges with fork tines.
9. Bake in preheated 400° F. oven 18 to 20 minutes, until golden.

Fried Zucchini Sticks

Makes 4 dozen

¾ cup fine dry bread crumbs
2 tablespoons Parmesan cheese
1 teaspoon onion salt
¼ teaspoon garlic powder
2 egg whites, well beaten

2 tablespoons water
about 1 quart corn oil
½ pound zucchini, cut into
   2 x ¼-inch sticks

1. Stir together bread crumbs, cheese, onion salt and garlic powder in medium bowl.
2. Stir together egg whites and water in small bowl.
3. Pour corn oil into heavy 3-quart saucepan or deep fryer, filling no more than ⅓ full.
4. Heat over medium heat to 375° F.
5. Dip zucchini sticks in egg mixture, then coat with crumbs.
6. Carefully add to oil in single layer. Fry about 1 minute, turning once, or until crisp and lightly browned.
7. Drain on paper towels and serve.

Vegetable Empanaditas
(Turnovers)

Makes 3 dozen appetizers

For the Pastry

2½ cups all-purpose flour
¾ cup corn meal
½ teaspoon salt

½ cup butter or margarine
⅓ cup vegetable shortening
½ cup plus 1 tablespoon cold water

1. Combine flour, corn meal and salt in a large mixing bowl.
2. Cut in butter and shortening until mixture resembles coarse crumbs.
3. Add water, 1 tablespoon at a time, stirring until mixture forms a ball. Set aside.

For the Filling

1 medium zucchini
water
1½ cups shredded sharp
  Cheddar cheese

1 medium tomato, diced
¼ cup minced onion
⅛ teaspoon Tabasco sauce
⅛ teaspoon salt

butter or margarine, melted

1. Trim ends from zucchini; cut into ¼-inch slices.
2. Combine zucchini and a small amount of water in saucepan. Cover and cook about 15 minutes, or until barely tender.
3. Drain and chop zucchini.
4. Combine zucchini with remaining ingredients except butter in small bowl.
5. Roll out half the pastry to ⅛-inch thickness on lightly floured surface.
6. Cut with 3¼-inch round cutter.
7. Place 2 teaspoons filling on half of each circle.
8. Moisten rim of pastry; fold circle over filling. Press edges together; crimp with tines of fork to seal.
9. Repeat, using remaining dough.
10. Place turnovers on greased cookie sheet. Brush tops with melted butter.
11. Bake in preheated 425° F. oven 15 minutes, or until golden brown. Serve hot.

NOTE: If desired, empanaditas can be tightly wrapped before baking and frozen up to 1 month before using. To bake: remove from freezer, let stand at room temperature about 30 minutes, brush lightly with butter, and bake as directed above.

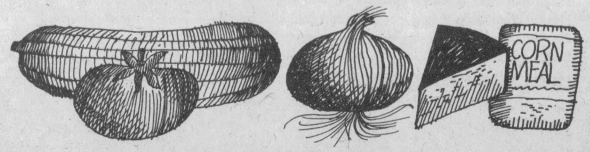

California Walnut Cheese Logs

Makes 2 dozen

1 pound soft Cheddar cheese
2 packages (3 ounces each) cream cheese
¼ pound blue cheese
¼ pound smoked cheese spread
1 tablespoon prepared yellow mustard
1 teaspoon grated onion
3 tablespoons port wine
cream
1 cup chopped California walnuts
assorted crackers

1. Grate Cheddar cheese; combine with 1 package cream cheese, blue cheese and smoked cheese.
2. Mix in mustard, onion and wine, using electric mixer or your hands.
3. Shape into logs about 1 inch in diameter.
4. Blend remaining cream cheese with enough cream to reach spreading consistency; spread over logs and roll in walnuts.
5. Wrap in aluminum foil and chill in refrigerator.
6. Slice and serve on assorted crackers.

Chutney-Cheese Spread

Makes 1 cheese ball

1 package (8 ounces) cream cheese, softened
⅓ cup super-chunk peanut butter
2 tablespoons chopped green onion
2 tablespoons chopped chutney
½ teaspoon curry powder
¼ cup toasted sesame seeds

1. Combine cream cheese and peanut butter until smooth in medium bowl.
2. Stir in onion, chutney and curry powder.
3. Shape into a ball. Roll in sesame seeds.
4. Refrigerate at least 1 hour before serving.

Crab Ball Appetizers

Serves 12 to 16

1 pound crab meat (all shell and cartilage picked out)
8 ounces cream cheese, softened
1 bottle (6 ounces) red cocktail sauce
assorted crackers

1. Mix ingredients; form into a ball.
2. Cover with plastic wrap and refrigerate 2 hours.
3. Serve with crackers.

Cheese Ball

Makes 3 cups

2 packages (8 ounces each) cream
  cheese
2 jars (5 ounces each) sharp
  Cheddar cheese spread
1 jar (5 ounces) process blue cheese
  spread

3 tablespoons wine vinegar
dash of garlic salt
1 cup chopped nuts
assorted crackers

1. Soften cheeses at room temperature.
2. Combine with vinegar and garlic salt; blend until smooth.
3. Refrigerate 30 minutes.
4. Shape into a ball. Roll in chopped nuts. Serve as spread for crackers.

Curried Papaya

Serves 4

2 packages (3 ounces each) cream
  cheese, softened
2 tablespoons minced chutney
1 tablespoon finely sliced scallion
¼ teaspoon curry powder
3 to 6 tablespoons milk

2 papayas, peeled, seeded and cubed
selection of condiment dips: chopped
  salted peanuts, toasted shredded
  coconut, chopped green pepper,
  chopped celery, sliced scallion,
  chopped toasted almonds

1. Combine cream cheese, chutney, scallion and curry powder.
2. Gradually beat in enough milk to make mixture desirable consistency for dipping.
3. Arrange papaya cubes, cheese mixture and condiments in papaya shells or separate
   bowls. Provide guests with picks or forks for dipping papaya into cheese mixture and
   then into condiments.

Danish Cheese Dunk

Serves 8 to 10

1 large Edam cheese
4 strips bacon, crisply cooked
¼ cup green onion, minced

¼ teaspoon garlic salt
1 half-pint heavy cream
1 fresh pineapple

1. Let cheese stand at room temperature at least 24 hours.
2. Remove wax covering; break cheese into small pieces and beat until creamy.
3. Crumble bacon; add to cheese along with green onion and garlic salt.
4. Whip cream until soft peaks form; fold into cheese. Set aside.
5. Cut pineapple into quarters lengthwise through the crown. Remove core. Cut into fruit
   with a curved knife.
6. Dice pineapple wedges; replace in shells. Serve with picks, along with cheese dunk.

Golden Party Cheese Ball

Makes 1¾ cups

2 ounces Swiss cheese
2 ounces blue cheese
2 ounces Camembert cheese

1 package (8 ounces) cream cheese
¼ cup walnut pieces
Golden Delicious apples

1. Bring cheeses to room temperature.
2. Place nuts in bowl of food processor with steel blade; chop coarsely. Remove nuts from bowl.
3. Cut cheeses into 1-inch cubes.
4. Place Swiss cheese in bowl of food processor with steel blade; process until finely chopped.
5. Add blue cheese; repeat.
6. Add Camembert cheese; mix until smooth.
7. Add cream cheese; process until light and creamy.
8. Stir in walnuts.
9. Chill mixture.
10. Shape into ball and serve with cored and sliced Golden Delicious apples.

Edam Cheese Spread

Makes about 1½ cups

1 pound Edam cheese, at room
    temperature
¼ cup real mayonnaise

¼ cup finely chopped sweet pickle
1 teaspoon minced onion
1 teaspoon finely minced pimiento

½ teaspoon cider vinegar

1. Make 8 slits through wax coating ¾ of the way down the cheese.
2. Peel back wax to form petals.
3. Scoop out cheese, leaving a ¼-inch shell; shred cheese.
4. Mix together shredded cheese, mayonnaise, pickle, onion, pimiento and vinegar in small bowl. Beat with fork, rotary beater or electric mixer until well blended and a spreadable consistency.
5. Turn into cheese shell; pull out wax petals slightly to resemble a tulip. Chill.
6. Serve at room temperature or slightly chilled.

Green Balls

Makes about 2 dozen

½ cup grated Swiss cheese
½ cup minced cooked ham
½ teaspoon prepared mustard
1 egg yolk

¼ teaspoon salt
dash white pepper
chopped fresh parsley or chives
sliced cucumber (optional)

1. Blend together cheese, ham, mustard, egg yolk, salt and pepper; chill thoroughly.
2. Form into balls; roll in parsley or chives.
3. Serve on a glass plate with thin slices of cucumber, if desired.

Melon & Cheese Appetizers

Serves 12

1¼ pound Cheddar cheese, shredded
12 ounces blue cheese
3 packages (3 ounces each) cream cheese
3 tablespoons grated onion

1 tablespoon original Worcestershire sauce
¾ cup chopped pecans or walnuts
honeydew melon, cantaloupe and watermelon, cut up

1. Soften cheeses at room temperature.
2. Combine Cheddar, blue and cream cheeses with onion and Worcestershire in a larg
bowl. Knead mixture like bread dough until well blended.
3. Shape into oblong pineapple-like form; sprinkle or roll in nuts.
4. Chill until firm.
5. Place in center of platter.
6. Cut tapered strips of honeydew melon and place on top of cheese, pineapple-leaf style
Surround with cut-up cantaloupe and watermelon.

Fresh Pears with Curried Cheese Ball

Makes 1⅓ cups

1 package (8 ounces) cream cheese, softened
2 tablespoons confectioners' sugar
½ teaspoon curry powder

⅓ cup flaked coconut
⅓ cup chopped pecans
maraschino cherry (optional garnish)

3 winter pears

1. Combine cream cheese, confectioners' sugar, curry powder, coconut and half o
pecans; mix well.
2. Place mixture in small round bowl lined with plastic wrap. Refrigerate until firm.
3. Unmold on serving tray or board; sprinkle with remaining pecans.
4. Garnish with maraschino cherry, if desired.
5. Core and slice pears; serve with curried cheese ball as an appetizer or dessert.

Walnut Cheese Bowl

Makes 1¾ cups

1 (10½ ounces) baby Gouda cheese
½ cup crumbled Roquefort cheese
1 package (3 ounces) cream cheese
2 tablespoons soft butter
½ teaspoon celery seed

⅛ teaspoon dried dill
1 teaspoon real mayonnaise
2 tablespoons brandy
½ cup chopped toasted
   California walnuts

1. Cut a thin slice from top of the Gouda. Scoop out inside, leaving about ¼-inch bowl or shell.
2. Grate cheese taken from inside.
3. Combine grated Gouda with Roquefort and cream cheese, butter, celery seed, dill and mayonnaise. Beat until smooth and well blended.
4. Stir in brandy and all but 1 tablespoon walnuts.
5. Refill Gouda shell, piling mixture high. (Save any extra filling for replenishing the bowl later.)
6. Sprinkle remaining walnuts on top; cover and chill.

Savory Cheese Snacks

Makes about 5 dozen

¾ cup grated sharp Cheddar cheese
¼ cup softened butter
½ cup wheat germ
⅓ cup all-purpose flour

½ teaspoon salt
1 tablespoon water
wheat germ, sesame seeds or poppy seeds
   (for topping)

1. Beat cheese with butter until well blended.
2. Mix in wheat germ, flour, salt and water.
3. Divide dough in half. Roll out each half on lightly floured surface to ⅛-inch thickness.
4. Cut into rounds with floured 1¾-inch cutter.
5. Place on ungreased baking sheets. Sprinkle with wheat germ, sesame seeds or poppy seeds.
6. Bake in preheated 350° F. oven 8 to 10 minutes until golden. (Watch carefully to avoid overbrowning.)
7. Transfer to racks; cool. Store in container with loose-fitting cover.

Roquefort-Brie & Walnut Spread

Makes 1 log

½ pound Roquefort cheese
½ pound Brie cheese
6 tablespoons butter, softened
½ cup ground walnuts

chopped parsley
crackers
fruit (apple wedges, pears)
pumpernickel bread

1. Cut Roquefort and Brie into cubes; blend in food processor along with butter until smooth.
2. Mix in nuts; shape in a log.
3. Cover and refrigerate until firm.
4. Garnish with additional nuts and parsley.
5. Serve with crackers, fresh fruits or pumpernickel bread.

Winter Pears with Camembert Cheese Ball

Makes about 1½ cups

½ pound Camembert cheese
¼ pound sweet butter, softened

¼ cup sherry wine
¼ cup chopped pecans

fresh, ripe pears, cut into wedges

1. Remove rind from cheese; soften at room temperature.
2. With an electric mixer, beat cheese and butter in a small bowl until creamy.
3. Slowly add sherry; continue beating on low speed until light.
4. Cover and refrigerate several hours or overnight.
5. Before serving, shape into ball and roll in chopped pecans.
6. Serve at room temperature with fresh pear wedges.

Wheat Germ Herb Balls

Makes 4½ dozen

2 cups grated sharp Cheddar cheese
1 cup butter, softened
¾ teaspoon thyme leaves, crushed

¼ teaspoon dry mustard
1¾ cups flour
½ cup wheat germ

wheat germ (for topping)

1. Beat cheese with butter, thyme and mustard until blended.
2. Mix in flour and wheat germ until combined. (Do not overbeat.)
3. Shape into 1-inch balls.
4. Dip half of each ball into wheat germ.
5. Place dipped side up on ungreased baking sheet. Bake in preheated 400° F. oven 1(to 12 minutes, or until lightly browned.
6. Remove from baking sheet. Cool on rack.

Super-Duper Dips

Sour Cream-Mayonnaise: Combine equal parts dairy sour cream and mayonnaise. Place in glass bowl. Dust top with paprika. Surround with raw vegetable dippers. Caloric, but wonderful!

Roquefort Cheese: Crumble two 1¼-ounce packages Roquefort cheese and mix well with 8 ounces cottage cheese. Season with 6 tablespoons dairy sour cream and ½ teaspoon onion juice. Nice and tart!

Cottage Cheese with Shrimps: Chop ½ pound cooked, deveined shrimps. Add to 1 package (8 ounces) cottage cheese, 3 tablespoons chili sauce, ½ teaspoon onion juice, ½ teaspoon lemon juice, ½ teaspoon original Worcestershire sauce and 4 tablespoons milk. Makes about 1½ cups.

Herbed Clam Dip: Blend together: 1 cup dairy sour cream; 1 package (3 ounces) cream cheese, softened; 1 can (10½ ounces) minced clams, drained; 2 tablespoons onion powder; ½ teaspoon garlic powder; ½ teaspoon basil leaves (crumbled); ¼ teaspoon ground red pepper; 1 tablespoon fresh lemon juice. Terrific with celery, carrots or chips. Makes 2 cups.

Parsley-Yogurt: Combine: 1 cup real mayonnaise; ½ cup minced parsley; 1 tablespoon Dijon-style mustard; 2 tablespoons minced onion; 1 clove garlic, pressed; 1 teaspoon salt; 1 cup plain yogurt or dairy sour cream. Chill several hours before serving. Makes 2½ cups. Tangy!

Steak 'n' Dip: Combine and whirl in blender: 1 cup real mayonnaise; 2 tablespoons chili sauce; 2 tablespoons capers; 2 tablespoons chopped parsley; 2 teaspoons prepared yellow mustard; 1 clove garlic. Cover and chill 1 hour. Use as marinade for meatballs or leftover cubed, cooked steak. Makes about 1 cup. Versatile and tasty!

Creamy Curry: Combine, blend and chill: 1 cup real mayonnaise; 2 tablespoons chili sauce; 1 teaspoon grated onion; 1 teaspoon tarragon vinegar; ½ teaspoon curry powder. Makes about 1 cup. Terrific with shrimp or raw vegetables!

Roquefort-Sour Cream Dip

Makes about 2 cups

½ pound Roquefort cheese,
  softened
½ small onion, peeled
  and grated
juice of ½ lemon

1 cup salad dressing or mayonnaise
½ cup dairy sour cream
½ teaspoon salt
potato chips or assorted raw
  vegetables

1. Beat all ingredients except potato chips in a blender or electric mixer until smooth.
2. Store in tightly-covered container in refrigerator.
3. Serve as dunking sauce for potato chips or raw vegetables, or served over crisp salad greens as a salad dressing.

Alaska Snow Crab Louis Dip

Makes 1⅔ cups

1¼ cups real mayonnaise
¼ cup chili sauce
¼ cup chopped pimiento-stuffed
  green olives

2 tablespoons chopped green onion
2 tablespoons fresh lemon juice
dash Tabasco sauce
Alaska Snow crab claws

1. Combine all ingredients except crab; chill thoroughly.
2. Serve as dip with crab.

NOTE: *Alaska Snow crab claws are available frozen in 10 to 12-ounce packages. Thaw before serving. This dip is also excellent served with Alaska Snow crab clusters, available frozen, by the pound.*

Green Goddess Dip

Makes about 1½ cups

1 cup chopped parsley
1 can (2 ounces) anchovies
  with oil
½ cup real mayonnaise

2 tablespoons instant minced onion
1 tablespoon tarragon
1 large clove garlic
2 tablespoons vinegar

3 to 4 tablespoons dairy sour cream

1. Combine all ingredients except sour cream in blender. Whirl until smooth.
2. Stir in sour cream.
3. Cover and chill several hours.
4. Serve with assorted vegetable dippers, crackers or cooked shellfish.

Avocado Herb Butter

Makes about 1 pound

1 fully ripe California avocado
1 pound butter, softened
2 tablespoons chopped parsley

½ teaspoon oregano
½ teaspoon ground savory
¼ teaspoon tarragon leaves

2 tablespoons fresh lemon juice

1. Halve avocado lengthwise, twisting gently to separate halves. Whack a sharp knife directly into seed and twist to lift out.
2. Peel avocado; mash with fork or electric mixer.
3. Whip butter with herbs and lemon juice.
4. Gradually beat in avocado until fluffy.

NOTE: *Buy fully ripe avocado or ripen at home at room temperature until soft to the touch.*

Avocado Parsley Dip

Makes about 2 cups

2 ripe California avocados
¾ teaspoon seasoned salt
1 tablespoon fresh lemon juice

dash Tabasco sauce
¼ cup minced parsley
1 tablespoon minced onion

¼ teaspoon original Worcestershire sauce

1. Mash avocados with fork or blender, or pass through sieve.
2. Blend in other ingredients.

Guacamole

Makes about 2 cups

2 soft California avocados,
  coarsely mashed
¾ teaspoon seasoned salt
1 tablespoon lemon or lime juice

¼ cup diced green chilies
¼ teaspoon original Worcestershire sauce
2 tablespoons freshly grated onion
fried tortilla chips

1. Mix ingredients except tortilla chips with a fork.
2. Cover closely and store in refrigerator.
3. Serve with tortilla chips.

Shrimp Dip à la Rose

Serves 12 to 14

1 envelope unflavored gelatin
¼ cup warm water
½ cup minced onion
¾ cup minced celery
1 cup mayonnaise
3 cans (7 ounces each) shrimp,
  rinsed and drained

1 package (8 ounces) cream cheese,
  softened
1 can (10¾ ounces) cream of tomato
  soup
parsley sprigs
crisp crackers

1. Soften gelatin in warm water.
2. Mix together onion, celery, mayonnaise and shrimp; blend well.
3. Heat cheese and soup together in small saucepan; add gelatin.
4. Combine all ingredients except parsley; pour into lightly oiled fish mold, and refrigerate until firm.
5. Unmold on a bed of parsley and serve with crisp crackers.

NOTE: This can be made with 1 pound fresh cooked and cleaned bay shrimp. If desired, make a "fish face," using pimiento-stuffed olive slice for eyes, slivers of green pepper for eyebrows, carrot for the mouth! The kids (of all ages) will applaud your efforts!

Banana Curry Dip

Makes 1¼ cups

1 cup dairy sour cream	bananas, peeled and cut in
¾ teaspoon curry powder	1-inch pieces
¼ teaspoon salt	cherry tomatoes
¼ cup mashed ripe banana	celery pieces
(½ small banana)	raw vegetables as desired

1. Mix together sour cream, curry powder, salt and mashed banana.
2. Chill 30 minutes to develop flavor.
3. Use as a dip with pieces of banana, cherry tomatoes, celery or other raw vegetable desired. For banana pieces, cocktail forks or picks are needed.

Garbanzo Bean Dip

Makes 1¼ cups

1 can (15½ ounces) garbanzo beans, drained (1½ cups)	1 tablespoon vinegar
⅓ cup corn oil	¼ cup chopped green onions
2 tablespoons water	¼ cup chopped parsley
	fresh vegetables (optional)

1. Place beans, oil, water and vinegar in blender container. Cover and blend on high speed 1 to 2 minutes or until puréed. (Stop blender often to push mixture into blades.)
2. Stir together bean mixture, onions, and parsley in small bowl.
3. Cover and refrigerate at least 4 hours to blend flavors.
4. If desired, serve with fresh vegetables.

Vegetable-Cottage Cheese Dip

Makes about 3 cups

¾ cup chopped green or red bell pepper	1 container (16 ounces) small curd cottage cheese, drained
2 tablespoons chopped green onions	assorted crackers (optional)
1 ripe tomato, seeded and chopped	potato chips (optional)
1 envelope (1.4 ounces) butter-milk salad mix	raw vegetables (optional)

1. Combine chopped vegetables and salad dressing mix; fold into cottage cheese.
2. Store in container with screw-top; chill well.
3. Serve with assorted crackers, chips or raw vegetables.

Hummus

Makes 1¼ cups

1 can (15½ ounces) garbanzo beans
⅓ cup toasted sesame seeds
¼ cup fresh lemon juice
½ to 1 teaspoon instant garlic powder
½ teaspoon salt

2 tablespoons corn or olive oil
dash Tabasco sauce
Pita bread or Armenian cracker bread
fresh vegetables: carrot and celery
   sticks, cucumber slices, cherry tomatoes

1. Drain beans.
2. Place sesame seeds in blender or food processor; process until finely ground.
3. Add drained beans; purée.
4. Add lemon juice, garlic powder and salt; process until smooth.
5. Blend in oil and Tabasco.
6. Spoon into a bowl; cover and let stand at room temperature 1 hour to blend flavors.
7. Serve with bread and vegetables for dipping.

NOTE: Cooked or canned Great Northern beans may be substituted for garbanzo beans. To toast sesame seeds: spread seeds in shallow pan, toast in preheated 350° F. oven 8 to 12 minutes, stirring frequently, until golden brown.

Zesty Red Dip for Snow Crab

Makes about 1½ cups dip

2 packages (12 ounces each) frozen
  Alaska Snow crab claws
1 cup chili sauce
⅓ cup dairy sour cream
1 tablespoon prepared horseradish

2 teaspoons fresh lemon juice
1 teaspoon sugar
¼ teaspoon salt
¼ teaspoon garlic powder
¼ teaspoon onion powder

1. Thaw crab.
2. Combine remaining ingredients; chill to blend flavors.
3. Serve as a dip with Alaska Snow crab claws.

Alaska Snow Crab Claws with Snappy Red Dip

Makes about 1¼ cups dip

2 packages (12 ounces each) frozen
  Alaska Snow crab claws
1 cup chili sauce

2 tablespoons fresh lemon juice
1 tablespoon grated onion
1 tablespoon prepared horseradish

1. Thaw crab.
2. Combine ingredients for dip; chill to blend flavors.
3. Serve as a dip with Alaska Snow crab claws.

Cocktail Sauce for Crudité
(Raw, Fresh Vegetables)

Serves 6 to 8

¾ cup catsup
¼ cup chili sauce
2 tablespoons minced celery
1 tablespoon minced onion
2 tablespoons fresh lemon juice
  or vinegar
1 teaspoon original Worcestershire sauce

dash Tabasco sauce
salt to taste
vegetable crudité:
  cucumber slices
  zucchini sticks
  carrot sticks
  radish roses
  celery sticks
  red pepper slices

1. Combine all ingredients except crudité.
2. Chill well.
3. Serve with crudité.

NOTE: A wonderful sauce to serve on cooked seafood too. Crudité served alone makes a terrific first course for dieters!

Cranberry-Pineapple Dunk

Serves 8

1 can (1 pound) cranberry sauce
2 teaspoons vinegar
½ teaspoon sharp prepared mustard

1 can (16 ounces) water-packed
  pineapple, drained
cooked ham, cubed

1. Press cranberry sauce through sieve.
2. Stir in vinegar and mustard.
3. Refrigerate until well chilled.
4. Use as dunk for pineapple chunks or cubes of cooked ham.

NOTE: Nice to use for holidays.

Fruit Dip

Makes 1½ cups

½ cup real mayonnaise
½ cup plain yogurt
⅓ cup apricot preserves
½ teaspoon grated orange rind

fresh fruit: cantaloupe,
  honeydew, bananas,
  strawberries, pineapple,
  apples

1. Combine ingredients except fruit; mix well.
2. Chill.
3. Serve with fresh fruit wedges.

Eggplant Party Dip

Makes 2 cups

1 eggplant (about 1½ pounds)	¼ teaspoon salt
½ cup real mayonnaise	¼ teaspoon garlic salt
½ small onion (optional)	2 teaspoons lemon juice
1 small dill pickle	2 hard-cooked eggs, chopped

assorted crackers

1. Bake eggplant in preheated 400° F. oven 45 minutes, or until soft.
2. Cool; remove skin and stem.
3. Purée in blender until smooth.
4. Add mayonnaise, onion, dill pickle, salt, garlic salt and lemon juice; blend just until smooth.
5. Stir eggs into eggplant mixture.
6. Chill.
7. Serve on assorted crackers.

Helen's Shrimp Spread

Serves 8 to 10

1 package unflavored gelatin	½ cup chopped onion
¼ cup warm water	½ cup chopped green pepper
1 package (3 ounces) cream cheese	1 cup real mayonnaise
1 can (10¾ ounces) cream	1 can (4½ ounces) shrimp,
of tomato soup (undiluted)	shredded
½ cup chopped celery	crackers or rye rounds

1. Dissolve gelatin in water.
2. Melt cheese and soup in small saucepan; beat until smooth.
3. Stir in gelatin.
4. Add remaining ingredients except crackers.
5. Mold in fish mold or small bowl.
6. Cover and chill at least 6 hours, or until set.
7. Unmold; serve with crackers and party rye rounds.

International Spread

Makes about ¾ cup

1 mashed ripe California avocado	3 dashes Tabasco sauce
	French bread (optional)
½ teaspoon garlic salt	crackers (optional)

raw vegetables (optional)

1. Blend avocado, garlic salt and Tabasco.
2. Serve as a spread over French bread (lightly broiled, if desired) or as a dip with crackers or raw vegetables (especially raw zucchini).

Smoky Salmon Cheese Spread for Bagels

Makes about 1½ cups spread

1 can (7¾ ounces) salmon	3 tablespoons sliced green onions
1 package (8 ounces) cream cheese, softened	1 dozen cocktail-size (2½-inch) bagels or 8 regular-size (4-inch) bagels
1 to 2 drops liquid smoke flavoring	butter or margarine

1. Drain and flake salmon, reserving 2 teaspoons salmon liquid.
2. Combine cream cheese, liquid smoke flavoring and salmon liquid; blend thoroughly.
3. Stir in green onions, then fold in salmon.
4. Refrigerate at least 2 hours, or overnight to blend flavors.
5. Just before serving, split, butter and toast bagels.
6. Spread bagel halves generously with cream cheese mixture.
7. Quarter large bagels for appetizer portions.
8. Serve open-faced as an appetizer.

NOTE: Recipe may be doubled, using 2 cans (7¾ ounces each) salmon or 1 can (15¼ ounces) salmon. If desired, chill until firm, 2 to 3 hours; shape into a ball and roll in ½ cup chopped parsley. Serve as a spread with bagels or crackers.

Curried Tuna Dipping Sauce

Makes 4½ cups

2 cans (7 ounces each) tuna, drained	¼ cup chopped chutney
1 cup plain yogurt	¼ cup chopped onion
1 cup cottage cheese	2 tablespoons raisins
¼ cup chopped almonds	1 tablespoon curry powder
	1 teaspoon salt

1 cup cored, chopped apple (do not pare)

1. Flake tuna in medium-size bowl.
2. Mix in remaining ingredients.
3. Chill 1 hour. Serve with Melba toast, breadsticks, crackers and/or carrot and celery sticks.

Foods To Serve on Picks: Cold & Quick

Ham and Cheese: Alternate cubes of boiled or baked ham and Swiss or American cheese on picks.

Ham and Melon: Alternate fresh cubes of cantaloupe or honeydew melon (dipped in lemon or lime) with cubes of ham or canned spiced luncheon meat on picks.

Shrimp Rolls: Place small shrimp in tiny lettuce leaf, spread inside with mayonnaise or horseradish. Roll up and fasten with picks.

Pickles in Blankets: Wrap thin slices of cooked tongue, corned beef or roast beef around tiny sweet-sour pickles or dill pickles. Secure with picks.

Onion and Cheese: Alternate tiny cubes of Swiss or American cheese with tiny pickled cocktail onion and pickle slices on each pick.

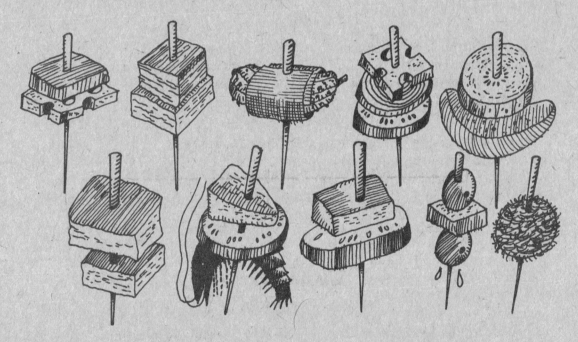

Banana-Orange: Alternate cubes of firm banana (rinsed in lemon to keep from turning brown) and orange segments on pick.

Roast Beef-Melon: Alternate cubes of leftover lean roast beef or lamb with cantaloupe cubes (rinsed in sherry) on pick.

Avocado-Cucumber-Shrimp: Spear cubes of avocado (dipped in lemon), cucumber and cooked, deveined shrimp on pick.

Turkey-Watermelon Pickle: Alternate cubes of leftover cooked or smoked turkey and watermelon pickles on pick.

Grapes 'n' Ham: Alternate large seedless grapes with ham chunks on picks.

Green Cheese Balls: Form cream cheese into balls and roll in chopped parsley or dust with paprika. Place on picks.

Tabbouli Appetizers

Serves 4 or 5

1 cup cooked kasha, whole
⅓ cup chopped green onions
15 fresh mint leaves, chopped
¼ cup chopped parsley
1 large tomato, seeded,
   chopped and salted to taste

1 tablespoon fresh lemon juice
1 tablespoon red wine vinegar
1 tablespoon corn or olive oil
mayonnaise
romaine lettuce leaves

1. Combine all ingredients except lettuce, using enough mayonnaise to moisten kasha.
2. Chill several hours before serving.
3. Place tabbouli in center of plate; surround with romaine leaves to be used as scoops.

Kasha

Makes about 3 cups

1 cup kasha (buckwheat groats)
1 egg, slightly beaten
1 teaspoon salt (use less if broth is
   highly seasoned)

¼ teaspoon pepper
2 cups boiling chicken broth
2 tablespoons butter

1. Combine kasha, egg and seasonings in a 2-quart saucepan.
2. Stir constantly over medium heat 2 minutes, or until egg is set and grains are separated.
3. Add boiling chicken broth.
4. Cover pan tightly and cook gently over low heat 15 minutes, or until kasha grains are tender.
5. If desired, stir in butter.

Tuna Dip

Makes about 1¾ cups

1 package (3 ounces) cream
   cheese, softened
⅔ cup dairy sour cream
1¾ teaspoons Italian seasoning
½ teaspoon salt
½ teaspoon onion powder
¼ teaspoon garlic powder

¾ teaspoon lemon juice
1 can (7 ounces) water-packed tuna,
   drained and flaked
chopped parsley (for garnish)
Italian bread sticks (optional)
vegetable dippers (optional)
crisp salad greens (optional)

1. Beat together cream cheese and sour cream in electric blender until fluffy.
2. Add Italian seasoning, salt, onion and garlic powders and lemon juice; mix well.
3. Blend in tuna.
4. Spoon into serving bowl; garnish with parsley.
5. Serve as dip with Italian bread sticks or vegetable dippers, or as salad dressing over crisp salad greens.

NOTE: Caloric but delightful!

Confetti Egg Salad Spread

Makes 2 cups

6 finely chopped hard-cooked eggs
½ cup minced peanuts
2 tablespoons minced pimiento
2 tablespoons minced ripe olives
1 tablespoon finely chopped parsley

¾ teaspoon salt
½ teaspoon white pepper
¼ cup real mayonnaise
1 tablespoon milk
½ teaspoon original Worcestershire sauce

crackers or bread

1. Combine eggs, peanuts, pimiento, olives, parsley, salt and pepper.
2. Blend in mayonnaise, milk and Worcestershire sauce.
3. Serve with crackers or bread.

Tasty Deviled Eggs

Makes 12 hors d'oeuvres

6 hard-cooked eggs
3 tablespoons real mayonnaise

1 tablespoon original Worcestershire sauce
⅛ teaspoon Tabasco sauce

1. Carefully halve eggs.
2. Remove yolks to a small bowl; reserve whites.
3. Blend mayonnaise, Worcestershire and Tabasco into yolks.
4. Spoon yolk mixture into whites. Chill.

Wheat Germ Pâté

Makes 1½ cups

1 tablespoon minced onion
6 tablespoons butter
2 eggs
⅔ cup vacuum-packed wheat
    germ, regular
¼ teaspoon salt

2 teaspoons lemon juice
½ cup chopped fresh parsley
½ cup plain yogurt
crackers, apple slices or
    zucchini strips

1. Sauté onion in 2 tablespoons butter until tender.
2. Add eggs; scramble to soft stage.
3. Place in blender with wheat germ, salt, lemon juice, parsley and yogurt. Whirl until smooth, scraping down sides often.
4. Cover and refrigerate until ready to use.
5. Serve on crackers, apple slices or zucchini strips.

Chicken Liver Paste

Serves 10 to 12

1 pound chicken livers
1 onion, sliced
water
¾ cup rendered chicken fat
   or melted butter or
   mayonnaise
4 tablespoons grated onion

2 teaspoons salt
½ teaspoon pepper
¼ teaspoon mace
1½ teaspoons dry mustard
⅛ teaspoon anchovy paste
1 tablespoon brandy
French bread

1. Wash livers carefully, removing any discolored areas.
2. Place livers in saucepan with sliced onion and water to cover.
3. Bring to a boil; cover and simmer 20 minutes.
4. Drain completely and discard onion.
5. Grind livers in a food chopper three times, or until very smooth.
6. Add chicken fat, grated onion, salt, pepper, mace, mustard, anchovy paste and brandy. Mix, blending well.
7. Place paste in a mold or other attractive dish, pressing it down until fairly firm. Chill at least 3 hours.
8. If in a mold, turn out onto a plate. Slice the paste about ¼ to ½-inch thick and serve on crusty French bread. Freshly ground pepper may be sprinkled on the top.

NOTE: This is also a fine way to use turkey livers.

Chicken Veronique Appetizers

Makes 45 to 50 appetizers

¾ pound cooked chicken breast,
   cut in ¾-inch cubes
2 tablespoons French dressing
¾ pound Thompson seedless green
   grapes

1 package (3 ounces) cream cheese,
   softened
2 tablespoons orange juice concentrate
3 tablespoons dairy sour cream
⅛ teaspoon Tabasco sauce

1. Toss warm chicken in French dressing; refrigerate 2 hours.
2. Drain well.
3. On frilled toothpicks, skewer 1 grape, 1 piece of chicken and 1 more grape. Arrange on platter.
4. Beat cream cheese until fluffy; beat in orange juice concentrate, sour cream and Tabasco sauce. Serve as a sauce on the side with skewered chicken and grapes.

Seviche

Serves 4 to 6

1 pound flounder or other firm
  white fish
¾ cup fresh lemon juice
1 large firm tomato, peeled
  and chopped

½ cup chopped green pepper
¼ cup chopped fresh parsley
1 clove fresh garlic, minced
1 teaspoon salt
¼ to ½ teaspoon Tabasco sauce
2 tablespoons corn oil

1. Cut fish into finger-length strips; place in glass bowl.
2. Add lemon juice; mix well.
3. Cover and refrigerate 6 to 8 hours. Drain well.
4. Mix together remaining ingredients; add to fish. Mix well and chill.

Seviche Supreme

Serves 4

1 pound red snapper, sea bass or
  sole fillets
grated peel of 1 lemon
juice of 3 lemons
2 large tomatoes, chopped
1 can (7 ounces) green chili salsa

⅓ cup sliced green onions
3 tablespoons chopped parsley
2 tablespoons corn oil
½ teaspoon dried oregano leaves, crushed
¼ teaspoon salt
corn or tortilla chips (optional)

1. Cut fish into ½-inch cubes.
2. Combine fish, lemon peel and juice in glass bowl.
3. Cover, chill, and marinate 8 hours or overnight, until fish is opaque and has a "cooked"
   look; stir occasionally.
4. Add remaining ingredients; chill 30 minutes.
5. Serve as dip with corn or tortilla chips or serve as an appetizer in cocktail glasses,
   garnishing each as desired with lettuce, avocado slices, lemon wedge, or parsley.

NOTE: Great for dieters!

Crab & Water Chestnut Appetizer

Serves 12

1 pound fresh crab meat,
  chopped
½ cup minced water
  chestnuts
2 tablespoons soy sauce

½ cup real mayonnaise
2 tablespoons green onions, minced
water biscuits, crisp wafers or
  wheat thins

1. Combine crab meat, water chestnuts, soy sauce, mayonnaise and green onions.
2. Serve with crisp crackers and your favorite libation.

Alaska King Crab with Sauce Verte

Makes about 1¼ cups sauce

For the Crab

1. Thaw and drain frozen Alaska King crab meat or split legs.
2. Slice into bite-size pieces with a sharp knife. Serve with Sauce Verte.

Sauce Verte

1 cup real mayonnaise	¼ teaspoon dry mustard
¼ cup minced spinach leaves	¼ teaspoon fines herbes
¼ cup minced parsley	1 teaspoon fresh lemon juice

1 tablespoon minced chives or 1 teaspoon freeze-dried chives

1. Combine mayonnaise with remaining ingredients; blend well.
2. Cover; chill at least 2 hours to blend flavors.
3. Serve as a dipping sauce to accompany Alaska King crab.

Crab Louie

Serves 2

½ head iceberg lettuce	2 hard-cooked eggs, peeled and
1½ cups finely shredded cabbage	quartered
2 to 3 cups flaked cooked crab,	Dressing
chilled	

1. Arrange lettuce and cabbage on 2 salad plates.
2. Arrange shrimp on lettuce; surround with egg.
3. Just before serving, top with Dressing.

Dressing

¾ cup mayonnaise	¼ cup chopped green onion
¾ cup plain yogurt	¼ cup chopped sweet pickle
⅓ cup chili sauce	salt to taste
¼ cup chopped green pepper	lemon juice to taste

oregano to taste

1. Mix together mayonnaise, yogurt, chili sauce, green pepper, green onion and sweet pickle.
2. Season to taste with salt, lemon juice and oregano.

King Crab Split Legs with Horseradish Dip

Makes 1¼ cups

1 cup real mayonnaise
¼ cup half-and-half
2 tablespoons fresh lemon juice
2 teaspoons prepared cream-style
    horseradish

2 teaspoons hot dry mustard
¼ teaspoon Tabasco sauce
¼ teaspoon salt
Alaska King crab legs, split
    and cut into 1-inch lengths

chopped parsley (optional garnish)

1. Combine all ingredients except crab; chill thoroughly.
2. Garnish with chopped parsley, if desired, and serve as a dip with the crab.

NOTE: Alaska King crab split legs are available frozen in 10- to 12-ounce packages. Thaw before serving.

New Orleans Crab Spread

Makes 2 cups

1 can (12 ounces) crab meat, frozen
¼ cup tarragon vinegar
⅓ cup real mayonnaise
3 tablespoons chopped pimiento
2 tablespoons chopped green onion

1 teaspoon salt
½ teaspoon freshly ground pepper
1 tablespoon drained capers
    (for garnish)
assorted chips, crackers or raw
    vegetables

1. Thaw frozen crab meat; drain when thawed. Remove any remaining shell or cartilage.
2. Flake the crab meat.
3. Pour vinegar over crab meat; chill for 30 minutes, then drain.
4. Add mayonnaise, pimiento, onion, salt, and pepper. Mix thoroughly.
5. Garnish with capers.
6. Serve with chips, crackers or vegetables.

Smoked Oysters

canned smoked oysters
crisp crackers (optional)

buttered toast (optional)
parsley or watercress (optional garnish)

1. Drain oysters.
2. Place on picks, or crisp crackers or fingers of buttered toast.
3. Garnish with parsley or watercress, if desired.

Shrimp Avocado Cocktail in Artichokes

Serves 4

⅔ cup chili sauce
⅔ cup catsup
4 teaspoons prepared horseradish
3 tablespoons fresh lemon juice
1 medium California avocado,
   peeled and diced

4 medium artichokes, cooked and
   chilled
¾ cup cooked, shelled small shrimp,
   or 1 package (6 ounces) frozen
   small shrimp, thawed, or 1 can
   (6 ounces) shrimp, drained

parsley (optional garnish)

1. Combine chili sauce, catsup, horseradish and 1 tablespoon lemon juice until well mixed. Chill.
2. Toss avocado with remaining lemon juice until well coated; drain.
3. Gently spread center leaves of chilled artichokes.
4. Spoon 1 tablespoon cocktail sauce into each artichoke center.
5. Stuff artichokes evenly with avocado and shrimp; top each with 1 additional tablespoon cocktail sauce.
6. Garnish with parsley, if desired.
7. Pass remaining cocktail sauce as dip for leaves. Serve immediately. Great as first course or supper main course!

Shrimp Pâté

Makes 3½ cups pâté

1 envelope unflavored gelatin
¼ cup fresh lemon juice
¼ cup water
2 cups dairy sour cream
¾ cup chili sauce

2 tablespoons horseradish
½ pound shrimp, shelled, cleaned,
   cooked and finely chopped
   (about 1½ cups)
assorted crackers and party-size breads

parsley (optional garnish)

1. Sprinkle gelatin over lemon juice and water in saucepan. Stir over low heat until gelatin dissolves, about 3 minutes; cool.
2. Blend in sour cream, chili sauce and horseradish.
3. Fold in shrimp.
4. Turn into 3½-cup loaf pan or oblong mold; chill until firm.
5. Unmold onto serving plate. Arrange crackers and party-size bread around pâté.
6. Garnish, if desired, with parsley.

Shrimp & Stuffed Celery Canapés

Serves 8

2 cups cooked or canned shrimp
½ cup diet French dressing
1 package (3 ounces) Roquefort cheese
1 package (3 ounces) cream cheese

1 tablespoon minced onion
¼ cup half-and-half
20 crisp celery sticks, about 3½ inches long

1. Remove black vein from shrimp.
2. Marinate shrimp 1 hour in French dressing in refrigerator.
3. Meanwhile, mash together Roquefort and cream cheeses, onion and half-and-half. Use the filling to stuff celery sticks.
4. Drain shrimp and insert a toothpick in each.
5. Arrange shrimp in center of a serving plate, with stuffed celery sticks around them.

Tower of Shrimp

Makes 8 canapés

2 pounds jumbo shrimp, parboiled 3 minutes with lemon juice to taste
1 garlic clove, crushed
¼ cup fresh lemon juice
1 cup olive oil

⅛ teaspoon cayenne
1 teaspoon salt
thin onion slices
thin slices of orange
black pitted olives
cherry tomatoes

parsley (for garnish)

1. Simmer shrimp, garlic, ¼ cup lemon juice and ¼ cup olive oil 5 minutes.
2. Discard garlic.
3. Combine remaining ingredients in bowl. Chill overnight.
4. To arrange centerpiece:
   a. Shell shrimp, leaving tails intact.
   b. Arrange a row of shrimp on toothpicks around the base of a styrofoam cone.
   c. Follow with a layer of pitted black olives, a layer of shrimp, and a layer of cherry tomatoes.
   d. Repeat to the top.
   e. Garnish with parsley.

Smoked Fish Pâté

Makes ⅔ cup

3 cups flaked, smoked fish
2 packages (8 ounces each) cream
    cheese, softened
3 tablespoons fresh lemon juice

2 tablespoons grated onion
3 tablespoons chopped parsley
parsley sprigs (for garnish)
assorted crackers

1. Remove skin and bones from fish; flake.
2. Combine cream cheese, lemon juice and onion; whip until smooth and fluffy.
3. Stir in fish and chopped parsley. Chill for 1 hour.
4. Garnish with parsley sprigs. Serve with crackers.

Spicy Gefilte Fish

Serves 6 to 7

2 pounds ground freshwater fish:
    white fish, yellow pike, carp,
    buffalo or any combination, plus
    heads and bones
2 cups onions, sliced
2 carrots, sliced
2 ribs celery, sliced

3 teaspoons salt
1 teaspoon Tabasco sauce
water
2 large onions, grated
1 carrot, grated
2 eggs
½ cup ice water

2 to 3 tablespoons matzoh meal

1. Combine fish bones and heads, sliced onion, sliced carrots, celery, 2 teaspoons salt, ½ teaspoon Tabasco and enough water to measure 4 inches deep in a large stockpot.
2. Bring mixture to a boil.
3. Combine ground fish, grated onion, grated carrot, eggs, ice water, remaining salt and remaining Tabasco sauce.
4. Add enough matzoh meal to form a mixture stiff enough to shape into balls; mix well.
5. Shape fish into balls; gently place in boiling water.
6. Simmer, partially covered, 2 hours.
7. Remove fish balls and carrots from stockpot; strain and reserve fish stock.
8. Store gefilte fish in stock.
9. Serve hot or cold with stock and additional Tabasco, if desired. Serve as an hors d'oeuvre or first course at a sit-down dinner.

Tuna Bites Superb

Makes 3 dozen appetizers

2 cans (7 ounces each) solid
  white albacore tuna, drained
4 ounces cream cheese, softened

1 ounce blue cheese, crumbled
2 tablespoons green onion, minced
¾ cup parsley, minced

cherry tomatoes (for garnish)

1. Combine tuna with cream cheese, blue cheese and green onion in large bowl; blend well.
2. Chill mixture 1 hour.
3. Form into small balls; roll in parsley.
4. Place in a flat dish; cover and chill until serving time.
5. Arrange on a platter; garnish with cherry tomatoes.

Tuna Mosaic Pâté

Yields 6 to 8 appetizer servings

2 cans (7 ounces each) tuna
½ cup soft bread crumbs
¼ cup milk
¼ cup fresh lemon juice
1 small onion, grated
2 eggs
½ teaspoon dried leaf tarragon

¼ teaspoon salt
dash pepper
3 thin lemon slices, peeled
14 whole, fresh green beans, uncooked
3 medium whole carrots, cooked
½ cup frozen peas, thawed
black olives (for garnish)

crackers, water biscuits, melba rounds or crudité

1. Drain tuna. Combine tuna with bread crumbs, milk, lemon juice, grated onion, eggs, tarragon, salt and pepper in large bowl of electric mixer; beat until tuna is finely flaked.
2. Center a row of lemon slices in bottom of a 7⅜ x 3⅝ x 2¼-inch loaf pan.
3. Spread thin layer of tuna mixture in pan.
4. Layer green beans lengthwise over tuna mixture, leaving spaces between beans.
5. Spread thin layer of tuna over beans, pressing mixture between the beans.
6. Arrange carrots lengthwise over tuna; cover with tuna mixture.
7. Add peas; cover with tuna, pressing down firmly.
8. Bake in preheated 375° F. oven 45 minutes.
9. Cool and refrigerate until chilled through.
10. Turn out onto serving plate; garnish with slivers of black olives. Serve with crackers, water biscuits, melba rounds, or crudité.

Happy Shrimps

Makes 10 to 14 appetizers

2 pounds medium shrimp, cooked
  cleaned and deveined
⅔ cup minced celery
¼ cup thinly sliced scallions
2 tablespoons minced chives
1 cup corn oil
⅓ cup chili sauce

3 tablespoons fresh lemon juice
1 tablespoon prepared horseradish
½ teaspoon prepared mustard
½ teaspoon paprika
½ teaspoon salt
⅛ teaspoon Tabasco sauce
rye rounds (optional)

assorted greens (optional)

1. Combine shrimp, celery, scallions and chives in large bowl or refrigerator container.
2. Combine remaining ingredients for sauce in separate bowl; mix well.
3. Pour sauce over shrimp-vegetable mixture; mix gently.
4. Cover securely; refrigerate 12 hours before serving.
5. Serve as an appetizer, chilled in large bowl with picks and plates for buffet service, or on hot toasted rye rounds, or as a salad on a bed of assorted greens.

NOTE: Everyone will smile when they eat these, hence the name!

Salmon Pâté

Serves 12

1 envelope unflavored gelatin
¾ cup cold water
1 cup salad dressing or
  mayonnaise
1 can (15½ ounces) red salmon,
  drained and flaked

½ cup minced celery
¼ cup minced green pepper
1 teaspoon minced onion
salt (optional)
pepper (optional)
½ cup heavy cream, whipped

crisp salad greens or watercress (for garnish)

1. Combine gelatin and cold water in small saucepan; stir until gelatin softens. Place over low heat, stirring until gelatin dissolves.
2. Let mixture cool.
3. Gradually add cooled gelatin mixture to salad dressing, blending well; chill until partially set.
4. Stir in salmon, celery, green pepper and onion; taste to correct seasonings, adding salt and pepper if necessary.
5. Fold in whipped cream; pour into a lightly oiled 1-quart mold or two 6 x 3½-inch loaf pans. Chill pâté until firm.
6. Unmold on serving plate garnished with greens or watercress.

NOTE: Terrific served with hot bread!

Beef Steak Tartare

Serves 12

1 pound freshly ground lean beef
  sirloin or round steak
½ cup minced onion
1 tablespoon original Worcestershire
  sauce

1 teaspoon salt
few drops Tabasco sauce
1 egg yolk
anchovy fillets (for garnish)
capers (for garnish)

melba toast, Swedish rye bread or crackers

1. Combine ground beef with onion, Worcestershire sauce, salt and Tabasco sauce.
2. Shape into mound on serving plate. Make indentation in center and fill with egg yolk.
3. Garnish with anchovy fillets and capers as desired. Spread on melba toast, thinly sliced dark Swedish rye bread or crackers.

Yogurt Beef Ball Appetizers

Makes 48 beef balls

1 pound lean ground beef
1 envelope onion soup mix
2 containers (8 ounces) plain
  yogurt

⅓ cup fine bread crumbs
1½ teaspoons basil, crumbled
½ teaspoon salt
1 tablespoon butter or margarine

1. Mix beef with ½ envelope soup mix, ¼ cup yogurt, bread crumbs, basil and salt. Form into 1-inch balls.
2. Brown a few balls at a time in butter over medium heat.
3. For dip, combine remaining yogurt with remaining soup mix; let stand 30 minutes.
4. Serve hot beef balls on toothpicks with cool yogurt dip.

Cherry Ham Canapés

Makes 16 canapés

1 package (3 ounces) cream cheese,
  softened
1 tablespoon orange juice
½ teaspoon grated orange peel

2 tablespoons finely chopped walnuts
16 slices party rye bread
4 slices thinly sliced ham
16 fresh sweet cherries, pitted

1. Combine cream cheese, orange juice, peel and walnuts.
2. Spread ½ tablespoon cheese mixture on each slice of bread.
3. Cut each slice of ham into 4 triangles; place one triangle on top of cream cheese mixture.
4. Top each canapé with a pitted cherry, secured with a toothpick.

Ground Ham Spread

Makes 4 cups

3 cups minced ham
1 package (8 ounces) cream cheese, at room temperature
⅓ cup chopped chutney

1¼ teaspoons Tabasco sauce
1 cup chopped pecans
pimiento strips
parsley

assorted crackers

1. Combine ham, cream cheese, chutney and Tabasco sauce in small bowl; mix until smooth.
2. Stir in ⅔ cup pecans.
3. Line a 4-cup mold with clear plastic wrap; pack ham mixture firmly into mold. Refrigerate 1 to 2 hours.
4. Turn mold out onto serving platter; remove plastic wrap.
5. Press remaining pecans on sides and top of mold. Decorate with strips of pimiento and parsley. Serve with assorted crackers around mold.

Oahu Appetizer

Makes 2 cups

2 packages (3 ounces each) cream cheese
1 can (4½ ounces) deviled ham
1 teaspoon prepared yellow mustard

2 cups shredded Cheddar cheese
2 tablespoons chopped chives
½ cup chopped macadamia nuts
paprika

assorted crackers

1. Beat together cream cheese, ham and mustard in a small mixing bowl.
2. Stir in Cheddar cheese and chives.
3. Chill to handling.
4. Shape in a ball; roll in nuts. Sprinkle with paprika. Serve with assorted crackers.

Salami Cornucopia

whole wheat bread
cream cheese, softened

salami slices
blue cheese

1. Cut ovals from whole wheat bread.
2. Spread with softened cream cheese.
3. Shape salami slices into cornucopias; fill with softened blue cheese through a star tube.
4. Place salami cornucopias on ovals of bread and pipe a border of cream cheese on edge of bread with pastry tube.

NOTE: A good leftover idea.

Easy Liverwurst Pâté

Makes 3½ cups

1 pound liverwurst, at room
   temperature
¼ cup bourbon
1 cup real mayonnaise
1 teaspoon unflavored gelatin
½ cup cold chicken or beef broth

2 teaspoons lemon juice
2 teaspoons original Worcestershire sauce
⅛ teaspoon pepper
⅛ teaspoon garlic powder
parsley or watercress (for garnish)
French bread

1. Grease an 8½ x 4½ x 2½-inch loaf pan or a 3½-cup mold. Set aside.
2. Mix liverwurst and bourbon until smooth. Stir in mayonnaise.
3. Sprinkle gelatin over broth in a small saucepan. Heat over low heat, stirring often, until gelatin is completely dissolved.
4. Stir broth into liverwurst mixture until blended.
5. Add lemon juice, Worcestershire sauce, pepper and garlic powder; mix well.
6. Turn mixture into greased pan. Cover and chill overnight.
7. Unmold and garnish with parsley or watercress. Serve with French bread.

Make-Ahead Assorted Canned Meat Platter

Serves 8

1 can (12 ounces) spiced ham
2 cans (12 ounces each) corned
   beef
1 medium-size jar tongue

crisp salad greens or watercress
   (for garnish)
assorted breads/soft rolls
condiments: mustard, mayonnaise,
   horseradish

1. Chill meats several hours for better slicing.
2. Use very sharp knife to cut ham and corned beef into thin, crosswise slices.
3. Lay tongue, flat-side down, on cutting board, with tip of tongue to your left. Cut thin, crosswise slices with sharp knife.
4. Arrange meats, fan-shaped, on platter; garnish with salad greens or watercress.
5. Serve with a basket of assorted breads or soft rolls and condiments (mustard, mayonnaise or horseradish).

NOTE: Nice for cocktail buffet when you are the cook-host!

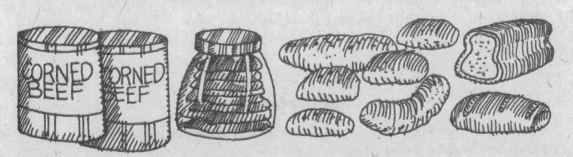

Frosted Tuna Party Loaf

Serves 8 to 10

Savory Tuna Sandwich Filling

1 can (6½ ounces) tuna, drained
 and flaked
¼ cup chopped celery

¼ cup mayonnaise
2 tablespoons pickle relish
2 tablespoons capers, chopped

Mix all ingredients well in a medium-size bowl; set aside.

Egg Salad Sandwich Filling

2 hard-cooked eggs, chopped
¼ cup chopped green or
 red pepper

¼ cup real mayonnaise
⅛ teaspoon salt
dash of pepper

dash dry mustard

Combine all ingredients in small bowl; blend well. Set aside.

To Assemble

1 cucumber, sliced paper thin
 (25 to 30 slices)
1 loaf white bread, unsliced
2 tablespoons butter or margarine,
 softened to room temperature

Savory Tuna Sandwich Filling
Egg Salad Sandwich Filling
2 packages (8 ounces each) cream
 cheese, softened to room
 temperature

⅓ cup chopped parsley

1. Place cucumber slices on paper towel to absorb excess moisture.
2. Cut all crusts from bread with sharp knife.
3. Place loaf on its side; cut into 5 even lengthwise slices.
4. Spread first slice with soft butter; cover with overlapping cucumber slices.
5. Spread second slice with half of Savory Tuna Sandwich Filling.
6. Spread third slice with Egg Salad Sandwich Filling.
7. Spread fourth slice with remaining Tuna Filling.
8. Stack slices; top with fifth slice of bread.
9. Beat cream cheese until smooth; spread on top and sides of loaf.
10. Gently press chopped parsley on sides of loaf.
11. Decorate with Flower Garnish.
12. Slice at the table.

Flower Garnish

Use strips of green pepper or cucumber skin for flower stems and circles of carrots, and radishes or black or green olives for flowers.

Ribbon Sandwiches

1. Trim crusts from 1 loaf each unsliced white and whole wheat sandwich bread.
2. Cut each loaf into 5 to 7 horizontal slices.
3. Spread butter or margarine and filling of your choice on 1 white slice and 1 dark slice. Stack.
4. Top with an unspread bread slice, the same color as the bottom slice.
5. Repeat with remaining slices, alternating colors.
6. Wrap tightly in foil or plastic wrap. Refrigerate or freeze 2 to 4 hours, or several days.
7. Partially thaw before cutting each stack into 15 to 20 crosswise slices; cut each slice in half for small sandwiches.
8. Cover and refrigerate until served.

Some Tips for Making Ribbon Sandwiches

- Use day-old bread and order it pre-sliced in lengthwise slices.
- Use compound butters (lemon flavored or anchovy-flavored butter) or cream-cheese-flavored spreads as alternates to softened butter for flavor accents. Cream cheese can also be tinted and studded with tiny morsels of candied ginger or candied cherries if "sweet-flavored" sandwiches are desired to go with tea.
- Do not use watercress or lettuce if bread is to be frozen. Egg yolks, meats, fish, poultry and butter and cream cheese spreads freeze the best.
- Keep in mind your guest list when planning party sandwiches. For example, you will have few takers if the majority of your guests are dieting. Plan accordingly. A crudite (raw vegetables) will probably be a better choice than ribbon sandwiches for weight-watchers!
- Sandwiches freeze better if stacked in single rows on flat baking sheet. If stacking is necessary, put double layer of waxed paper between items and package in airtight freezer containers or moisture-proof freezer bags or wrap.
- Garnish service plate around sandwich with edible items such as cherry tomatoes, parsley, cucumber, etc.

Open-Face Sandwiches

Trim crusts from 1 loaf each unsliced whole wheat and white bread. Cut each loaf into 5 to 7 horizontal slices. (Bakeries will do this for you if you order a few days ahead.) Use cookie cutters in various shapes to cut into various shapes to suit the occasion. For example: bells and hearts for weddings, animal designs for children's parties or baby showers, trees and balls for Christmas. Spread surface with softened butter or cream cheese before adding a filling. Allow about ¼ pound softened butter or margarine for every 1-pound loaf of bread. Work with a small amount at a time as bread dries out quickly. Keep covered or refrigerated until ready to use. If desired, use pastry tube to pipe edges of sandwiches to give a finish or border. Individual garnishings make attractive morsels to please the palate as well as the eye. Some to include: cucumber, pimiento-stuffed olives, mushrooms, hard-cooked eggs, carrots, radishes, pickles, parsley or watercress sprigs. (Slice thinly and press into each sandwich.) Sandwiches can be made about an hour or two in advance, then refrigerated until ready to use.

Assorted Fillings for Cream Puffs & Stacked Sandwiches

Crab Filling: Mix together 2 packages (3 ounces each) softened cream cheese, 1½ tablespoons dry white wine, 1 teaspoon lemon or lime juice, dash seasoned salt, ½ teaspoon grated onion, 1 can (6 ounces) drained crab meat (picked over and flaked), and 1 teaspoon real mayonnaise (to moisten). Makes 1 cup.

Tuna Filling: Combine and blend 1 can (6½ ounces) tuna (drained and flaked), ⅓ cup real mayonnaise, ⅓ cup minced celery and 1 tablespoon chopped pickle. Makes about 1½ cups.

Chicken or Turkey Filling: Combine 2 cups ground, cooked or smoked chicken or turkey with ⅓ cup minced celery, ⅓ cup real mayonnaise and a dash each of salt and white pepper. Makes 1½ cups.

Corned Beef Filling: Combine 2 cups cooked corned beef (minced), 1 tablespoon prepared yellow mustard, 2 teaspoons prepared horseradish, 2 teaspoons minced sweet pickle and ½ cup real mayonnaise. Makes 2⅓ cups.

Egg Salad Filling: Combine 1 to 2 hard-cooked eggs (minced), ¼ cup chopped celery, ¼ cup chopped parsley, 2 tablespoons plain yogurt, 2 tablespoons real mayonnaise. Makes about 1 cup.

Blue Cheese Filling: Combine 1½ packages (8 ounces each) softened cream cheese, 4 ounces blue cheese (crumbled), ¼ cup real mayonnaise, ¼ teaspoon onion powder, ¼ teaspoon thyme, and ¼ teaspoon white pepper. Makes 2 cups.

Chicken and Mushroom Spread: Combine 1 cup cooked chopped chicken or turkey, ½ cup chopped almonds, 1 tablespoon minced celery, handful chopped mushrooms and about ⅓ cup real mayonnaise (to moisten). Makes about 1½ cups.

Cream Cheese with Avocado: Soften 5 ounces cream cheese and combine with 1 medium avocado (peeled and mashed), ¼ teaspoon onion juice and a dash of salt. Makes about 2 cups.

Watercress Cream Cheese: Cream 6 ounces cream cheese with 1 tablespoon fresh lemon or lime juice, ¼ teaspoon minced onion and ¼ teaspoon celery salt. Chop in 1 small bunch watercress. Blend well and refrigerate 1 hour (allows flavors to marry) before using. Makes about 1½ cups.

Stuffed French Bread

Makes about 40

1 loaf French bread (20 inches)
2 packages (8 ounces each)
   cream cheese, softened
½ cup real mayonnaise
½ teaspoon seasoned salt
⅛ teaspoon garlic powder
1 jar (4 ounces) diced pimientos,
   well drained

¼ cup chopped parsley

1. Cut bread crosswise. With fork, hollow out center, leaving ½-inch shell; set aside.
2. In medium bowl, with mixer set at high speed, beat remaining ingredients until well blended.
3. Pack mixture into bread.
4. Wrap in plastic wrap; chill at least 3 hours.
5. Just before serving, cut into ½-inch slices.

Chicken Stacks

Makes about 40 stacks

For Chicken Salad Mixture

½ cup minced toasted almonds
2 cups minced cooked chicken
½ cup minced water chestnuts
2 tablespoons lemon juice
½ cup mayonnaise
salt to taste
white pepper to taste
rosemary to taste

thyme to taste

Combine ingredients; chill until ready to make sandwiches.

To Assemble

1 loaf whole wheat bread
1 loaf white bread
whipped butter
Chicken Salad Mixture
softened cream cheese
pimiento-stuffed olives, sliced
   (for garnish)

1. Cut whole wheat bread and white bread into same-size rounds; cut round opening in center of white bread rounds.
2. Spread wheat rounds first with whipped butter, then with Chicken Salad Mixture.
3. Spread white rounds with butter and place on top of chicken mixture.
4. Cut olive slices in half; place half an olive, cut-side up, in center of each sandwich.

Avocado Mousse

Serves 8

1 envelope unflavored gelatin
¼ cup water
1 cup dairy sour cream
1 ripe avocado, peeled and mashed
¼ cup chopped green onions

2 teaspoons fresh lemon juice
⅛ teaspoon Tabasco sauce
cucumber slices, carrot sticks,
   radish roses, or cooked shrimp,
   or assorted crackers

1. Soften gelatin in water; heat and stir until dissolved. Cool.
2. Combine sour cream, avocado, green onions, lemon juice and Tabasco. Stir in gelatin.
3. Pour into greased 2-cup mold; chill until firm.
4. Unmold and serve with raw vegetables, shrimp or crackers.

Stuffed Celery with Variations

1 bunch celery (select
   only tender white stalks,
   showing no discoloration)
¼ cup minced toasted almonds
1 package (3 ounces) cream cheese

1 tablespoon chili sauce
1 teaspoon curry powder (less,
   if desired)
salt to taste
white pepper to taste

parsley sprigs (optional)

1. Wash celery and leave tips of leaves on stalks or remove leaves from coarse outer stalks.
2. Crisp in ice water; dry thoroughly on paper towels before stuffing.
3. Combine almonds, cream cheese, chili sauce, curry powder, salt and pepper; with a pastry tube, fill celery grooves.
4. Arrange on serving plate; garnish with parsley, if desired.

Avocado Filling (Variation)

Mash ripe peeled avocado. Sprinkle with fresh lemon or lime juice (to prevent discoloration). Season avocado pulp to taste with salt and white pepper. If desired, add chopped pimiento-stuffed olives. Moisten slightly with mayonnaise. Stuff celery as directed.

Crab Meat-Cream Cheese Filling (Variation)

Drain 1 can (6½ ounces) crab meat. Remove cartilage. Mash crab meat with 1 package (3 ounces) softened cream cheese. Flavor with Marsala wine to taste. Season to taste with salt and freshly ground black pepper. Stuff celery as directed.

Ham-Egg Filling (Variation)

Soften contents of 1 small can deviled ham with one chopped hard-cooked egg. Add enough mayonnaise to moisten. Stuff celery as directed.

NOTE: Stuffed celery makes a popular finger food at cocktail parties or buffets. It's a great way to use leftovers too, such as minced cooked chicken, turkey or ham. You can also use minced clams, tuna, pickles, pimiento and your choice of condiments to add flavors.

British Glazed Nuts

Makes about 2½ pounds glazed nuts

2 cups granulated sugar
1 cup corn syrup
½ cup water
1 tablespoon Angostura aromatic
   bitters

1 cup butter
3 cups assorted shelled nuts:
   pecans, filberts, walnuts, etc.
1 teaspoon baking soda

1. Combine sugar, syrup and water in a large saucepan.
2. Add Angostura and butter; boil until a candy thermometer registers 300° F., or until a small amount, when dropped into cold water, forms a lollipop-like ball.
3. Heat nuts in a 250° F. oven until warm, about 15 minutes.
4. Stir nuts and baking soda into syrup; stir quickly to blend.
5. Divide mixture equally between two well-buttered 15 x 10 x 1-inch pans. Using two greased forks, spread out nuts into a single layer. Cool.
6. Break into pieces and store in an airtight container in a cool, dry place.

Cucumber Sherbet

Serves 8 to 10

2 cups tomato juice
1 teaspoon gelatin, softened in
   1 tablespoon cold water
½ teaspoon salt
1 teaspoon sugar
1 teaspoon prepared horseradish

1 medium cucumber, peeled and
   grated
2 egg whites, stiffly beaten
1 teaspoon onion juice
grated rind of 1 lemon
chilled lettuce

8 to 10 cooked, deveined shrimp (for garnish)

1. Bring tomato juice to a boil; remove from heat.
2. Add softened gelatin; stir until dissolved.
3. Add salt, sugar and horseradish; cool quickly.
4. Freeze to a mush in ice cube tray.
5. Place ½ of frozen sherbet in chilled bowl; beat until fluffy with rotary beater.
6. Fold in cucumber, stiffly beaten egg whites, onion juice and lemon rind.
7. Return to ice cube tray (with remaining sherbet). Set control to coldest point. Freeze 30 minutes.
8. Beat again, return to tray and freeze, undisturbed, for 2 hours.
9. Serve on beds of crisp lettuce in sherbet glasses, garnished with shrimp.

Duchesses
(Small Cocktail Cream Puffs)

Makes about 4 dozen small puffs

½ cup butter
⅛ teaspoon salt
1 cup boiling water

1 cup sifted all-purpose flour
3 large eggs, unbeaten (if small, use
   4 eggs)

1. Add butter and salt to boiling water in saucepan; stir over medium heat until mixture reboils.
2. Reduce heat, add flour all at once; beat vigorously until mixture leaves sides of pan. (Mixture should be smooth.)
3. Remove from heat. Add eggs, one at a time, beating thoroughly after each addition.
4. Use 1 teaspoon paste to shape each puff (very small).
5. Bake on lightly greased cookie sheets in preheated 450° F. oven about 8 minutes, or until points of puff begin to brown.
6. Reduce heat to 350° F. and continue baking 10 to 12 minutes longer.
7. When cool, cut a small slit carefully on one side; open and fill with crab meat salad or filling of your choice (see page 88). Makes a delicious morsel!

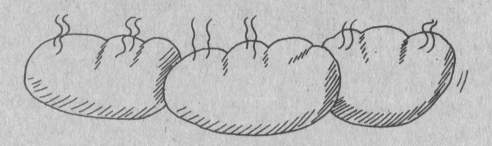

Melon on Skewers

Serves 6

1 cup cantaloupe balls or cubes
1 cup watermelon balls or triangles
1 cup honeydew balls or wedges

1 cup Persian or Crenshaw melon
   cut in cubes or balls
Mint Marinade

1. Place prepared melons in bowl.
2. Add Mint Marinade and chill, covered, for a few hours.
3. Drain and thread on skewers, alternating shapes and colors.

Mint Marinade

¼ cup white crème de menthe
¼ cup fresh lemon juice

1 teaspoon poppy seeds
¼ cup dry white wine

Combine all ingredients; pour over melons.

Munch-Crunch

Makes 7¼ cups

4 cups puffed rice or wheat cereal
1 cup raw almonds
1 cup raw hulled pumpkin seeds
1 cup raw sunflower seeds
¾ cup grated Parmesan cheese
¼ cup corn oil
⅓ cup water

4 teaspoons chili powder
½ teaspoon onion powder
1 teaspoon ground coriander
½ teaspoon garlic powder
1 teaspoon dried oregano, finely crushed
2 teaspoons salt
dash Tabasco sauce

1. Mix together cereal, nuts and seeds in a large bowl.
2. Sprinkle mixture with cheese; shake bowl to distribute.
3. Mix oil, water and spices in a jar with lid. Cover jar; shake well.
4. Pour spiced liquid over nut mixture; stir to coat very well.
5. Spread mixture onto 2 rimmed baking sheets; bake in preheated 350° F. oven 20 to 25 minutes, or until toasted.
6. Cool; store refrigerated in covered cans or jars.

Cool Italian Mushroom Dip

Makes about 25 servings

1 pint dairy sour cream
2 tablespoons grated Parmesan cheese
1 tablespoon dried sweet basil

½ teaspoon onion salt
¼ teaspoon garlic salt
⅛ teaspoon pepper
1 pound fresh mushrooms

parsley (for garnish)

1. Combine sour cream, Parmesan cheese and seasonings in a small bowl; chill until serving time.
2. Rinse mushrooms and pat-dry; trim ends of stems and thickly slice mushrooms.
3. Arrange mushroom slices on a serving plate; garnish with parsley.
4. Serve with sour cream dip.

Marinated Mushroom Hor d'Oeuvres

Makes 2 cups

⅔ cup corn oil
⅔ cup white wine vinegar
¼ cup water
1 large clove garlic, sliced

1 bay leaf
10 peppercorns
½ teaspoon salt
1 pound small fresh mushrooms
chopped parsley (for garnish)

1. Mix together corn oil, vinegar and water in 2-quart saucepan.
2. Add garlic, bay leaf, peppercorns and salt; cover and simmer 10 minutes. Add mushrooms; cover and simmer 5 minutes, stirring occasionally. Remove from heat; cool.
5. Chill several hours or overnight.
6. Drain before serving. Sprinkle with chopped parsley.

Elegant Mushroom Pâté

Serves 10

2 pounds coarsely chopped mushrooms
1 cup chopped green onions
1 large clove garlic, minced
½ teaspoon ground nutmeg
2 tablespoons butter
½ pound pork sausage
¼ pound liverwurst, diced

3 eggs, slightly beaten
1 tablespoon plus 1 teaspoon water
½ teaspoon original Worcestershire sauce
¼ teaspoon ground black pepper
⅛ teaspoon salt
½ cup fresh bread crumbs
⅓ cup chopped parsley
1 sheet frozen puff pastry, thawed

1. Cook mushrooms and onions with garlic and nutmeg in butter in large, heavy pan until liquid evaporates; stir often.
2. Combine mushroom mixture, sausage, liverwurst, eggs, 1 tablespoon water, Worcestershire sauce, pepper and salt in electric blender. Blend until smooth.
3. Stir in bread crumbs and parsley.
4. Pour pâté mixture into a buttered 8½ x 4½ x 2½-inch loaf pan. Bake in preheated 375° F. oven 45 minutes, or until done.
5. Unmold on cookie sheet. Set aside.
6. Meanwhile, increase oven temperature to 400° F. while placing puff pastry sheet on lightly floured board.
7. Roll pastry with rolling pin into rectangle 13 x 9½ inches.
8. Cover top and sides of pâté loaf with pastry; decorate top with additional pastry cut in leaf shapes, if desired.
9. Combine remaining egg and water; brush on pastry.
10. Bake 20 minutes more, or until golden brown.
11. Cool. Serve at room temperature.

Mushroom Tidbits

Makes 2 dozen hors d'oeuvres

1 can (7 ounces) tuna, drained
   and flaked
¼ cup real mayonnaise
3 tablespoons chopped watercress

1 tablespoon sesame seed
1 tablespoon soy sauce
½ teaspoon ground ginger
24 small mushroom caps

1 hard-cooked egg yolk (for garnish)

1. Mix together tuna, mayonnaise, watercress, sesame seed, soy sauce and ginger.
2. Stuff each mushroom cap with generous teaspoon of tuna mixture.
3. Garnish with sieved egg yolk and chill.

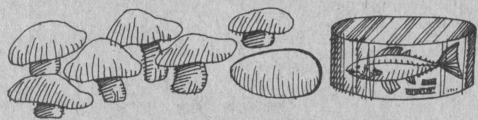

Walnut Mushroom Pâté

Makes 10 to 12 slices

½ cup minced onion
1 clove garlic, minced
12 ounces mushrooms, minced
2 tablespoons butter
3 tablespoons dry sherry
1 tablespoon salt
¾ teaspoon rosemary
⅛ teaspoon white pepper

2 cups minced fresh spinach
1⅓ cups minced walnuts
⅓ cup minced fresh parsley
¼ teaspoon nutmeg
1 cup cottage cheese
2 eggs
crisp lettuce leaves
scallion curls (for garnish)

1 loaf thinly sliced dark bread

1. Sauté onion, garlic and mushrooms in butter in skillet until onion is limp.
2. Stir in sherry, salt, rosemary and pepper. Cook, stirring often, several minutes, or until most of liquid is absorbed.
3. Transfer mixture to large bowl. Add spinach, walnuts, parsley and nutmeg.
4. Purée cottage cheese and eggs together in blender or food processor until smooth. Add to mixture in bowl and blend well.
5. Spread mixture evenly in greased 9 x 5-inch loaf pan.
6. Bake in preheated 375° F. oven about 1¼ hours.
7. Cool on rack 30 minutes.
8. Cover pâté with foil. Let stand 1 hour to firm up.
9. Chill several hours before serving.
10. Unmold and invert on lettuce-lined plate. Garnish with scallion curls and accompany with thinly sliced dark bread.

NOTE: A vegetarian's delight!

Potato Chips

Makes about 6 cups

3 large baking potatoes,
   peeled

1 quart corn oil
salt

1. Using a vegetable slicer or large slicing slot of a grater, slice potatoes crosswise into ve
   thin slices.
2. Soak 2 hours in ice water, changing water several times.
3. Drain potatoes well on paper towels.
4. Pour oil into heavy 3-quart saucepan or deep-fryer, filling no more than ⅓ full. He
   over medium heat to 375° F.
5. Place potatoes, ⅓ at a time, in fryer basket. Carefully lower into oil; stir.
6. Fry 2 minutes, or until golden brown.
7. Drain on paper towels. Sprinkle with salt.

NOTE: *Chips do not remain crisp for long periods.*

Snack Mix

Makes 30 cups

10 cups bite-size toasted wheat
   (15-ounce package)
10 cups bite-size toasted rice
   (8-ounce package)
10 cups unsalted popped popcorn

1 cup corn oil
¼ cup original Worcestershire sauce
1 tablespoon dried basil leaves
2 teaspoons onion salt
2 teaspoons garlic salt

1. Toss together cereals and popcorn in large bowl.
2. Stir together oil, Worcestershire, basil, onion salt and garlic salt in small bowl.
3. Pour over cereal-popcorn mixture. Toss gently until well coated.
4. Place mixture in large baking pan. Bake in preheated 250° F. oven, stirring
   occasionally, 30 minutes.
5. Cool before serving.

NOTE: *Great for appetizer, or a TV or after-school snack!*

Walnuts Parmisano

Makes 1 pint

2 cups California walnut halves
   or large pieces
½ cup shredded Parmesan cheese

¼ cup butter, melted
hickory smoke salt

1. Stir walnuts with melted butter in a large skillet. Continue stirring over moderate heat
   until lightly toasted.
2. Sprinkle walnuts lightly with hickory smoke salt; sprinkle cheese on it.
3. Continue to heat and stir until cheese melts and clings to walnuts.
4. Cool; store in covered jar in cool place. Makes a delightful snack with drinks.

Soups

Introduction

Soup is a year-round favorite, from jellied madrilene for torrid temperatures to hearty chowders or cream-style soups when icy winds blow. Hot or cold, consommé or hearty peasant soup, the varieties are limitless. Soup makes a lovely prelude to an elegant dinner, or it can become a meal in itself.

In old-fashioned households, the stockpot was a necessity. The stock derived from chicken or meat gave the essence to the soup; fresh garden vegetables in season and a variety of herbs added rich flavor as well as vitamins to the stock. Now, thanks to modern technology, soup can be prepared not in hours, but in minutes. Food processors and blenders make quick work of laborious shopping or puréeing. But for those who still like "to get the marrow out of the bone" remote-control cooking can be accomplished while you are away at work, thanks to the cook-all-day, energy-saving crockpots! Popular with people from all nations, young or old, soup remains an all-time favorite dish with such versatility that it even appears as a dessert on Scandinavian tables!

Why is soup so popular? Obviously because it incorporates so many tasty ingredients that it pleases many palates. Soup is:

- Inexpensive, a boon to contemporary cooks who are constantly trying to solve the problem of spiraling food costs.
- Available in so many different guises that it never goes out of style, even with increasing emphasis on low-calorie, low-cholesterol and low-sodium cooking for health-minded Americans.

- A marvelous way to use up leftovers. Many cooks maintain that the best part of a roast is the leftover bones or the turkey carcass.
- A simple solution to the age-old question: "What's for dinner?" People never tire of it. With the addition of crusty bread, a crisp green salad and a simple dessert, you have a simple but delicious meal, fit for family or company dining.
- Nutritious, thanks to the infinite variety of non-cooking soups such as gazpacho, which features salad-type ingredients (lettuce, tomatoes, onions, cucumbers and herbs). It's a great way for health-minded Americans to get their vitamins and minerals. Soups are also a fine answer to vegetarians who eat their protein in rich lentil soups.
- Fun to make, whether you are using recipes based on foreign cuisines or your mother's old-fashioned vegetable soup. In many homes, the old adage still persists: The hallmark of a good cook is her soup! And thanks to shortcuts such as dried herbs; instant chicken, vegetarian, or beef bouillon cubes; freeze-dried herbs, onion and garlic; soup starters (dried vegetables); and a limitless variety of excellent canned products (chicken broth, beef stock or consommé), it need not take all day to turn out good soup.
- A "comfort" food, whether it's Mother's chicken "penicillin" soup, popular in Kosher households, or Italian minestrone, thick with fresh garden vegetables. There's nothing more homey than the aromatic smell of homemade soup wafting through the kitchen, whether it's an all-modern steel kitchen in a Manhattan penthouse or an old-fashioned kitchen in a rustic log cabin!

Because of the limitless varieties of soups, a few guidelines will serve as a jumping-off point to understanding the categories:

- Soups which contain vegetable purée (vegetables forced through a sieve, food mill, processor or blender) usually separate on standing, with the thick part settling to the bottom, unless they are slightly thickened with flour — a process called "binding the soup."
- Soups should be well seasoned with a little of various seasonings (herbs or spices) than with a lot of one.
- In making soup stocks, cut meat or poultry into small pieces, put on to cook in cold water, and cook slowly for several hours.
- Soups made with clear meat broth or stock are known as bouillons and consommé. These, however, can be duplicated easily with high-quality canned or powdered products.
- Consommé made from two or three kinds of meat is highly seasoned, cleared and strained. It may be served cold or jellied (usually called madrilene).
- Bouillon is made from lean meat or poultry and delicately flavored.
- The water in which vegetables are cooked and the leftover vegetables themselves give flavor and added nutrients to soup.
- Soups become heartier with the addition of grains, noodles, or legumes, making a convenient meal-in-one.
- Chowders are usually thick soups made with onions and potatoes, often with the addition of milk or cream.
- Cream-type soups refer to the texture of the soup. Cream sauce, milk, half-and-half or cream give the soup its creamy texture. Fresh vegetables are often puréed and added to creamed soup or chicken broth. Both can be served hot or cold.
- Bisque was the name originally given by French chefs to game soups. From the 19th century on, the name was extended to include thick shellfish or fish soups.
- Bouquet garni refers to a bunch of herbs (usually 3 sprigs parsley, thyme and 1 small bay leaf) tied in a cheesecloth bag.

So, call it chowder, bisque, bouillon, potage or just plain soup, take it from here!

Homemade Chicken Stock

Makes 2 quarts stock

1 cleaned stewing hen, weighing
  about 5 pounds
2½ quarts water
2 large onions, chopped
¾ cup sliced celery (including
  tops)

¾ cup chopped carrots
½ cup peeled and sliced turnips
1 bouquet garni: 1 bay leaf, ¼ teaspoon
  whole black peppercorns (bruised)
  and ½ bunch parsley stems, tied
  loosely in a cheesecloth bag

1. Place chicken in large saucepot. Cover with cold water and bring to a boil.
2. Drain. Add 2½ quarts cold water, or enough to cover chicken.
3. Bring to a boil. Reduce heat and simmer 1 hour.
4. Add onion, celery, carrots, turnips and bouquet garni.
5. Simmer 1 hour longer, or until chicken and vegetables are tender.
6. Remove chicken. (Reserve for salads or casseroles.)
7. Strain stock through a fine strainer or sieve.
8. When stock cools, cover and refrigerate until fat layer forms on surface.
9. Pick off fat layer. (Reserve for cooking.)
10. Use stock immediately or freeze. Stock is very perishable and should be used within 1 to 2 days. Delicious!

NOTE: *This makes a wonderful beginning to many heavenly homemade soups or sauces! Stock can also be made from a turkey carcass in much the same way.*

Homemade Beef Stock

Makes 2 quarts

8 pounds beef shank bones, cut
  into pieces
3 to 3½ quarts water
2 cups chopped tomatoes (fresh
  or canned)
1 large white onion, chopped
¾ cups sliced celery
  (with leaves)

½ bunch parsley
2 small bay leaves
¼ teaspoon thyme, crumbled
10 to 12 bruised peppercorns
2 whole cloves
½ small clove garlic, pressed
  (optional)

1. Place bones in roaster pan. Bake in preheated 450° F. oven 1 hour, turning often to brown on all sides. (This gives color and flavor to stock.)
2. Remove bones from oven and place in large stockpot with enough water to cover.
3. Bring to a boil; remove any foam that is formed.
4. Cover and simmer slowly 2 hours.
5. Add remaining ingredients; simmer 2 hours longer.
6. Strain through fine strainer or sieve.
7. Cool to room temperature before refrigerating. Remove hard fat layer that forms on top. Use at once, or freeze for future use. Stock is highly perishable and should be used within 2 days.

Cream of Avocado Soup

Serves 6

2 California avocados, peeled and seeded
1 can (13 to 14½ ounces) evaporated milk
½ teaspoon celery salt

½ teaspoon garlic salt
¼ teaspoon salt
⅛ teaspoon white pepper
2 cups milk
1 cup chicken broth

watercress (optional garnish)

1. Mix ingredients in blender or mixer until smooth.
2. Chill well for several hours.
3. Serve garnished with watercress, if desired.

NOTE: Soup can also be served hot. Heat gently, but do not boil. Serve warm, with garlic croutons, if desired.

Crab-Lettuce Soup

Serves 6

1 head iceberg lettuce
2 cups cooked crab meat
1¼ cups rich chicken broth
1½ cups half-and-half or milk
1 tablespoon fresh lemon juice

1 teaspoon onion powder
¼ teaspoon salt
⅛ teaspoon white pepper
2 drops Tabasco sauce, or to taste

1. Cut up lettuce into small pieces to measure 2 cups.
2. Place lettuce in blender or food processor with 1 cup crab meat and remaining ingredients. Process until mixture is smooth.
3. Chill mixture until very cold.
4. Serve topped with pieces of remaining crab.

NOTE: Delightful for a hot summer day.

Frosted Crab Soup

Serves 4

1 can (6½ ounces) crab meat
2 tablespoons butter
1 can (10¾ ounces) condensed cream of mushroom soup, undiluted
1 cup light cream

½ teaspoon salt
⅛ teaspoon white pepper
2 tablespoons pale dry sherry
2 tablespoons fresh lemon juice
parsley (for garnish)

1. Sauté crab meat in butter until golden.
2. Blend together with remaining ingredients except parsley.
3. Chill 3 hours.
4. Garnish with parsley and serve, preferably on a bed of crushed ice.

Curried Apple Onion Soup

Serves 6

3 tablespoons butter or
  margarine
1 large onion, peeled and
  chopped
2 large tart apples, peeled,
  cored, and sliced

2 cans (13 ounces each) beef
  consommé
¾ teaspoon curry powder
½ cup heavy cream
chopped chives or parsley
  (optional garnish)

1. Melt butter in large saucepan.
2. Add onion and cook slowly 5 minutes, stirring often.
3. Add apples; cook 5 minutes longer, stirring to prevent scorching.
4. Pour in beef consommé, add curry powder, and simmer 5 minutes.
5. Purée mixture in blender or food processor; blend in cream at the end.
6. Refrigerate until well chilled.
7. Stir before serving. Garnish with chopped chives or parsley.

NOTE: *May also be served warm.*

Health Soup

Serves 6 to 8

1½ cups coarsely chopped carrots
1½ cups peeled and seeded
  chopped tomatoes
1½ cups peeled and seeded
  chopped cucumber
1½ cups chopped green pepper
1 cup coarsely shredded zucchini
1 cup chopped celery
1 cup chopped red onion

2 cloves garlic, minced or pressed
3 cups tomato juice
½ cup corn oil
2 tablespoons red wine vinegar
1 tablespoon salt
1 tablespoon fresh lemon juice
1 teaspoon Tabasco sauce
½ teaspoon dried oregano leaves
½ teaspoon dried basil leaves

croutons

1. Reserve ¼ cup each carrots, tomatoes, cucumber, green pepper and zucchini for garnish.
2. Stir together remaining carrots, tomatoes, cucumber, green pepper, zucchini, celery, onion, garlic, tomato juice, corn oil, vinegar, salt, lemon juice, Tabasco, oregano and basil.
3. Cover and refrigerate 2 hours.
4. To serve, garnish with reserved chopped vegetables. Serve with croutons.

NOTE: *For blended Health Soup: Follow recipe for Health Soup. Place 2 cups vegetable mixture in blender container. Cover and blend at high speed 10 seconds, or until vegetables are minced. Repeat until all vegetables are blended. Chill 2 hours before serving. A nice variation of gazpacho!*

Chilled Blueberry Bisque

Makes 3⅓ cups; serves 3 to 4

1 tablespoon chopped shallots
1 tablespoon butter or margarine
1 can (10¾ ounces) condensed
  chicken broth
1 pint (about 2 cups) blueberries,
  washed and sorted

½ cup heavy cream
¼ cup Kirschwasser or other
  sherry-flavored liqueur
1 teaspoon sugar
strawberries (for garnish)
lemon slices (for garnish)

1. Cook shallots in butter in saucepan until tender.
2. Add broth and blueberries.
3. Cover and bring to a boil.
4. Pour into electric blender; blend until smooth.
5. Return mixture to saucepan.
6. Add cream, liqueur and sugar; heat, stirring occasionally.
7. Chill 6 hours or longer.
8. Garnish with strawberries and lemon slices.

Gazpacho

Serves 6

3 large cloves fresh garlic
3 tablespoons tarragon flavor
  wine vinegar
1 teaspoon salt
1 teaspoon corn oil
1 medium green pepper, halved
  and seeded

1 cucumber, pared
2 stalks celery
2 medium tomatoes, scalded
  and peeled
1 can (24 ounces) vegetable
  juice cocktail
ice cubes

toasted croutons

1. Put garlic through press into blender jar with vinegar, salt and oil; blend smooth.
2. Coarsely cut half each of the green pepper and cucumber, 1 stalk celery and 1 tomato into blender jar.
3. Add 2 cups vegetable juice cocktail and blend smooth.
4. Turn out and combine with remaining cup vegetable juice.
5. Finely chop remaining vegetables and add to blended mixture. Chill thoroughly.
6. To serve, portion soup into bowls and add an ice cube to each serving.
7. Top with croutons and serve at once.

NOTE: If thinner soup is preferred, add ½ cup water or broth or white table wine before portioning into bowls.

Consommé Madrilene

Serves 4 to 6

2 cups tomato juice
celery leaves
1 slice lemon
1 slice onion
1 cup cold water
2 envelopes unflavored
  gelatin

2 cups chicken consommé or stock
2 teaspoons lemon juice
2 teaspoons Angostura aromatic
  bitters
sliced lemon (optional garnish)
minced parsley (optional garnish)
sour cream (optional garnish)

1. Combine tomato juice, celery leaves, lemon, onion and ½ cup water.
2. Simmer over low heat 10 minutes; strain.
3. Soften gelatin in ½ cup water.
4. Add strained tomato juice and chicken consommé.
5. Add lemon juice and Angostura.
6. Pour into bowl and chill until set.
7. Beat with fork and pile into chilled bouillon cups.
8. Garnish with your choice of sliced lemon, minced parsley, or sour cream.

Sengalese Soup

Serves 4 to 6

4 cups milk
2 eggs, slightly beaten
2 teaspoons chicken bouillon
  cubes, crumbled
½ teaspoon curry powder

½ teaspoon salt
½ cup chopped celery
2 cups chopped cooked chicken
1 container (8 ounces) pineapple
  yogurt
watercress (for garnish)

1. Combine 2 cups milk, eggs, bouillon cubes, curry and salt.
2. Add celery.
3. Cook, stirring constantly until slightly thickened.
4. Remove from heat; add remaining milk and chicken.
5. Chill. Just before serving, stir in yogurt. Garnish with watercress.

Herbed Buttermilk Soup

Serves 6

2 cans (10½ ounces each)
  cream of tomato soup, undiluted
2 soup cans buttermilk
1 teaspoon basil leaves, crumbled
½ teaspoon sugar

½ teaspoon salt
¼ teaspoon freshly ground
  black pepper
2 tablespoons dairy sour cream
  (for garnish)
paprika (for garnish)

1. In mixing bowl combine soup, buttermilk, basil, sugar, salt and pepper.
2. Mix well and chill.
3. At serving time, garnish each serving with 1 teaspoon sour cream and dash of paprika.

August Soup

Serves 2 to 3

1 can (10½ ounces) condensed
   cream of chicken soup
1 soup can milk

¼ cup chopped cucumber
1 teaspoon chopped fresh dill
1 teaspoon chopped green onion

1. Combine soup, milk, cucumber, dill and green onion in bowl.
2. Refrigerate for at least 4 hours.
3. Serve in chilled bowls.

Russian Yogurt Soup

Serves 3 to 4

1 can (10½ ounces) condensed
   Scotch broth
1 cup plain yogurt (8-ounce
   container)
2 teaspoons sugar

2 teaspoons fresh chopped dill
   weed or 1 teaspoon dried dill
   weed, crushed
½ teaspoon pepper
1 cup milk

chopped dill, parsley or green onion (optional garnish)

1. Combine broth, yogurt, sugar, dill and pepper in blender; blend until smooth.
2. Pour mixture into saucepan; gradually stir in milk and heat; stirring occasionally.
3. Remove from heat and chill 6 hours or more.
4. If desired, garnish with additional chopped dill, chopped parsley or chopped green onions.

Iced Pea & Potato Soup

Serves 6

¾ cup minced scallions
2 thinly sliced leeks
2 tablespoons butter
3 cups chicken stock (page 95)
2 cups green peas

2 cups peeled, diced potatoes
½ teaspoon salt
¼ teaspoon celery salt
2 cups light cream
paprika

1. Cook scallions and leeks in butter in skillet until vegetables soften.
2. Add chicken stock, peas, potatoes, salt and celery salt; cook until vegetables are tender.
3. Purée vegetables and their liquid in blender or force them through a fine sieve.
4. Cool soup; stir in cream.
5. Chill before serving; dust with paprika.

Chilled Tomato-Carrot Soup

Serves 6

2 tablespoons butter or margarine
1 pound carrots, peeled and thinly
  sliced
1 cup chopped onion
1 clove garlic, minced or pressed
8 medium fresh California tomatoes
  (about 2 pounds), peeled
  and chopped

1 can (14½ ounces) chicken broth
½ teaspoon basil, crushed
½ teaspoon thyme, crushed
½ teaspoon salt
⅛ teaspoon pepper
⅛ teaspoon nutmeg
1 cup milk
chopped fresh parsley

1. Melt butter in large saucepan.
2. Add carrots, onion and garlic; cook 5 minutes.
3. Add 7 of the tomatoes, chicken broth, basil, thyme, salt, pepper and nutmeg. Bring to boil.
4. Reduce heat; cover and simmer 30 minutes, or until vegetables are tender.
5. In food blender or food processor fitted with metal blade, purée tomato mixture thoroughly in batches.
6. Pour into large bowl and stir in milk. Chill thoroughly.
7. Stir in remaining chopped tomato. Sprinkle with parsley.

Avocado & Ginger Vichyssoise

Serves 6

½ cup butter
1 medium onion, minced
1 ounce fresh grated ginger root
  or 1 tablespoon powdered ginger
1 large ripe avocado, mashed

2 cups chicken stock (page 95)
1 teaspoon salt
1 teaspoon freshly ground black
  pepper
½ cup light cream

1 stalk scallion, minced (for garnish)

1. Melt butter in saucepan.
2. Add onion and grated ginger; sauté 2 minutes.
3. Add mashed avocado and chicken stock; mix well. Simmer slowly 10 to 15 minutes.
4. Add salt, pepper and cream.
5. Stir and chill for at least 1 hour.
6. Garnish each soup cup or bowl with scallions.

NOTE: This soup is a favorite at the Hotel Inter-Continental Ocho Rios in Jamaica.

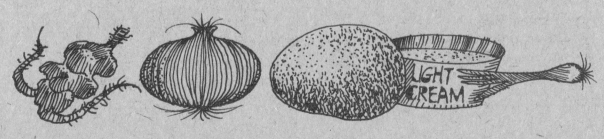

Vichyssoise

Serves 8

4 leeks, white part only
1 medium onion
¼ cup butter or margarine
5 medium potatoes, finely
   sliced

4 cups chicken stock (page 95)
salt to taste
2 cups milk
2 cups cream
chopped chives

1. Finely chop leeks and onion.
2. Brown lightly in butter in saucepan.
3. Add potatoes, chicken stock and salt. Cook, covered, 35 minutes.
4. Put through sieve and return to heat.
5. Add milk; heat but do not boil.
6. Cool. Add cream.
7. Chill thoroughly.
8. Top with finely chopped chives.

NOTE: Vichyssoise is delightful served in a soup cup set in a bed of crushed ice.

Banana Vichyssoise

Serves 6 to 8

1 broiler-fryer chicken, cut
   into quarters
about 1 quart water
3 bananas, sliced
1 cup tart apples, diced and peeled
2 cups potatoes, peeled
   and chopped

½ cup celery
½ teaspoon salt
2 tablespoons butter
½ teaspoon curry powder
1 cup instant non-fat dry
   milk powder
chopped chives (for garnish)

banana slices (for garnish)

1. Combine chicken, water, bananas, apples, potatoes, celery and salt in large soup kettle. Bring to boil.
2. Cover, reduce heat, and simmer 30 minutes, or until chicken is tender.
3. Remove chicken. (Cool, then refrigerate to use for chicken salad.)
4. Pour 2 cups chicken broth (unstrained) into container of electric blender. Blend on moderate speed 1 minute.
5. Add butter, curry powder and ½ cup milk powder. Cover and blend 1 minute, or until smooth.
6. Pour into bowl.
7. Repeat process, using remaining chicken broth and milk powder.
8. Cover and chill several hours until very cold.
9. To serve, garnish with chopped chives and fresh banana slices. Delightfully refreshing.

NOTE: If soup seems a little thick, dilute with a little cold water.

Spanish Cream of Almond Soup

Serves 6

½ cup butter or margarine
4 teaspoons flour
2 tablespoons chicken stock
  granules

1 quart boiling water
1 cup ground almonds
⅛ teaspoon white pepper
1 cup heavy cream

salted whipped cream (for garnish)

1. Melt butter in saucepan over low heat.
2. Stir in flour, blending well. Cook and stir 2 minutes.
3. Dissolve chicken granules in boiling water; gradually add to flour mixture. Stir until smooth.
4. Add ground almonds and white pepper. Cook slowly 10 minutes, stirring often.
5. Gradually add cream and continue cooking over low heat until heated through.
6. Garnish with salted whipped cream and additional ground almonds, toasted.

Elegante Cream of Asparagus Soup

Serves 4

2 pounds cleaned tender asparagus,
  chopped
½ cup minced onion
3 tablespoons butter
1 cup low-fat cottage cheese
1 cup skim milk

5 cups vegetable or chicken broth
scant teaspoon curry powder
salt to taste
pepper to taste
minced parsley or dill (for garnish)
lemon or lime wedges (for garnish)

1. Sauté asparagus and onion in butter about 8 minutes.
2. Put half of sautéed vegetables into blender container with cottage cheese and milk. Whirl until smooth.
3. Heat broth in saucepan; stir in remaining sautéed vegetables.
4. Gradually blend in vegetable-milk mixture; heat through.
5. Add curry powder and seasonings to taste.
6. Garnish with parsley accompanied by lemon wedges.

Crab Bisque

Serves 8

1 can (10¾ ounces) condensed
  mushroom soup
1 can (10¾ ounces) condensed
  tomato soup

1 can (5 ounces) crab meat
1 soup can milk
paprika to taste
curry powder to taste

1. Combine all ingredients, beating with rotary beater until well blended.
2. Heat in top of double boiler until ready to serve.

NOTE: If desired, a tablespoon sherry can be added to bisque just before serving.

Artichoke-Shrimp Bisque

Serves 10 to 12

6 artichokes, prepared as
 directed below
6 cups vegetable bouillon
2 pounds fresh or frozen shelled,
 deveined shrimp
⅓ cup chopped scallions
2 tablespoons instant minced onion

1 teaspoon onion salt
⅛ teaspoon white pepper
2 cups heavy cream
⅔ cup all-purpose flour
2 egg yolks, slightly beaten
1 can (1 pound) small whole
 carrots, undrained

1. Scrape pulp from artichoke leaves. Remove and discard chokes (thistle portions).
2. Force artichoke bottoms and pulp from leaves and blend in electric blender; set aside.
3. Heat bouillon to boiling.
4. Add shrimp, scallions, onion, onion salt and white pepper; cook 10 minutes, or until shrimp are tender.
5. Add artichoke purée and cook 5 minutes.
6. Add cream to flour and blend; beat in egg yolks.
7. Stir cream mixture into artichoke mixture. Cook over low heat, stirring constantly, until thickened.
8. Add carrots and heat to serve.

NOTE: Great with crackers or melba toast.

Cream of Artichoke Soup

Serves 4

1 jar (6 ounces) marinated
 artichoke hearts
3 large cloves fresh garlic
½ cup chopped onion
2 tablespoons flour

2 cans (10¾ ounces each) condensed
 chicken broth
1 cup half-and-half
finely chopped fresh parsley
 (for garnish)

1. Drain marinade from artichoke hearts into a 2-quart saucepan.
2. Crush garlic with press; add to marinade.
3. Add onion and cook, covered, 10 minutes over low heat.
4. Blend in flour.
5. Slowly stir in 1 can broth; heat to boiling, stirring. Boil 1 minute, or until mixture thickens.
6. Turn artichoke hearts into blender jar or food processor bowl. Add hot mixture, and blend smooth. Strain into saucepan.
7. Add remaining broth and half-and-half. Heat just to serving temperature; do not boil. Sprinkle each serving with parsley.

Chicken Asparagus Soup

Serves 4

1 package (10 ounces) frozen asparagus
vegetable water and milk to make
  1 cup
2 sprigs parsley
½ teaspoon salt

⅛ teaspoon pepper
¼ teaspoon dry mustard
1 can (10½ ounces) cream of
  chicken soup
1 cup half-and-half

1. Cook asparagus according to package directions until tender-crisp.
2. Drain vegetable water into 1-cup measure and add milk to make 1 cup.
3. Cut cooked asparagus into 1-inch lengths.
4. Place asparagus, milk mixture, parsley, salt, pepper and dry mustard in blender container. Cover and blend for 30 seconds.
5. Return to saucepan in which vegetables were cooked. Add chicken soup and half-and-half; stir in with wooden spoon or rotary beater.
6. Serve hot or cold.

German Beef & Corn Soup

Serves 6

⅛ cup minced onion
3 tablespoons bacon fat
1 jar (5 ounces) dried beef,
  shredded

1½ tablespoons flour
¼ teaspoon pepper
1½ cups beef broth (page 95)
1 can (17 ounces) cream-style corn

1 can (13 ounces) evaporated milk

1. Sauté onion in bacon fat 5 minutes, or until tender.
2. Add beef; cook until edges of meat begin to curl.
3. Blend in flour and pepper.
4. Slowly stir in beef broth, stirring constantly, until mixture thickens and boils. Boil gently 2 minutes.
5. Stir in cream-style corn; stir in evaporated milk to which water has been added to make 2 cups.
6. Heat through, but do not boil. Taste to correct seasonings.

Cream of Chicken Bisque

Serves 4 to 6

4 tablespoons butter
4 tablespoons flour
1¼ cups rich chicken broth
½ teaspoon salt
1 onion, cut into halves
1 stalk celery, cut in halves

2 cups milk
¾ cup minced cooked chicken
dash garlic powder
1 egg yolk
⅓ cup dry sherry
whipped cream (optional)

paprika (optional)

1. Mix butter and flour in skillet over low heat, stirring until smooth and bubbling.
2. Add broth, salt, onion and celery. Stir until creamy.
3. Cover and cook over low heat 15 minutes, stirring as necessary to prevent lumping.
4. Strain liquid into pot; add milk, minced chicken and garlic powder. Cook until creamy.
5. Mix a little soup into egg yolk, stirring to blend, then blend into soup pot.
6. Stir in sherry. Do not boil after addition of egg and wine.
7. If desired, serve topped with dollops of whipped cream dusted with paprika.

Cream of Pheasant Soup

Serves 4

2-pound pheasant, cooked
  and boned
¼ pound fresh mushrooms
2 cups cubed carrots
¼ cup chopped onion
½ teaspoon thyme leaves, crushed
1 small bay leaf

2 tablespoons butter or margarine
1 can (10¾ ounces) condensed golden
  mushroom soup
¼ cup water
1 can (10¾ ounces) condensed chicken
  broth
½ cup heavy cream

mushrooms (optional garnish)

1. Chop pheasant. Set aside.
2. Brown mushrooms, carrots, onion, thyme and bay leaf in butter until vegetables are tender.
3. Remove bay leaf. Add mushroom soup and water.
4. Pour into electric blender; blend until smooth.
5. Return mixture to saucepan.
6. Combine pheasant meat and chicken broth in electric blender; blend until smooth.
7. Add to soup mixture.
8. Gradually stir in cream and heat, stirring occasionally.
9. Garnish with mushrooms if desired.

NOTE: A gourmet's delight!

Baked Garlic Soup

Serves 4 to 6

butter
2 cups diced fresh tomato
1 can (15 ounces) garbanzo beans, undrained
4 to 5 summer squash, sliced
2 large onions, sliced
½ green pepper, diced
4 to 5 cloves fresh garlic, minced

1½ cups dry white wine
1 bay leaf
2 teaspoons salt
1 teaspoon basil
½ teaspoon paprika
1¼ cups grated Monterey Jack cheese
1 cup grated Romano cheese
1¼ cups heavy cream

1. Butter inside of a 3-quart baking dish.
2. Combine all ingredients except cheeses and cream in ovenproof dish.
3. Cover and bake in preheated 375° F. oven 1 hour.
4. Stir in cheeses and cream. Lower heat to 325° F. and bake 10 to 15 minutes without allowing soup to boil.

Hearty Lentil-Pumpkin Soup

Serves 6 to 8

2 cups onions, sliced
3 tablespoons sweet butter
½ cup lentils
5 cups chicken stock (page 95)
1½ cups canned pumpkin
⅛ teaspoon marjoram

¼ teaspoon ground thyme
½ teaspoon curry powder
¼ teaspoon ground white pepper
2 to 3 tablespoons Tabasco sauce
1 cup light cream
salt to taste

⅓ cup coarsely chopped pine nuts (for garnish)

1. Sauté onions in butter in large saucepan until limp.
2. Stir in lentils and chicken stock.
3. Add pumpkin, marjoram, thyme, curry powder, white pepper and Tabasco.
4. Cover and simmer 1½ hours, or until lentils are tender.
5. Cool to room temperature.
6. Purée mixture in blender.
7. Refrigerate until ready to serve.
8. Reheat. Add cream slowly, stirring.
9. Taste to correct seasonings.
10. Serve in soup bowls or cups. Garnish with pine nuts.

Clam Coriander Tomato Bisque

Serves 2

1 can (8 ounces) minced clams
¼ cup chopped onion
¼ cup chopped leeks
2 tablespoons chopped shallots
¼ teaspoon ground coriander seed

¼ teaspoon fennel seed
2 tablespoons olive oil
1 can (11 ounces) condensed tomato
  bisque
½ cup water

garlic croutons (for garnish)

1. Drain clams, reserving juice.
2. Cook onion, leeks, shallots, coriander and fennel in olive oil in saucepan until vegetables soften.
3. Add soup, clam juice and water.
4. Pour into electric blender; blend until smooth.
5. Return mixture to saucepan; add minced clams. Heat, stirring occasionally.
6. Garnish with garlic croutons.

Cream of Tomato-Dill Soup

Serves 6 to 8

2 pounds ripe tomatoes
2 teaspoons sugar
¼ cup sweet butter
2 tablespoons minced green onion
2 tablespoons minced parsley
⅓ cup minced fresh dill

4 cups homemade chicken stock (page 95)
3 tablespoons flour
1 quart milk
1 cup dairy sour cream
salt to taste
white pepper to taste

1. Immerse tomatoes in boiling water 20 to 30 seconds; remove with slotted spoon.
2. Plunge tomatoes immediately into ice water. Skins should peel off very easily.
3. Remove stem and flower ends from tomatoes; chop into fine cubes. Set tomatoes aside.
4. Melt butter in pan; add onion and cook until golden.
5. Add tomatoes, parsley and half the dill; cook slowly over medium heat 10 minutes, stirring occasionally.
6. Add chicken stock; bring to a boil. Simmer slowly 30 minutes to reduce slightly in volume.
7. Using wire whisk, blend flour with milk until lump-free.
8. Slowly add flour-milk mixture to soup, stirring constantly with whisk.
9. Bring mixture to a boil; reduce heat and stir. Taste to correct seasonings.
10. Mix a few tablespoons hot soup with sour cream, stirring. Return this mixture to soup, stirring constantly.
11. Heat through but do not boil, stirring.
12. Ladle soup into soup plates. Garnish with remaining fresh dill. Serve piping hot.

NOTE: This soup has a nice fresh flavor. It will have small lumps of fresh tomato.

Mussels & Mushroom Soup

Serves 2

2 tablespoons chopped onion
generous dash crushed tarragon
  leaves
2 tablespoons butter or margarine
10 mussels, cleaned

2 tablespoons Chablis or other
  dry white wine
1 can (10¾ ounces) condensed cream
  of mushroom soup
¼ cup heavy cream

1. Cook onion with tarragon in butter in saucepan until tender.
2. Add mussels and wine; steam until mussels open.
3. Discard shells; add soup.
4. Pour mixture into electric blender; blend until smooth.
5. Return mixture to saucepan; gradually stir in cream. Heat, stirring occasionally.

NOTE: *Wonderful, especially on a cold winter day. A Basque-influenced soup.*

Sherried Seafood Bisque

Serves 8

5 cups water
5 medium-size potatoes,
  peeled and quartered
½ cup coarsely chopped onion
4 teaspoons original Worcestershire sauce
1 clove garlic, crushed
½ teaspoon thyme leaves,
  crumbled

½ teaspoon salt
1 can (10½ ounces) minced clams,
  undrained
2 cups cooked, flaked fish
1 can (4½ ounces) medium-size shrimp,
  drained
2 tablespoons dry sherry
2 egg yolks
½ cup light cream

paprika (optional garnish)

1. Bring water to a boil in large saucepan.
2. Add potatoes, onion, 2 teaspoons Worcestershire, garlic, thyme and salt. Bring to a boil.
3. Reduce heat and simmer, uncovered, until potatoes are almost soft, about 20 minutes.
4. Stir in clams, fish, shrimp, sherry and remaining Worcestershire. Cook until seafood is hot, 5 minutes.
5. Remove from heat. Combine egg yolks and cream; stir into fish mixture. Heat only until hot. Do not boil.
6. Serve hot or cold. Garnish with paprika, if desired.

Winter Potage

Serves 6

3 medium tomatoes, peeled
1½ cups diced potatoes
1 tablespoon chopped onion
2 teaspoons salt

pepper
4 cups boiling water
1 cup dairy sour cream
2 tablespoons flour

1. Dice tomatoes into saucepan; add potatoes, onion, salt and a few grains pepper.
2. Add boiling water; cook until potatoes are tender.
3. Mix sour cream and flour together in double boiler; cook over hot water stirring constantly, until thickened.
4. Stir sour cream mixture gradually into tomato-potato mixture; season to taste with additional salt and pepper. Reheat but do not boil.

Harvest Potato Soup

Serves 6 to 8

½ cup chopped green onion
1 onion, chopped
1 tablespoon butter
4 cups chicken stock (page 95)
3 cups pared and diced Washington
  Russet potatoes

2 medium carrots, pared and thinly sliced
1 cup zucchini, diced in ½-inch
  pieces
3 cups finely shredded spinach
salt to taste
white pepper to taste

1. Sauté onions in butter in saucepan.
2. Cook over low heat, covered, about 5 minutes.
3. Add remaining ingredients except spinach, salt and white pepper.
4. Simmer, covered, 20 minutes.
5. Add spinach and seasonings to taste. Heat thoroughly.

Creamy Spinach Curried Soup

Serves 6

1 cup minced onions
1 small clove garlic, pressed
2 tablespoons corn oil
4 cups chicken broth (canned
  or homemade)
2 packages (10½ ounces each)
  fresh spinach, finely chopped

½ cup evaporated milk
1 teaspoon curry powder
1 teaspoon salt
⅛ teaspoon white pepper
2 cups cooked brown rice
1 lemon, thinly sliced

1. Sauté onions and garlic in oil until tender; add chicken broth and bring to a boil.
2. Stir in spinach; cover and simmer 10 minutes.
3. Pour mixture into blender; purée.
4. Return puréed mixture to saucepan; add milk, seasonings, and rice. Heat thoroughly.
5. Serve with a twist of lemon.

Onion Veloute

Serves 3

1½ cups thinly sliced
  onions
2 tablespoons chopped celery
2 tablespoons chopped green
  onions
3 tablespoons butter or
  margarine
1 tablespoon flour

1 can (10¾ ounces) condensed
  chicken broth
1 teaspoon original Worcestershire sauce
⅛ teaspoon white pepper
½ cup light cream
½ cup milk
1 green onion, sliced (for garnish)

paprika (for garnish)

1. In saucepan, cook sliced onions, celery and green onions in butter until tender.
2. Blend in flour; cook a few minutes, stirring constantly.
3. Remove from heat; add broth, a little at a time, stirring until smooth after each addition.
4. Add Worcestershire and white pepper.
5. Pour mixture into blender; blend until smooth.
6. Return mixture to saucepan; gradually stir in cream and milk. Heat, stirring occasionally.
7. Garnish with sliced green onion slices and paprika.

Potage Printanier

Serves 8

2 leeks, white part only, sliced
1 medium onion, sliced
3 tablespoons corn oil margarine
2 cups chopped raw potatoes
1 thinly sliced carrot
6 asparagus stalks, cut into
  1-inch pieces

½ teaspoon salt
dash white pepper
6 cups water
5 packages instant chicken
  broth
¼ cup uncooked rice
1 cup heavy cream

1. Sauté leeks and onion in margarine until tender.
2. Add potatoes, carrot, asparagus, salt, white pepper, water, chicken broth and rice. Bring to a boil.
3. Simmer, covered, 25 minutes.
4. Remove vegetables and purée with ⅔ cup vegetable stock.
5. Return to pot and blend well.
6. Add heavy cream and heat through.

Fresh Tomato Seafood Soup

Serves 6

1 large onion, chopped
3 pounds Italian plum tomatoes, chopped
½ teaspoon salt
⅛ teaspoon white pepper

⅓ cup hot water
2 cups clam juice or fish stock
1 cup heavy cream
½ pound poached bay scallops
1 tablespoon fresh chives, chopped

1. Add onion, tomatoes, salt, white pepper and water to a large stockpot. Bring to a boil; simmer over medium heat 5 minutes.
2. Add clam juice; simmer 10 minutes longer.
3. Taste to correct seasonings.
4. Purée contents of pot, then strain to remove peel and seeds.
5. Chill 4 to 5 hours.
6. Mix cream into cold soup.
7. Place scallops in bottom of tureen or serving bowls, pour in soup, and top with chives.

NOTE: Scallops can be poached by cooking them in clam juice diluted with water or a wine-water broth flavored with bouquet garni (thyme, parsley, peppercorns and a small piece of lemon — all wrapped in a cheesecloth bag).

Old-Fashioned Tomato Bisque

Serves 8

2 cans (1 pound each) tomatoes
2 beef bouillon cubes
1 tablespoon sugar
2 teaspoons salt
1 teaspoon onion powder
¼ teaspoon basil leaves

¼ teaspoon white pepper
1 bay leaf
½ cup 100% corn oil margarine
½ cup unsifted flour
4 cups skim milk
chopped parsley (for garnish)

1. Measure 1 cup drained tomatoes; cut into large pieces and set aside.
2. Combine remaining tomatoes and liquid in saucepan with bouillon cubes, sugar, salt, onion powder, basil leaves, pepper and bay leaf. Simmer 30 minutes.
3. Remove bay leaf.
4. Force mixture through food mill or sieve.
5. Melt margarine in large saucepan over low heat.
6. Blend in flour until smooth.
7. Gradually stir in milk. Cook over medium heat, stirring constantly, until mixture comes to a boil.
8. Remove from heat. Gradually blend in tomato mixture, stirring briskly. Add tomato pieces.
9. Return to heat. Stir constantly until hot.
10. Serve garnished with parsley.

Creamy Sweet Potato Soup

Serves 6

2 tablespoons butter or margarine
1 cup chopped onion
2 cups chicken broth
1¾ pounds sweet potatoes
   (yam variety), peeled and cut
   into chunks

2 cups sliced carrots
1½ teaspoons salt
¼ teaspoon mace
¼ teaspoon garlic powder
⅛ teaspoon pepper
2 cups milk

1. Melt butter in large saucepan. Add onion and cook until tender.
2. Add broth and bring to a boil.
3. Add sweet potatoes, carrots, salt, mace, garlic powder and pepper. Return to a boil.
4. Reduce heat and cover; simmer 20 minutes, or until sweet potatoes are tender.
5. Purée soup, in batches, in blender or food processor.
6. Return to saucepan. Stir in milk and cook over low heat, stirring frequently until hot.
   Wonderful served with hot cornbread!

Rock Lobster Corn Soup Stew

Serves 6 to 8

2 packages (8 ounces each) frozen
   South African rock lobster tails
¼ cup butter or margarine
1 small onion, minced
½ cup chopped celery
½ cup chopped fresh mushrooms

¼ cup flour
1 quart milk
1 can (1 pound) cream-style corn
salt to taste
pepper to taste
cayenne to taste

paprika

1. Thaw lobster tails. With scissors, remove underside membrane. Pull out meat in one piece and cut into crosswise slices. Set aside.
2. Heat butter and sauté onion, celery and mushrooms until tender but not brown.
3. Stir in flour. Gradually stir in milk.
4. Cook over low heat, stirring constantly until soup thickens slightly.
5. Add corn and lobster slices.
6. Season to taste with salt, paprika and cayenne.
7. Cook over low heat, stirring, until lobster slices are white and opaque.
8. Sprinkle with paprika at serving time.

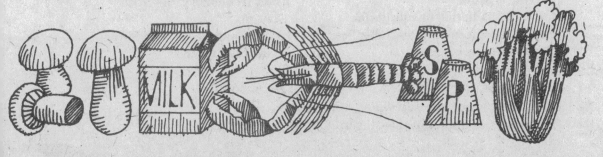

Chili Corn Chowder

Serves 8 to 10

3 cups diced raw potatoes
3 cups water
3 tablespoons bacon fat or
vegetable oil
1 tablespoon salt
2 cans (1 pound each) whole
kernel corn

1 can (10¾ ounces) condensed
cream of tomato soup
¼ cup instant minced onion
1½ teaspoons chili powder
¼ teaspoon garlic powder
⅛ teaspoon ground black pepper
¾ cup evaporated milk

1. Combine potatoes, water and bacon fat in saucepan; bring to a boil.
2. Reduce heat and simmer, covered, until potatoes are tender.
3. Add corn, soup, minced onion, chili and garlic powders and black pepper. Bring just to boiling point.
4. Add milk and heat. Serve hot as a main dish soup.

Classic French Onion Soup

Serves 6

4 cups thinly sliced sweet
onions
1 clove garlic, minced
¼ cup butter or margarine
5½ cups water
⅓ cup dry sherry or white
wine or water

8 teaspoons beef-flavored instant bouillon
or 8 beef-flavored bouillon cubes
6 slices (¾-inch thick) French
bread, buttered and toasted
6 slices (8 x 4-inch) Swiss cheese,
cut in half crosswise

1. Cook onions and garlic in butter until golden.
2. Add water, sherry and bouillon; bring to a boil.
3. Reduce heat; cover and simmer 30 minutes to blend flavors.
4. Place soup in 6 ovenproof soup bowls. Top each serving with a bread slice and cheese.
5. Broil until cheese melts. Serve at once.

Frankfurter Creole Chowder

Serves 4

1 pound frankfurters, cut in
½-inch slices
¼ teaspoon basil or thyme
leaves, crushed
2 tablespoons butter or margarine
1 can (11½ ounces) condensed split
pea with ham soup

1 can (10¾ ounces) condensed
cream of potato soup
½ soup can water
1 can (8 ounces) tomatoes,
cut up
1 can (8 ounces) whole kernel
corn, undrained

1. Brown frankfurters with basil in butter in large saucepan.
2. Add soups; gradually add water, stirring.
3. Add tomatoes and corn. Heat, stirring often.

Boston Clam Chowder

Serves 6 to 8

1 quart shucked, soft-shell
   clams, with liquor (2 dozen)
¼ pound salt pork, sliced
2 medium onions, sliced
3 cups pared, cubed potatoes

1¼ teaspoons salt
¼ teaspoon pepper
2 cups boiling water
1 quart scalded milk
2 tablespoons butter or margarine

pilot crackers (optional)

1. Pick over clams carefully; removing any bits of shell.
2. Drain off liquor; strain and reserve.
3. Separate hard part from clams and chop fine.
4. Dice salt pork; cook in kettle until brown and crisp.
5. Add sliced onions; continue cooking, stirring often, until tender.
6. Add potatoes, salt, pepper, chopped hard part of clams and boiling water. Simmer until potatoes are tender.
7. Add milk, soft part of clams and butter; heat.
8. Add clam liquor. Serve with or without crackers.

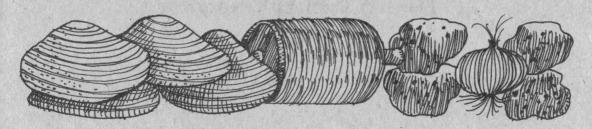

Nor'easter Fish Chowder

Serves 6

6 ounces salt pork, cubed
1 cup flour
1½ teaspoons salt
1 teaspoon pepper
1 cup raw haddock, cubed

2 cups diced potatoes
1 cup minced onions
2 quarts milk
1 tablespoon minced parsley
salted crackers

1. Put salt pork cubes in heavy soup kettle; fry until crisp.
2. Remove pork pieces.
3. Mix together flour, salt and pepper.
4. Layer fish, potatoes and onions in pork drippings in kettle, sprinkling each layer generously with seasoned flour.
5. Add milk; cover and simmer 35 minutes, stirring gently 2 or 3 times.
6. Add browned pork cubes and parsley. Simmer 5 minutes longer.
7. Taste to correct seasonings.
8. Serve with crackers.

NOTE: A classic New England soup at its best!

Jiffy Tuna-Potato Chowder

Serves 6 to 8

¼ pound lean sliced bacon,
  diced
½ cup chopped onion
2 cans (10½ ounces each) tomato
  soup, undiluted
2¼ cups water
2 medium-size potatoes, peeled
  and diced

1 can (7 ounces) tuna, drained
  and flaked
2 tablespoons chopped parsley
⅛ teaspoon thyme leaves
⅛ teaspoon ground black pepper
½ cup sliced pimiento-stuffed
  green olives
dash of Tabasco (optional)

1. Cook bacon and onion together in skillet until bacon is crisp and onion tender.
2. Pour off excess drippings.
3. Add remaining ingredients. Heat to a boil; reduce heat.
4. Simmer 20 minutes, or until potatoes are tender, stirring often.
5. Taste to correct seasonings, using Tabasco if desired.

Mom's Turkey Chowder

Serves 6 to 8

1 bunch parsley
1 bay leaf
1 large rib celery
4 pounds turkey wings
water
4 tablespoons butter or margarine
1 cup diced celery
½ cup diced green or red
  pepper

1 cup chopped onion
2 tablespoons salt
½ teaspoon freshly ground
  black pepper
1 can (20 ounces) creamed corn
1 can (20 ounces) whole kernel corn
2 egg yolks, beaten
1 cup heavy cream or
  half-and-half

1. Tie parsley, bay leaf and celery rib together in cheesecloth bag; set aside.
2. Wash turkey wings; cover with water in large stockpot.
3. Bring to boil; simmer 4 minutes. Pour off water (to get rid of fat).
4. Melt butter in large stockpot.
5. Add diced celery, green or red pepper, onion and 1 tablespoon salt. Cook over medium heat, stirring until vegetables are golden.
6. Reduce heat. Add turkey wings, remaining salt, black pepper and parsley bouquet.
7. Add about 2 quarts water. Cover and simmer 2½ hours until wings are tender.
8. Remove wings and cool. Remove and discard parsley bouquet.
9. Remove turkey meat from bones; discard bones.
10. Return turkey meat to soup with both cans of corn. Simmer, uncovered, 10 minutes.
11. Mix beaten egg yolks with cream; place in bottom of large soup tureen.
12. Add a few tablespoons hot chowder to mixture, stirring constantly.
13. Add more hot liquid, then pour in all chowder.
14. Serve piping hot.

Fisherman's Chowder

Serves 8

1 cup chopped onions
½ cup carrots, diced
½ cup celery, chopped
2 tablespoons corn oil
2 tablespoons flour
2 cups water
1 can (1 pound tomatoes)

2 packages (12 ounces each) frozen
   haddock fillets, thawed and
   cut into 1-inch pieces
1 tablespoon original Worcestershire sauce
scant teaspoon salt
¼ cup chopped fresh parsley
oyster crackers

1. Sauté onions, carrots and celery in oil in large saucepan until vegetables are limp.
2. Blend in flour; cook and stir for 2 minutes.
3. Add water and tomatoes; bring to boiling point.
4. Add fish, Worcestershire and salt. Reduce heat; simmer, uncovered, 15 minutes.
5. Stir in parsley.
6. Serve with oyster crackers.

Pennsylvania Dutch Ham & Apple Soup with Dumplings

Serves 4

1 ham hock weighing 3 pounds
water
2 tablespoons brown sugar
¼ teaspoon whole cloves

1 small onion, minced
6 green cooking apples,
   cored and quartered
Dumplings

1. Brown ham in soup pot; cover with water and simmer 1½ hours.
2. Stir in brown sugar.
3. Put cloves in cheesecloth bag; drop into soup.
4. Toss in onion and apples.
5. Simmer 2 hours longer, adding water as necessary.
6. Remove spice bag before serving. Taste to correct seasonings.
7. Serve with Dumplings

Dumplings

20 salted crackers rolled
   into fine crumbs
1 tablespoon baking powder
1 teaspoon salt

¼ teaspoon black pepper
3 tablespoons melted butter or
   margarine
2 eggs, separated
⅓ cup milk

1. Combine cracker crumbs, baking powder, salt and pepper and butter in mixing bowl.
2. Beat egg yolks with milk; add to dry ingredients.
3. Beat egg whites until stiff; fold into cracker mixture.
4. Drop by spoonfuls into soup; cover and steam 15 minutes without removing cover.

Vegetable Clam Chowder

Serves 6

6 small carrots
1 large potato
1 large onion
3 sprigs parsley
2 cans (8 ounces each) minced clams
1½ quarts water
1 can (19 ounces) tomatoes

1 cup canned or frozen lima beans
1½ teaspoons salt
¼ teaspoon freshly ground black pepper
2 teaspoons thyme
2 tablespoons corn oil
3 tablespoons flour

1. Scrape carrots; set aside.
2. Peel potato and cut into small pieces; set aside.
3. Peel onion and cut into thin slices; set aside.
4. Chop parsley.
5. Drain clams and reserve juice; set aside.
6. Bring water to a boil in large saucepan. Add carrots, potatoes, onions, tomatoes, lima beans, salt, pepper and thyme, Cook until vegetables are tender.
7. Heat oil in skillet; stir in flour.
8. Add clam juice, mixing until thick.
9. Stir clam juice and oil into vegetable mixture; cook and stir until slightly thickened.
10. Add clams and parsley. Taste to correct seasonings.

Vegetable Chowder

Makes 3½ quarts

¼ cup corn oil margarine
1 cup chopped onion
1 clove garlic, minced
1 cup chopped celery
4 cups beef bouillon
3 cups peeled, cubed potatoes
1 can (16 ounces) tomatoes

1 can (17 ounces) corn, undrained
2 cups sliced carrots
½ teaspoon salt
½ teaspoon ground thyme
½ teaspoon celery seed
2 tablespoons cornstarch
¼ teaspoon water

1. Melt margarine in Dutch oven over medium heat.
2. Add onion and garlic; cook until transparent.
3. Add celery, bouillon, potatoes, tomatoes, corn, carrots, salt, thyme and celery seed Bring to a boil over medium heat.
4. Cover and simmer 30 minutes, or until vegetables are tender.
5. Stir together cornstarch and water until smooth.
6. Add to soup.
7. Bring to boil over medium heat, stirring constantly; boil 1 minute.

NOTE: Use leftover cooked roast beef to make soup heartier. Makes a wonderful meal-in-one, with thick slabs of dark bread.

Cheese-Shrimp Chowder

Serves 8

1 pound shrimp
water
1 box (5 ounces) pre-cooked rice
2 medium onions
4 stalks celery
2 tablespoons butter or margarine
2 cups cut green beans

1 teaspoon salt
½ teaspoon pepper
½ teaspoon thyme
1 cup boiling water
4 cups milk
½ pound Cheddar cheese, grated
¼ cup sherry

1. Cook shrimp in boiling water (to cover) about 5 minutes, or until they start to turn pink.
2. Drain shrimp, remove shells, and devein.
3. Cook rice according to box instructions; set aside.
4. Peel and cut onions into thin slices. Wash celery; cut into small pieces and set aside.
5. Melt butter in saucepan; add onions and cook until tender, but not browned.
6. Add celery, green beans, salt, pepper, thyme and boiling water to onions; cover and cook gently 15 minutes, or until celery is tender.
7. Heat milk in large saucepan until scalded; add cheese, shrimp and celery mixture, stirring until cheese is melted. Add sherry.
8. Place cooked rice in bottom of soup dishes; spoon chowder over rice; serve piping hot.

Indonesian Fish Chowder with Pineapple

Serves 8 to 10

1 pound cleaned carp, pickerel
  or eel
2 dozen mussels
2 dozen large shrimps
3 cloves garlic, peeled and minced
¼ cup peanut oil
2 bay leaves
1 strip dried orange peel
1 fresh red chili pepper,
  with seeds removed

water
¼ cup rice wine (sake)
6 white onions, peeled and sliced
3 or 4 threads saffron
2 cups fresh or canned pineapple
  sticks, cut 2 to 3 inches long
2 tablespoons cornstarch
soy sauce
hot cooked rice (optional)

1. Cut fish into small portions; wash mussels and shrimps, cutting off heads. Set aside.
2. Fry garlic in peanut oil in skillet; add bay leaves, dried orange peel and red chili pepper. Heat through, stirring.
3. Add 1 cup water and rice wine.
4. Transfer garlic-sake mixture to a large stockpot; add 3 quarts of water and onions. Bring mixture to a brisk boil.
5. Add fish pieces; boil a few minutes.
6. Add mussels and shrimps; cover and simmer gently, about 12 to 15 minutes. (If red chili pepper makes soup taste too hot, remove it.)
7. Add saffron, soaked in 3 tablespoons hot water, pineapple, and cornstarch diluted in ¼ cup cold water; let soup come to slow boil to thicken slightly.
8. Remove soup from heat; serve in tureen. Pass soy sauce at the table to season the stock. (Can be served with cooked rice in separate bowl, if desired.)

Baked Portuguese Egg Soup

Serves 10 to 12

¼ cup corn oil
¼ cup olive oil
3 cups thinly sliced onions
1 tablespoon paprika
⅓ cup dry bread crumbs
2 cloves garlic, pressed
2 cans (28 ounces each) diced or chopped tomatoes, undrained

1 bay leaf
1 teaspoon sugar
1 teaspoon oregano leaves, crushed
½ teaspoon black pepper
3 beef bouillon cubes
3 cups tomato juice
10 to 12 eggs (1 per serving)

1. Pour corn and olive oils into large soup kettle; heat over medium heat.
2. Add onions and paprika; sauté until onions are light brown.
3. Add remaining ingredients except eggs, stirring to blend. Heat to boiling, stirring occasionally.
4. Reduce heat, cover, and simmer 45 minutes.
5. Place individual ovenproof soup bowls on heavy cookie sheet in preheated 350° F. oven for 5 to 10 minutes, or until heated.
6. Remove from oven. Ladle 6 ounces soup into each bowl.
7. Break an egg into center of each bowl. Ladle an additional 2 ounces soup over each egg.
8. Return to oven; bake 6 to 8 minutes, or until whites are cooked but yolk is still liquid.
9. Allow to cool slightly before serving. Serve with thick slabs of dark bread.

NOTE: This is an excellent choice when the cupboard is bare, as you are likely to have all these ingredients on hand.

Chicken-Corn Soup with Egg Dumplings

Serves 4 to 6

1 can (12 ounces) whole kernel corn
1 can (10½ ounces) chicken rice soup
2 chicken bouillon cubes
3 soup cans water
salt to taste

pepper to taste
¾ cup sifted flour
½ teaspoon salt
1 tablespoon margarine or butter
1 egg
½ cup cold water

1. Combine corn, soup, and bouillon cubes in large saucepan.
2. Add 3 soup cans water.
3. Bring to a boil; season to taste with salt and pepper.
4. Sift together flour and salt; cut in margarine.
5. Add egg to ½ cup water; beat with fork enough to blend.
6. Add egg mixture to flour mixture; beat with spoon until smooth.
7. Drop by spoonfuls into soup. Cover and cook 10 to 15 minutes, or until dumplings are cooked.

Beef Savory Soup with Spaetzle

Serves 6

1½ pounds boneless lean stewing beef, cut into ½-inch pieces
1 tablespoon corn oil
3 cups boiling water
1 large onion, chopped
1 tablespoon instant beef bouillon
1 clove garlic, minced
½ teaspoon celery seed
½ teaspoon savory
freshly ground black pepper
  to taste

1 can (29 ounces) tomatoes
pinch sugar (optional)
¼ teaspoon seasoned salt
¾ cup all-purpose flour
½ teaspoon salt
⅛ teaspoon baking powder
¹⁄₁₆ teaspoon ground nutmeg
1 egg, beaten
cold water
2 to 3 tablespoons minced fresh
  parsley

1. Brown beef quickly in oil in Dutch oven; pour off excess fat.
2. Add boiling water, onion, bouillon, garlic, celery seed, savory and pepper. Bring to a boil.
3. Reduce heat, cover and simmer 1¼ hours.
4. Add tomatoes, sugar, and seasoned salt.
5. Continue cooking, covered, 45 minutes, or until meat is fork-tender.
6. Meanwhile, prepare spaetzle:
   a. Combine flour, ½ teaspoon salt, baking powder and nutmeg.
   b. Add egg and about 4 to 5 tablespoons cold water; beat until batter is a thick paste.
   c. Add parsley.
   d. Place batter into a large-holed colander; quickly press batter through colander into simmering soup.
7. Cook 1 to 2 minutes until spaetzle float to the top.

Country-Style Chicken Noodle Soup

Serves 6

1 cleaned stewing hen,
  weighing about 4 pounds,
  cut up
2½ quarts water
2 teaspoons salt

1 teaspoon peppercorns, bruised
1 small onion, sliced
1 carrot, sliced
1 bay leaf
1 tablespoon parsley, chopped

3 cups cooked noodles

1. Bring hen to a boil in water, adding water as needed.
2. Skim off fat.
3. Add remaining ingredients except noodles; boil 20 minutes.
4. Add noodles and cook 20 minutes longer.
5. Taste to correct seasonings. Serve piping hot.

NOTE: If desired, boil hen and cool to room temperature. Then chill until fat layer forms on top. Remove fat layer before reheating to finish soup as directed.

Chicken Soup with Kreplach

Serves 6

Soup

1 cleaned stewing hen, weighing 3 to
  4 pounds, cut up
2 quarts water
1 tablespoon salt
1 tablespoon soy sauce

2 onions, peeled and quartered
2 carrots, peeled and sliced
2 stalks celery, sliced
6 to 8 parsley sprigs
½ teaspoon dill weed

1. Place all ingredients in large soup kettle; cover and bring to a boil.
2. Reduce heat and simmer 1 to 1½ hours, or until chicken is tender.
3. Remove chicken; strain soup and skim off excess fat.

Kreplach Filling

1 tablespoon soy sauce
1 teaspoon instant minced onion
1 egg, beaten

1½ cups ground cooked
  chicken or beef

1. Combine soy sauce and onion; let stand 10 minutes.
2. Mix in egg and chicken.

Kreplach Dough

2 cups all-purpose flour
⅔ teaspoon salt

2 eggs, slightly beaten
cold water

1. Sift together flour and salt.
2. Add eggs and enough cold water to make a stiff dough.
3. Turn out onto lightly floured board; knead until smooth.
4. Roll out very thin; cut into 3-inch squares.

To Assemble

1. Place 1 tablespoon filling in center of each square.
2. Moisten edges with a little water. Fold over diagonally; seal edges well.
3. Drop into simmering soup and cook 20 minutes. Serve at once.

NOTE: Canned chicken broth can be easily substituted for soup. In lieu of making prepared
dough, use 3-inch won-ton wraps (available in Oriental food sections of supermarkets o
Oriental markets).

Danish Beer & Bread Soup

Serves 6

½ pound stale whole wheat bread
½ pound stale pumpernickel
4½ cups water
4½ cups dark beer
⅓ cup sugar

pinch salt
1-inch piece cinnamon stick
rind of ¼ lemon, thinly shaved
1 egg yolk (optional)
heavy cream

1. Soak breads in water overnight.
2. Put bread-water mixture in covered saucepan. Cook, stirring from time to time, over very low heat, until a thick paste is formed.
3. Add beer, sugar, salt, cinnamon stick and lemon rind; cook a few minutes longer, stirring.
4. Beat yolk and add to soup if more thickening is needed.
5. Serve in soup plates with chilled cream or whipped cream in center. (This is served as porridge in the morning or as supper dish.)

NOTE: *This unusual "soup" is also popular as an appetizer, served with herring and anchovies.*

Greek Liver Soup

Serves 6

1½ pounds lamb liver
3 cups water
½ cup onion, chopped
½ cup fresh dill, minced
½ cup fresh parsley, minced
⅓ cup sweet butter

lamb or chicken broth (page 95)
½ cup rice
salt to taste
white pepper to taste
Avgolemono (page 124)

1. Simmer liver in 3 cups water for 15 minutes.
2. Remove from heat, strain broth, and set aside.
3. Mince liver; set aside.
4. Cook onion, dill and parsley in butter until soft and transparent.
5. Add liver and cook 5 minutes over moderate heat, stirring often.
6. Add reserved liver broth and enough chicken broth to make 2 quarts liquid; bring to a boil.
7. Add rice. Reduce heat, cover and cook until rice is tender, about 25 minutes.
8. Taste to correct seasonings.
9. Remove from heat; blend with Avgolemono.

Greek Chicken Soup
with Avgolemono (Lemon Egg Sauce)

Serves 6

1 cleaned stewing hen, weighing
   about 4 pounds
2 quarts water
1½ teaspoons salt
1 small yellow onion, sliced

½ cup chopped celery
1 cup rice
pepper
Avgolemono

1. Cover hen with salted water; add onion and celery.
2. Cook until chicken is tender, about 1½ hours, adding more water as needed.
3. Remove chicken from broth and set aside on warm platter.
4. Strain broth and cool to room temperature, skimming off any fat that floats on top.
5. Reheat broth to boiling temperature; stir in rice.
6. Cover and simmer until rice is tender.
7. Season to taste with pepper and additional salt.
8. Cool soup slightly and blend with Avgolemono. Serve at once.

Avgolemono

4 large eggs (at room temperature),
   separated

2 tablespoons cold water
juice from 1 large lemon

1. Beat egg whites until stiff.
2. Blend in yolks; add water and lemon juice, beating until thick.
3. Spoon a small amount of hot soup into the egg mixture, blending quickly.
4. Pour mixture into soup; stir well.

Zucchini Soup with Rice

Serves 6

½ cup chopped onions
1 clove garlic, minced
1 tablespoon chicken fat, butter
   or margarine
1 quart chicken broth
2 cups (12 ounces) zucchini

½ teaspoon salt
¼ teaspoon coarsely ground black
   pepper
¼ teaspoon ground thyme
½ cup uncooked rice
grated Parmesan cheese

1. Cook onions and garlic in fat until soft but not brown.
2. Add remaining ingredients except cheese.
3. Bring to a boil, stirring once or twice.
4. Lower heat and simmer 15 to 20 minutes, or until rice is tender.
5. Add more salt if needed.
6. Ladle into bowls and sprinkle with Parmesan cheese.

Hungarian Goulash Soup
with Pinched Noodles

Serves 4 to 6

½ cup minced onion
3 tablespoons corn oil
1 pound soup meat, cut into
   1-inch cubes
1½ teaspoons salt
1 teaspoon paprika
¼ teaspoon caraway seed, crushed

1 clove garlic, peeled and stuck
   on pick
½ green pepper, cut in strips
2 small ripe tomatoes or 1 cup canned
4 cups beef stock (page 95)
2 medium potatoes
Pinched Noodles

1. Sauté onion in oil in Dutch oven until limp.
2. Add meat and brown lightly on all sides.
3. Add 1 teaspoon salt, paprika and caraway seed, stirring to blend.
4. Add garlic, green pepper, tomatoes and 2 cups stock. Bring to a boil.
5. Reduce to simmer. Cover and cook 1 hour, adding more stock to keep meat well covered.
6. Meanwhile, prepare Pinched Noodles.
7. Peel and dice potatoes into ½-inch pieces.
8. Add potatoes to soup with remaining salt and stock. Simmer until potatoes are done, about 25 minutes.
9. Remove soup from heat and let stand few minutes.
10. Remove garlic. Skim off most of the fat that floats on the surface.
11. Stir in cooked noodles. Bring soup back to simmering and serve piping hot.

Pinched Noodles

1 cup sifted all-purpose flour
½ teaspoon salt

1 egg
1 tablespoon corn oil

1. Mix together flour and salt.
2. Add egg and oil. Stir with wooden spoon to form a stiff dough.
3. Sprinkle with few drops cold water if dough seems too stiff.
4. Turn out on lightly floured board. Knead until smooth.
5. Let dough rest 30 minutes.
6. Flatten with hands, a little at a time, between floured palms, or roll out to ⅛-inch thickness on board.
7. Pinch off pieces slightly smaller than a dime and drop into rapidly boiling salted water. Cook until tender, about 15 minutes.
8. Drain and rinse; add directly to soup.

Italian Bread Soup

Serves 6 to 8

2 small cloves garlic, minced
1 tablespoon fresh basil or
   1 teaspoon dried, crushed basil
2 tablespoons olive oil
1 can (1¾ ounces) whole tomatoes
salt to taste

pepper to taste
1 loaf sour dough bread, cut or
   torn into chunks
2 cups vegetable broth
½ cup freshly grated Romano
   cheese

2 tablespoons butter, melted

1. Sauté garlic and basil in olive oil in large saucepan until golden.
2. Add tomatoes; season to taste with salt and pepper.
3. Cook, breaking up tomatoes with a fork.
4. Soak bread in water to cover; squeeze dry.
5. Add bread, broth and half the cheese to tomato mixture; bring to a boil.
6. Simmer slowly 1 hour, or until most of liquid is absorbed.
7. Add butter and remaining cheese. Soup should thicken to consistency of porridge.

NOTE: This is a popular peasant soup.

Tuna Won-Ton Soup

Serves 8 to 10

1 can (7 ounces) tuna, drained
   and flaked
¼ cup minced celery
2 teaspoons grated lemon peel
2 teaspoons minced green onion
1 package (10 ounces) won-ton
   wrappers

3 cans (10¾ ounces each)
   condensed chicken broth
5 cups water
2 medium zucchini, thinly sliced
¼ pound mushrooms, sliced
½ cup shredded carrot
½ lemon, thinly sliced

1 tablespoon soy sauce

1. Combine tuna, celery, lemon peel and green onion in small mixing bowl. Mix well.
2. Lightly dampen edges of each won-ton wrapper with water.
3. Place 1 teaspoon filling in center of each won-ton.
4. Fold in half to top edge to form rectangle. Fold again to within ⅛ inch of top edge. Press sides to seal in filling.
5. Dampen ends with water.
6. Lay rectangles on flat surface and form into a horseshoe shape. Overlap ends and press to seal.
7. Heat chicken broth and water in large saucepan. Bring to a boil.
8. Add won tons and simmer gently, about 6 minutes, stirring occasionally.
9. Reduce heat. Add zucchini, mushrooms and carrot.
10. Simmer 4 to 5 minutes longer, adding lemon slices for the last 2 minutes.
11. Add soy sauce. Serve piping hot.

Mona's Chicken Soup with Meatballs & Dumplings

Serves 8 to 10

2 cleaned stewing hens, each weighing about 4 pounds, cut into serving pieces
3 teaspoons salt
1 teaspoon pepper
1 teaspoon basil
2 sprigs parsley, chopped

1 teaspoon thyme
3 quarts chicken broth
6 small carrots, peeled and cubed
4 leeks (leaves only), cut in large pieces
Meatballs
Dumplings

1. Arrange chicken, salt, pepper, basil, parsley and thyme in large soup kettle.
2. Add broth; bring to a boil.
3. Reduce heat and simmer, covered, until chicken is tender, about 1½ hours.
4. Remove chicken to platter.
5. Add carrots and leeks to soup; drop in meatballs when soup is simmering.
6. Continue simmering, covered, 45 minutes. Add dumplings during last 10 minutes and simmer, uncovered.
7. Just before serving, return chicken to soup kettle and reheat. Spoon soup, meatballs and dumplings into soup plates.

Meatballs

1½ cups minced onion
2 pounds lean ground beef
1½ cups milk

⅔ cup flour
2 eggs
1 teaspoon seasoned salt

½ teaspoon pepper

Mix together all ingredients; form into walnut-size balls and set aside.

Dumplings

4 tablespoons butter or margarine
3 cups flour
2 teaspoons baking powder

1 teaspoon salt
2 eggs
2 cups milk
1 tablespoon minced fresh parsley

1. Melt butter; set aside.
2. Sift together flour, baking powder and salt.
3. Beat eggs until light; add milk and melted butter.
4. With wooden spoon, stir egg-milk mixture into dry ingredients in bowl; stir in parsley.
5. Ten minutes before serving time, shape batter into small dumplings with spoon; drop into simmering soup.

African Bean & Peanut Soup

Serves 8

3 tablespoons margarine
½ pound lean ground beef
2 cups thinly sliced carrots
3 quarts boiling water
1 cup dry black-eyed peas
1 cup dry navy beans
1 cup diced green pepper

3½ teaspoons salt
⅛ teaspoon crushed red pepper
1 cup salted peanuts, chopped
2 tablespoons onion powder
1 tablespoon basil leaves, crushed
1½ teaspoons ground coriander
chopped fresh parsley

1. Melt margarine in large stockpot. Add beef and carrots; cook 5 minutes, or unt
   browned.
2. Add water, black-eyed peas, navy beans, green pepper, salt and crushed red pepper
   (Add more water, if necessary, to cover ingredients.)
3. Cook, covered, until ingredients are tender (1½ to 2 hours).
4. Add peanuts, onion powder, basil and coriander during last 10 to 15 minutes o
   cooking.
5. Taste to correct seasonings.
6. Sprinkle with chopped parsley to serve. Soup should be thick and hearty.

NOTE: If desired, a ham hock can be added to soup at the beginning for added flavor.

Golden Cauliflower Soup ·

Makes about 2 quarts

2 packages (10 ounces each) frozen
  cauliflower or 1 small head
  fresh cauliflower, separated
  into small flowerets
2 cups water
½ cup chopped onion
⅓ cup margarine or butter
⅓ to ½ cup unsifted flour

2 cups milk
2 tablespoons chicken-flavored
  instant bouillon
2 cups (8 ounces) shredded mild
  Cheddar cheese
⅛ teaspoon ground nutmeg
chopped green onion or parsley
  (for garnish)

1. Cook cauliflower in 1 cup water in saucepan until tender.
2. Reserve 1 cup cooked flowerets; blend remaining cauliflower and liquid in blender. Se
   aside.
3. Cook onion in margarine in heavy saucepan until tender.
4. Stir in flour.
5. Gradually add remaining water, milk and bouillon; cook and stir until well blended and
   thickened.
6. Add cheese, puréed cauliflower, reserved flowerets and nutmeg; cook and stir unti
   cheese melts and mixture is hot. (Do not boil.)
7. Garnish with green onion or parsley.

Barley Vegetable Soup

Makes 3 quarts

5 cups water
1 can (16 ounces) whole tomatoes, undrained
3 beef bouillon cubes
⅔ cup regular barley
1 cup carrot slices
1 cup chopped white turnips

1 cup fresh green beans, cut into 1-inch pieces
¾ cup chopped onion
⅔ cup chopped green pepper
1 bay leaf
1 to 2 teaspoons sugar
¼ teaspoon basil leaves, crushed

1. Combine water, tomatoes and bouillon cubes in a 4-quart Dutch oven.
2. Bring to a boil, stirring occasionally, until bouillon cubes are dissolved.
3. Cut tomatoes into bite-size pieces with wooden spoon.
4. Stir in barley; reduce heat.
5. Cover and simmer about 20 minutes.
6. Stir in remaining ingredients.
7. Cover and simmer 40 minutes, or until vegetables are tender.

NOTE: *If desired, meat can be added to the soup. Use a nice soup bone with meat to make a heartier version.*

Beef Barley Vegetable Soup

Makes about 3 quarts

1 pound beef shanks, cracked
7 to 8 cups water
3 tablespoons beef-flavored instant bouillon
1 can (16 ounces) stewed tomatoes, undrained

¾ cup chopped onion
½ teaspoon basil leaves
1 bay leaf
½ cup regular barley
1½ cups chopped carrots
1½ cups chopped celery

1. Combine shanks, water, bouillon, tomatoes, onion, basil and bay leaf in large kettle. Bring to a boil.
2. Reduce heat; cover and simmer 1 hour.
3. Remove shanks from stock. Cut meat into ½-inch pieces.
4. Skim fat from stock.
5. Add meat and barley to stock; bring to a boil.
6. Reduce heat and add carrots and celery.
7. Cover and simmer 30 minutes longer. Remove bay leaf before serving.

Black Bean Soup I

Serves 6

1 pound dried black beans	1 teaspoon instant minced garlic
10 cups water	1 teaspoon oregano leaves
¼ pound salt pork	½ teaspoon cumin seed
¾ teaspoon powdered mustard	¼ teaspoon ground black pepper
¾ teaspoon warm water	2 tablespoons lemon juice
⅓ cup instant minced onion	1 teaspoon salt
¼ cup sweet pepper flakes	2 tablespoons parsley flakes

hard-cooked egg (optional garnish)

1. Combine beans, water and salt pork in Dutch oven or large heavy stockpot. Bring to a boil.
2. Reduce heat; cover and simmer 2½ hours, or until beans are tender.
3. Combine mustard with warm water in cup; let stand 5 minutes for flavor to develop.
4. Add mustard water to cooked beans along with onion, pepper flakes, garlic, oregano, cumin and black pepper.
5. Cover and simmer 30 minutes longer, or until beans are very tender. (If soup is too thick, add more water.)
6. Stir in lemon juice and salt. Sprinkle with parsley flakes.
7. Garnish with hard-cooked egg, if desired.

Black Bean Soup II

Serves 12

2 cups black beans	3 small onions, minced
3 quarts water	3 cloves
¼ pound salt pork	¼ teaspoon mace
½ pound lean beef, cut in small pieces	dash red pepper
	3 hard-cooked eggs, sliced
1 carrot, diced	1 lemon, sliced

½ cup sherry

1. Wash and clean beans; soak overnight.
2. In morning, sort beans carefully and put in stockpot with 3 quarts water; add salt pork, beef, carrot, onions, cloves, mace and red pepper.
3. Cover and cook slowly 3 hours, or until beans are very soft.
4. Rub through sieve.
5. Place hot bean liquid and purée in a tureen; add egg slices, lemon slices and sherry.

Camper's Corn Chowder

Serves 4

1 cup thinly sliced pepperoni
2 teaspoons corn oil
2 cups water
⅔ cup non-fat dry milk powder

1 can (16 ounces) whole kernel corn, undrained
¼ cup instant potato granules
¼ teaspoon salt
¼ teaspoon thyme

1. Brown pepperoni lightly in oil in saucepan.
2. Add remaining ingredients; stir and heat to a boil.
3. Reduce heat and simmer 5 minutes, stirring occasionally.

Cheese Vegetable Soup

Serves 8 to 10

½ cup minced onion
¼ cup butter or margarine
1½ tablespoons cornstarch
¼ cup flour
4 cups rich chicken stock
4 cups milk

½ cup cooked, minced carrots
½ cup cooked, minced celery
¼ teaspoon paprika
½ pound processed cheese, grated
salt to taste
pepper to taste

minced fresh parsley

1. Sauté onions in butter until tender and golden brown.
2. Add cornstarch and flour, blending well.
3. Add stock and milk slowly, stirring until well blended; bring to a boil, stirring constantly.
4. Add carrots, celery, paprika and cheese. Cook slowly, stirring, until cheese melts.
5. Add salt and pepper to taste.
6. Serve hot with parsley floating in each soup bowl.

Chicken & Ham Gumbo

Serves 6

2 tablespoons corn oil
2 pounds chicken wings
1 cup diced cooked ham
2 cups boiling water
2 teaspoons salt
1 bay leaf

2 cups canned tomatoes
1 cup sliced okra
¼ cup sweet pepper flakes
¼ cup onion flakes
1 teaspoon ground thyme
¼ teaspoon ground black pepper

1. Heat corn oil in soup kettle; add chicken wings and ham; cover and cook slowly for 15 minutes, turning chicken to cook uniformly.
2. Add boiling water, salt and bay leaf; cover and cook 30 minutes, or until chicken is tender.
3. Twenty minutes before cooking time is completed, add tomatoes, okra, sweet pepper flakes, onion flakes, thyme and black pepper.
4. Serve piping hot in soup bowls.

Chicken & Snow Pea Soup

Serves 4

4 cups chicken broth (page 95)
1 tablespoon fresh lemon juice
1 teaspoon salt
½ teaspoon marjoram
6 peppercorns
3 whole cloves
¼ teaspoon thyme

1 bay leaf
2 tablespoons rendered chicken fat
   or vegetable oil
1 package (7 ounces) frozen snow
   peas, chopped
2 green onions, white and
   green parts, chopped

1 cup cooked chicken, diced

1. Mix together chicken broth, lemon juice, salt, marjoram, peppercorns, cloves, thyme and bay leaf in large saucepan.
2. Cover and bring to a boil; simmer 15 minutes.
3. Place rendered chicken fat in frying pan; heat over medium temperature.
4. Add snow peas and green onions; stir-fry 3 minutes.
5. Add diced chicken; heat thoroughly.
6. Add chicken to broth mixture; simmer 5 minutes.
7. Remove bay leaf before serving.

Chicken Zucchini Soup

Serves 4

2 tablespoons olive oil
3 scallions, chopped
1 clove fresh garlic, minced
½ teaspoon basil

4 cubes chicken bouillon dissolved
   in 4 cups hot water
4 cups zucchini, finely grated
freshly grated Parmesan cheese

rye or whole wheat rounds

1. Combine olive oil, scallions, garlic and basil in saucepan.
2. Cook over medium heat 10 minutes, or until vegetables soften.
3. Add dissolved bouillon and zucchini; cover and cook over medium heat 35 minutes, or until zucchini is tender.
4. Top with grated cheese.
5. Serve with toasted thin rounds of rye or whole wheat bread.

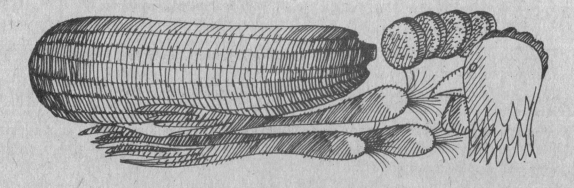

Corned Beef & Cabbage Chowder

Serves 6

¼ cup corn oil margarine
1 cup thinly sliced celery
½ cup chopped green onion
2 cloves garlic, minced
3 cups chicken broth
2 cups shredded cabbage

1 cup thinly sliced carrots
¼ pound cooked corned beef, cut into
  thin strips (1¼ cups)
½ teaspoon salt
¼ teaspoon pepper
3 tablespoons cornstarch

1 cup milk

1. Melt margarine over medium heat in 3-quart saucepan.
2. Add celery, green onion and garlic; sauté 5 minutes, or until tender.
3. Add chicken broth, cabbage, carrots, corned beef, salt and pepper. Cover and bring to boil.
4. Reduce heat and simmer, stirring occasionally, 20 minutes, or until vegetables are tender.
5. Stir together cornstarch and milk; gradually stir into vegetable mixture.
6. Bring mixture to a boil, stirring constantly over medium heat; boil 1 minute. Serve at once.

Crockpot Inflation-Fighter Five-Bean Soup

Serves 6

¼ cup pinto beans
¼ cup garbanzo beans
¼ cup red beans
¼ cup lentils
¼ cup black-eyed peas or
  green split peas
¼ cup raw rice
1 ham hock, weighing 1½ pounds
2 large onions,
2 cloves garlic, mashed

2 cups chopped celery, including
  tops
2 cups chopped carrots
1 cup chopped parsley
1 cup mushrooms
1 teaspoon crushed thyme
¼ teaspoon crushed red pepper flakes
1 cup red table wine
salt to taste
1 cup dry red table wine

1. Place all ingredients in crockpot; add enough water to cover.
2. Cook on low heat 6 to 8 hours, or until beans are cooked. (The taste gets better the longer the soup cooks.)

Creole Gumbo

Serves 6 to 8

1½ pounds fresh okra or 2 packages
(10 ounces each) frozen okra
¼ cup corn oil
2 cups chopped onion
1 cup chopped celery
¼ cup chopped shallots
4 large cloves fresh garlic, minced
1 teaspoon salt

½ teaspoon freshly ground black
pepper
1 can (16 ounces) tomatoes
6 cups water
2 pounds medium shrimp, shelled
and deveined
1 pound crab meat, fresh or frozen
hot cooked rice (optional)

1. Rinse and dry okra; cut into ½-inch pieces.
2. Sauté okra in corn oil until sap from okra is absorbed.
3. Remove okra from pan; place in strainer and set aside.
4. Use oil from okra pan to sauté onion, celery, shallots, garlic, salt and pepper for 5 minutes.
5. Add tomatoes and water; bring to a boil.
6. Stir in reserved drained okra. Reduce heat and simmer gently, uncovered, 1 hour, stirring often.
7. Stir in shrimp and crab meat; cook 15 minutes longer.
8. Serve over hot cooked rice, if desired.

Creole Shrimp Gumbo

Serves 6

2 pounds shrimps in shells
3 quarts water
6 ounces salt pork, sliced thin
1½ pounds okra or 2 packages
frozen okra
1 green pepper, minced

1 onion, minced
1 clove garlic, minced
½ teaspoon thyme
1 teaspoon black pepper
1 teaspoon salt
2 fresh tomatoes, cubed

2 tablespoons minced fresh parsley

1. Wash and peel shrimps; do not discard shells.
2. Put shells in 3 quarts water in heavy kettle; simmer 30 minutes.
3. Meanwhile, devein shrimp; set aside.
4. Drain and discard shells, saving 6 cups shrimp stock.
5. Fry pork in same heavy kettle until brown and crisp.
6. Remove pork and set aside.
7. Sauté okra, green pepper, onion and garlic in pork fat for 5 minutes.
8. Add thyme, black pepper, salt, tomatoes and reserved shrimp stock. Simmer 1 hour.
9. Add shrimp, pork and parsley; simmer 5 minutes longer. Serve piping hot.

Garbanzo Chili Pot

Serves 4 to 6

½ pound dry garbanzos (chick peas)
2½ pounds short ribs of beef
1 quart hot water
2 cans (1 pound 12 ounces each)
  whole tomatoes

2 onions, chopped
2 cloves garlic, minced
½ teaspoon freshly ground black pepper
2 teaspoons salt (less if desired)
1 teaspoon chili powder (or more to taste)

salted crackers

1. Wash garbanzos. Cover with warm water, soak overnight, then drain.
2. Brown short ribs in soup pot; cover with hot water.
3. Add garbanzos and simmer 2 hours, adding more water as needed.
4. Add remaining ingredients except crackers; cook 1 hour longer.
5. Serve with salted crackers.

Chili Bean Soup

Serves 4

1 pound pink, red or pinto beans
6 to 8 cups boiling water
1 teaspoon garlic salt
1 teaspoon onion salt
¼ teaspoon thyme
¼ teaspoon marjoram

1 can (10½ ounces) beef or chicken
  broth
1 can (16 ounces) stewed tomatoes
1 package (1⅛ ounces) chili
  seasoning mix or 1 can (7 to 10 ounces)
  green chili salsa

1. Rinse, sort and soak beans. Drain and empty them into large pot.
2. Add boiling water, garlic and onion salt, thyme and marjoram. Cover and simmer until beans are tender, 2½ to 3 hours, adding hot water as needed. (Do not let beans boil dry.)
3. Spoon out 3 cups of cooked beans to use another day in another way. Mash the rest of the beans with their liquid.
4. Add remaining ingredients, plus 1 cup hot water. Heat at least 10 minutes to blend flavors.

NOTE: *Those spooned-out beans make a great salad. Just cool them, cover with French dressing and refrigerate until needed.*

Curry-Pumpkin Soup

Serves 8 to 10

3 tablespoons bacon fat
1 large onion, chopped
2 cloves fresh garlic, minced
2 teaspoons curry powder
1 can (1 pound 13 ounces) whole tomatoes

6 cups chicken broth
5 cups peeled and diced pumpkin
1 teaspoon salt
⅛ teaspoon pepper
1 can (16 ounces) whole kernel corn, drained

1. Heat bacon fat in a large saucepan.
2. Add onion and garlic; sauté until tender.
3. Blend in curry powder; cook 1 minute.
4. Add tomatoes, chicken broth, pumpkin, salt and pepper; bring to a boil.
5. Reduce heat and simmer, covered, 30 minutes.
6. Add corn; simmer 5 minutes longer.

Esau's Pottage

Serves 8 to 10

3½ cups sliced onion
½ cup peanut oil
1 pound ground lamb
3 cups stewed tomatoes
1⅓ cups diced celery
1 cup sliced carrots

1 cup diced parsnips
1 cup diced green pepper
1 quart water
1 pound lentils
1 tablespoon salt
½ teaspoon ground pepper

1. Sauté onion in peanut oil; add lamb and brown.
2. Stir in remaining ingredients; bring to a boil.
3. Reduce heat, cover, and simmer 1½ hours, or until lentils are tender.
4. Taste to correct seasonings.

NOTE: *Lentil pottage is the world's oldest-known soup, dating back to the time when Esau sold his birthright for "that red, red pottage."*

Georgia Peanut Soup

Serves 6 to 8

¼ cup butter or margarine
¼ cup finely chopped onion
¼ cup finely chopped celery
1 cup creamy-style peanut butter

1 tablespoon flour
4 cups beef bouillon
2 teaspoons lemon juice
½ cup chopped cocktail peanuts (for garnish)

1. Melt butter in large saucepan.
2. Add onion and celery; sauté until tender.
3. Stir in peanut butter and flour; blend well.
4. Gradually stir in beef bouillon and lemon juice until smooth.
5. Cook over medium heat 20 minutes, stirring occasionally.
6. To serve, garnish with chopped peanuts.

Flaming Onion Soup

Serves 4 to 6

6 to 8 large onions, peeled
  and thinly sliced
½ cup butter or margarine
Irish whiskey
4½ cups beef stock

salt to taste
pepper to taste
French or Italian bread
freshly grated Romano or
  Parmesan cheese

1. Sauté onions in butter over low heat until golden.
2. Add ⅓ cup Irish whiskey and ignite.
3. When flame dies down, add beef stock gradually.
4. Season to taste with salt and pepper.
5. Simmer, uncovered, 45 minutes.
6. Pour into heat-proof tureen or individual soup bowls.
7. Top soup with toasted bread sprinkled with Romano cheese and run under the broiler until golden.
8. At the table, pour a jigger of whiskey over cheese toast and ignite.

Halloween Witches' Brew

Serves 10 to 12

½ pound lean bacon
3 pounds lean ground beef
1½ cups chopped onions
2 cans (26¼ ounces each) spaghetti
  in tomato sauce with cheese
1 can (16 ounces) tomatoes
2 cans (16 ounces each) kidney
  beans
2 cans (4 ounces each) mushrooms
  with liquid

1 teaspoon garlic salt
1 teaspoon celery salt
1 tablespoon original Worcestershire
  sauce
2 to 3 tablespoons catsup (more
  if desired)
2 cans (10½ ounces each) beef broth
4 cups water (more if needed)
salt to taste
pepper to taste

1. Brown bacon in large stockpot.
2. Drain off most of the fat.
3. Add beef and onions, cooking until onions are limp.
4. Add remaining ingredients; simmer 30 minutes, or until flavors blend.
5. Taste to correct seasoning.

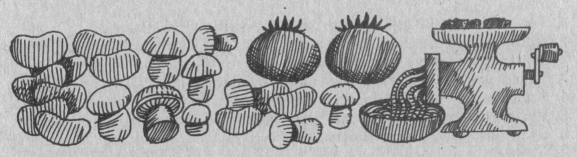

Ham & Garbanzo Bean Soup

Serves 6 to 8

1 pound dried garbanzo beans
  (chick peas)
water
meaty ham bone
1½ cups chopped onions
½ teaspoon dried leaf thyme

½ teaspoon dried sage
½ teaspoon dried marjoram
1 bay leaf
1¼ cups chopped carrots
1 cup chopped celery
2 teaspoons salt

½ teaspoon Tabasco sauce

1. Wash beans; discard any stones or shriveled beans; drain.
2. Place beans in large kettle; add 6 cups water. Cover and soak overnight.
3. Drain beans, reserving soaking liquid.
4. Add enough water to soaking liquid to make 9 cups.
5. Combine beans, soaking liquid, ham bone, onions, thyme, sage, marjoram and bay leaf in large kettle; bring to a boil.
6. Reduce heat and simmer 1½ hours.
7. Add carrots, celery, salt and Tabasco. Cover and bring to a boil.
8. Reduce heat and simmer 1½ hours, or until beans are tender.
9. Remove meat from ham bone and return to soup; discard bone.
10. Remove and discard bay leaf.
11. Heat soup to serving temperature.

Ham & Three-Bean Soup

Serves 6

½ cup dried red kidney beans
½ cup dried white navy beans
½ cup dried pinto beans
water
1 smoked ham shank, weighing
  about 2 pounds

¼ cup diced onions
1½ teaspoons salt
1 bay leaf
3 tablespoons original Worcestershire sauce
2 cups diced carrots

1. Wash beans. Soak 3 to 4 hours, or overnight in water to cover; drain.
2. Combine beans in a large, heavy saucepan with ham, onions, salt, bay leaf, 2½ quarts water and Worcestershire sauce. Bring to a boil.
3. Reduce heat and simmer, covered, until beans are almost tender, about 2 hours.
4. Stir in carrots. Cover and simmer until beans and vegetables are tender, about 1 hour.
5. Remove ham shanks. Cut off and discard fat; cut meat into chunks.
6. Return meat to pot. Heat and serve.

Hearty Ham & Bean Soup

Serves 10

1 smoked ham shank (2 pounds)
2½ quarts water
½ cup dried red kidney beans
½ cup dried white kidney beans
½ cup dried pinto beans

¼ cup chopped onion
3 tablespoons original Worcestershire sauce
1 bay leaf
2 cups sliced carrots

1. Combine ham, water, beans, onion, Worcestershire and bay leaf in large stockpot. Bring to a boil.
2. Reduce heat and simmer, covered, until beans are almost tender, about 2 hours.
3. Stir in carrots.
4. Cover and simmer until beans are tender, about 1 hour longer.
5. Remove ham shank; cut off skin from bone and discard.
6. Cut meat into chunks and return to stockpot. Heat until hot.

Hearty Meatball & Vegetable Soup

Makes about 5 cups

2 tablespoons onion flakes
½ teaspoon instant minced garlic
water
1 pound lean ground beef
1½ teaspoons marjoram leaves, crushed
2 tablespoons corn oil

1 tablespoon cider vinegar
6 whole cloves
½ teaspoon thyme leaves, crushed
⅛ teaspoon ground black pepper
1 large potato, peeled and diced (1 cup)
2 cups shredded cabbage
1 large tomato, diced (1 cup)

1 tablespoon parsley flakes

1. Combine onion flakes and minced garlic with 2 tablespoons water; let stand 10 minutes to soften. Set aside.
2. Mix beef with ½ teaspoon marjoram; shape into ½-inch balls.
3. Heat oil in saucepan. Add meatballs a few at a time; brown on all sides. Remove meatballs and set aside.
4. Add reserved onion and garlic to oil; sauté 2 minutes.
5. Add 2½ cups water, vinegar, cloves, thyme, black pepper and remaining marjoram. Bring to a boil, stirring to scrape drippings from bottom of pan.
6. Return meatballs to pan.
7. Add potato; reduce heat and simmer, covered, 10 minutes.
8. Add cabbage and tomato. Return to a boil.
9. Reduce heat and simmer, covered, until vegetables are tender, about 10 minutes.
10. Sprinkle with parsley flakes and serve.

Herbed Vegetable Soup

Serves 10 to 12

2 cups lentils (about ¾ pound)
2 quarts water
¼ cup onion flakes
2 bay leaves
2 cups diced tomatoes
2 cups sliced carrots

2 cups shredded cabbage
2 cups sliced zucchini
¼ cup soy sauce
1 tablespoon salt
¼ teaspoon ground black pepper
2 teaspoons basil leaves

1. Combine lentils with water in a large saucepan. Heat to a boil.
2. Reduce heat and simmer 2 minutes. Remove from heat and let soak 1 hour.
3. At end of hour, add onion flakes, bay leaves, tomatoes and carrots. Heat to a boil.
4. Reduce heat, cover, and simmer 1½ hours, or until lentils are tender.
5. Add cabbage, zucchini, soy sauce, salt and pepper. Cover and simmer 8 minutes, or until cabbage and zucchini are crisp-tender.
6. Stir in basil leaves; cover and simmer 5 minutes longer.
7. Remove bay leaves before serving.

Irish Cockaleekie Soup

Serves 8

1 cleaned stewing chicken,
   weighing 3 to 4 pounds
1 tablespoon salt
¼ teaspoon white pepper

2 celery tops
2 small bay leaves
about 3½ quarts water
3 leeks, sliced

1 cup rice

1. Place chicken in large kettle.
2. Add 2 teaspoons salt, pepper, celery tops, bay leaves and water. Bring to a boil.
3. Cover, reduce heat, and simmer 1½ hours, or until chicken is tender.
4. Remove chicken; strain broth.
5. Cool stock; chill, then remove fat layer that forms on top.
6. Reheat broth. Add additional salt (if needed). Add leeks and rice.
7. Bring to a boil, cover, and simmer 30 minutes longer, or until rice is done.

Irish Haddock Soup

Serves 6 to 8

1 pound haddock fillets, cut into
   ½-inch pieces
½ cup instant minced onions
1 tablespoon parsley flakes
1 teaspoon salt
½ teaspoon crumbled thyme leaves

1 small bay leaf
1/16 teaspoon ground nutmeg
1/16 teaspoon ground black pepper
4 cups boiling water
¼ pound diced salt pork
2 tablespoons flour

1. Combine haddock, instant minced onions, parsley flakes, salt, thyme, bay leaf, nutmeg, pepper and water in a large saucepan.
2. Cover and simmer 10 minutes.
3. Brown salt pork in separate skillet; blend in flour.
4. Add salt pork mixture to fish mixture; cook 5 minutes longer.

Hot Borscht

Serves 12

1½ pounds fresh brisket of
    beef, cut into ½-inch pieces
1 pound beef marrow soup bones
2 quarts water
1 tablespoon salt
1 can (1 pound) slivered beets
1 can (1 pound) tomatoes, broken up
3 tablespoons original Worcestershire
    sauce

3 cups shredded cabbage
1 cup shredded carrots
1 cup chopped onions
5 sprigs parsley
2 bay leaves
1 teaspoon sugar
dairy sour cream
dill sprig (optional garnish)

1. Combine beef, bones, water and salt in large saucepan; bring to a boil.
2. Skim off foam.
3. Reduce heat and simmer, covered, 1½ hours.
4. Meanwhile, strain beets from liquid; set both aside.
5. Stir beet liquid, tomatoes and 2 tablespoons Worcestershire into beef broth.
6. Add cabbage, carrots, onions, parsley, bay leaves and sugar. Bring to a boil.
7. Reduce heat and simmer, covered, 20 to 30 minutes longer.
8. Stir in reserved beets and remaining Worcestershire.
9. Serve with a dollop of sour cream and a sprig of dill, if desired.

Luscious Lentil Soup

Serves 8

2 cups dry lentils
4 cans (10¾ ounces each)
    condensed beef consommé
4 cups water
2 large onions, peeled and chopped
2 tablespoons butter or margarine

3 sprigs parsley
1 teaspoon dried thyme
1 bay leaf
salt to taste
freshly ground black pepper
    to taste

6 hot dogs, cooked and thinly sliced

1. Wash lentils. Cover with cold water and soak overnight.
2. Discard water. Place lentils in large saucepan; add consommé and water. Simmer slowly 1½ hours, or until lentils are tender.
3. Sauté onions in butter until golden.
4. Add onions to soup.
5. Add parsley, thyme and bay leaf; season to taste with salt and pepper.
6. Simmer ½ hour longer.
7. Add hot sliced hot dogs. Serve soup in large soup tureen, casserole or individual soup plates.

Lamb Mulligatawny Soup

Serves 6

2 pounds lamb neck bones
2 quarts water
salt
2 onions, minced

2 tablespoons butter or margarine
2 teaspoons curry powder
½ cup peas
3 tablespoons chopped pine nuts

lemon slices

1. Put lamb, water and salt in large stockpot.
2. Simmer 3 to 4 hours, or until meat falls off the bones, adding more water if needed to keep lamb covered as it cooks.
3. Remove meat and bones from stock. Set meat aside; discard bones.
4. Simmer liquid to reduce to 6 cups; set aside.
5. Sauté onions in butter until golden; remove onions.
6. Add curry powder to pan drippings; cook, stirring, over medium heat until dark brown.
7. Add curry mixture and onions to reserved broth.
8. Add peas. Taste to correct seasonings.
9. Add reserved lamb; simmer 15 minutes, or until peas are done.
10. Serve in individual soup bowls. Sprinkle with pine nuts and lemon slices.

NOTE: A tasty and inexpensive soup. Can be made with leftover lamb.

Lamb Vegetable Soup

Serves 4 to 6

6 cups water
½ cup barley, washed
½ cup chopped onion
½ cup chopped celery
2 tablespoons chopped parsley
1 teaspoon salt

½ teaspoon dried leaf thyme
¼ teaspoon Tabasco sauce
bones from 5- to 6-pound leg of New Zealand spring lamb
2 cups tomato juice or mixed vegetable juice

1 package (10 ounces) frozen mixed vegetables

1. Combine all ingredients except tomato juice and frozen vegetables in 4-quart saucepan; bring to a boil.
2. Cover, reduce heat, and simmer 30 minutes longer.
3. Remove bones.
4. Add tomato juice and frozen vegetables. Cover and simmer 10 minutes longer.
5. Meanwhile, remove any meat from bones; add to soup and heat.

Lentil-Spinach Soup

Serves 8

1 cup dried lentils
2 cups chopped onions
2 quarts water
½ tablespoon salt

¼ teaspoon black pepper
2 cups chopped raw spinach
  or Swiss chard
1 tablespoon olive oil

3 tablespoons fresh lemon juice

1. Soak lentils overnight as directed on package label.
2. Next morning, wash lentils thoroughly several times in cold water.
3. Cook onions and lentils in water with salt and pepper until lentils are tender, about 1½ hours.
4. Add spinach, olive oil and lemon juice; cook 20 minutes longer, or until spinach is tender.

Senate Bean Soup I

Serves 6

2 pounds white Michigan beans
water

1 smoked ham hock
salt to taste

pepper to taste

1. Pick over beans. Soak overnight in cold water. Drain and re-cover with water.
2. Add ham hock and simmer slowly 4 hours, or until beans are tender.
3. Add salt and pepper to taste.
4. Just before serving, press beans with soup ladle enough so texture of soup is cloudy.

NOTE: If desired, sweeten cooking water with a little chopped onion and carrot browned in small amount of butter before adding to stock. Cut meat from bone and add to soup.

Senate Bean Soup II

Serves 6

1½ cups dry Great Northern
  beans
water
1 smoked ham hock
1 medium potato, finely diced

1 onion, diced
¼ cup celery, sliced
½ cup garlic, minced
salt to taste
pepper to taste

chopped parsley

1. Soak beans overnight in 1 quart water. (Or for quick soak, heat beans and water to a boil; cook 2 minutes. Cover and let stand 1 hour.)
2. Drain beans; measure liquid. Add enough water to make 2 quarts.
3. Combine beans, water and ham hock in soup kettle; cover and simmer 2 hours.
4. Add potato, onion, celery and garlic; simmer 1 hour.
5. Remove ham hock; cut up meat and set aside.
6. Remove 1 cup beans and some liquid; purée in blender or food processor.
7. Return meat and purée to soup; heat.
8. Season to taste with salt and pepper; sprinkle with parsley. Serve piping hot.

Mom's Split Pea Soup with Croutons

Serves 10 to 12

2 cups dry green peas
10 cups cold water
1 large onion, chopped
2 carrots, chopped
bacon fat
1 ham bone or two smoked
  ham hocks

2 cloves fresh garlic, minced
½ teaspoon salt
1 teaspoon freshly ground black pepper
½ teaspoon marjoram
3 hot dogs, sliced in 1-inch pieces
  (optional)
Hot Buttered Croutons

1. Soak peas in water overnight.
2. Next day, sauté onion and carrots in bacon fat until tender.
3. Add ham bone, garlic, salt, pepper and marjoram; bring to a boil.
4. Reduce heat, cover, and simmer 3 hours, stirring often.
5. Remove ham bone, trim off meat, and return meat to soup.
6. Adjust seasonings.
7. Add hot dog slices. Serve with Hot Buttered Croutons.

Hot Buttered Croutons

1. Cube any bread into ½-inch cubes; sauté in butter or margarine until golden.
2. Sprinkle croutons sparingly with garlic powder while still hot; toss.
3. Float on top of soup.

Jamaican Pumpkin Soup

Serves 6

2 quarts cold water
1½ pounds boneless stewing beef
½ pound bacon slices,
  cut in half
2 cloves garlic, crushed
2 pounds pumpkin, sliced
2 medium white potatoes, diced

½ green or red pepper, diced
1 medium tomato, diced
1 medium onion, sliced
2 stalks scallion, sliced
2 sprigs thyme or 1 teaspoon
  powdered thyme
salt to taste

1. Put water, beef, bacon and garlic in a large saucepan; bring to a rapid boil.
2. Simmer until meat is tender, about 1 hour.
3. Add pumpkin and potatoes; stir and simmer 15 minutes.
4. Add pepper, tomato, onion, scallions and thyme. Stir thoroughly and simmer 20 minutes longer, or until vegetables are cooked.
5. Taste to correct seasonings, adding salt if necessary (bacon gives soup a saltiness already). Serve piping hot.

NOTE: For best results, use Caribbean pumpkin. It can be obtained at many supermarkets, in the tropical foods section, or in Spanish food shops. This delicious soup is served at the Hotel Inter-Continental in Ocho Rios, Jamaica.

Philadelphia Pepper Pot Soup

Serves 6

1½ pounds honeycomb tripe
water
salt
1 veal knuckle (about ½ pound)
1½ quarts water
1 tablespoon red pepper, diced
1 tablespoon green pepper, diced
1 tablespoon powdered thyme
6 bruised peppercorns

2 large bay leaves
3 whole cloves
3 to 4 tablespoons chopped parsley
2 large stalks celery, chopped
3 carrots, diced
2 tomatoes, peeled and cut up
4 onions, thinly sliced
1 piece pimiento, minced
4 potatoes, diced

1. Wash and scrub tripe; put in large stockpot and cover with cold water. Bring to a boil.
2. Add 1 teaspoon salt for each quart water. Simmer, covered, until tripe is tender (becomes clear and jelly-like in appearance), 3 to 4 hours. Do not boil. (This is the secret to making tripe tender.)
3. Drain and dice tripe into ½-inch squares.
4. Meanwhile, add veal knuckle to another stockpot with 1½ quarts water.
5. Add remaining ingredients except potatoes. Simmer 1 hour.
6. Add potatoes and cook until tender, about 1 hour.
7. Cut meat from bones and add together with tripe to vegetables.
8. Taste to correct seasonings.
9. Heat to serve.

NOTE: Great with hunks of dark bread.

Pork Soup-Stew, Polish Style

Serves 4 to 6

1 pound boneless pork shoulder,
    cut into 1-inch cubes
1 tablespoon shortening
1 tablespoon flour
1½ cups carrots, cut into
    1-inch lengths
1 cup sliced onion

1 can (10 ounces) tomatoes,
    undrained and cut up
1 cup water
1½ teaspoons salt
½ teaspoon caraway seed
4 cups coarsely chopped red
    cabbage

chopped parsley

1. Brown pork cubes in hot shortening.
2. Sprinkle with flour; stir to coat evenly.
3. Add carrots, onion, undrained tomatoes, water, salt and caraway seed; bring to a boil.
4. Cover, reduce heat, and cook slowly for 30 minutes.
5. Stir in cabbage. Cover and cook slowly until pork and vegetables are tender and flavors are blended, about 30 minutes.
6. Sprinkle with parsley. Serve with small boiled potatoes and/or crusty bread.

NOTE: Dish becomes "soupier" with the addition of more water.

Polish Mushroom Soup

Serves 4 to 6

¾ pound fresh mushrooms
2 tablespoons corn oil
1 package (1 pound) sauerkraut
water
2 cans (16 ounces each) whole
   tomatoes, broken up

¼ pound kielbasa (Polish sausage),
   sliced, then cut into halves
scant 1 teaspoon salt
1 teaspoon caraway seeds
1 bay leaf

1. Rinse, pat-dry and slice mushrooms.
2. Heat oil in large saucepan. Add mushrooms and cook until tender.
3. Meanwhile, place sauerkraut in a bowl. Cover with cold water; let stand 10 to 15 minutes.
4. Drain well and squeeze out water. Set aside.
5. Add tomatoes, 1 cup water, kielbasa, salt, caraway seeds and bay leaf to mushrooms bring to a boil. Reduce heat and simmer, covered, 15 minutes.
6. Add reserved sauerkraut. Simmer, covered, 15 minutes.

Russian Vegetable & Fish Soup

Serves 8

2 pounds whole fish
½ lemon
3 carrots, cut in strips
3 medium potatoes, peeled and sliced
1 cup instant minced onion

2 quarts water
1 bay leaf
1 tablespoon salt
6 whole black peppercorns
¼ teaspoon ground black pepper

1. Rub fish with lemon.
2. Place carrots, potatoes, onion, water, bay leaf, salt, peppercorns and black pepper in large stockpot. Cover and simmer 1 hour.
3. Add fish. (For easier handling, tie fish in cheesecloth.) Simmer 20 minutes.
4. Remove fish from soup, lift out bones, and remove and discard skin, fins and head.
5. Return fish to soup. Cook 1 minute. Serve piping hot.

Dilled Split Pea Soup

Serves 6

2 quarts water
1 cup dried split peas
½ cup finely diced fresh carrots
¼ cup instant minced onion

½ teaspoon salt
¼ teaspoon instant minced garlic
¹⁄₁₆ teaspoon ground black pepper
½ teaspoon dill weed, crushed

1. Bring water to a boil in large saucepan; add split peas, carrots, onion, salt, garlic and black pepper.
2. Simmer, covered, until thick, about 2½ hours.
3. Add dill weed; simmer 5 minutes longer.

Sauerkraut Soup

Serves 10

2 pounds pork shanks, ham hocks or pig's feet
1 quart water
1 medium onion, peeled and sliced
1 bay leaf
5 peppercorns
1 sprig parsley or ¼ teaspoon dried parsley leaves
1 pound sauerkraut
2 cups meat broth, bouillon or meat stock

few slices bacon, fried crisp, drained and diced, (optional)
handful raisins (optional)
3 tablespoons shortening or margarine (at room temperature)
1 tablespoon flour
½ teaspoon salt
¼ teaspoon ground black pepper
boiled potatoes or potato dumplings (optional)

1. Cook pork shanks in water in 5-quart kettle for 20 minutes. Skim off foam.
2. Add onion, bay leaf, peppercorns and parsley. Cook 45 minutes, or until meat is tender.
3. Remove meat from broth; strain broth. Return broth to kettle.
4. Remove meat from bones; discard skin and bones. Dice meat.
5. Rinse sauerkraut with cold water; drain.
6. Add to broth diced meat, drained sauerkraut, and, if desired, a little lean, diced bacon and raisins. Simmer 1 hour.
7. Mix shortening with flour to form smooth paste; stir into simmering soup.
8. Cook and stir over medium heat until thickened.
9. Mix in salt and pepper.
10. Serve with plain boiled potatoes or potato dumplings, if desired.

Seafood Soup

Serves 4 to 6

1 cup cooked cellophane noodles, cut in 2-inch noodles
1 can (10¾ ounces) condensed chicken soup
1 can (10¼ ounces) condensed oyster stew

1 soup can water
1 pound fillet of flounder, cut up
4 cups (¼ pound) chopped fresh spinach
½ cup drained bamboo shoots

1. Soak noodles in warm water 20 minutes to soften; drain.
2. Combine soups, water and fish in electric wok. Bring to a boil, stirring.
3. Reduce to simmer and cook 5 minutes.
4. Stir in spinach and bamboo shoots. Cover and cook 5 minutes over medium heat, stirring now and then.

NOTE: Substitute 1 cup cooked fine egg noodles for cellophane noodles.

South American Black Bean Soup

Serves 8

1 pound (2½ cups) dried
   black beans
water
1 meaty ham bone, weighing
   1 to 1½ pounds
2 cups chopped onion
1 cup chopped celery
1 cup chopped carrot
¼ cup snipped parsley
1 tablespoon original Worcestershire
   sauce

½ teaspoon dry mustard
2 bay leaves
3 whole cloves
½ teaspoon crushed dried thyme
3 tablespoons dry sherry
salt to taste
pepper to taste
2 hard-cooked eggs, chopped
   or sliced (for garnish)
several thin lemon slices
   (for garnish)

1. Rinse beans. Place in large pot with 6 cups cold water. Bring to a boil.
2. Reduce heat and simmer 2 minutes.
3. Remove from heat; cover and let stand 1 hour.
4. Drain beans; discard liquid.
5. Add ham bone, onion, celery, carrot, parsley, Worcestershire, mustard, bay leaves, cloves and thyme.
6. Stir in 7 cups water. Bring to a boil.
7. Reduce heat; simmer, covered, 2 to 2½ hours, or until beans are tender.
8. Remove ham bone; cut off meat and dice. Discard bone.
9. Place 2 cups bean mixture in blender container; cover and blend until smooth.
10. Return bean mixture to soup with diced ham and sherry. Heat through, then taste to correct seasonings.
11. Garnish with egg and lemon. Serve with hunks of chewy bread.

NOTE: *Beans are obtainable in Spanish markets or speciality stores. They are sometimes called "turtle beans."*

Split Pea Soup Supreme

Serves 8

2 cups dry split peas
2 quarts water
1 ham hock
½ cup celery, chopped

½ cup carrots, peeled and chopped
1 teaspoon onion, minced
salt to taste
pepper to taste

1. Place all ingredients in large soup kettle. Boil gently 2 hours, or until the consistency desired for soup.
2. Remove ham hock.
3. If desired, press peas through a coarse sieve to purée.
4. Chop meat from bone and return to soup.
5. Season with salt and pepper to taste. Add water to taste.

NOTE: *For a superb flavor and to strengthen the quantity, add a can of cream of potato soup and reheat. Wonderful with homemade bread for a winter meal!*

Hearty Turkey Soup

Serves 6

2 cans (13¾ ounces each)
   chicken broth
2½ cups cooked turkey pieces
2 cloves garlic, minced
1 cup chopped onion
3 tablespoons butter or margarine
¼ cup flour
1½ teaspoons seasoned salt

½ teaspoon rosemary, crumbled
dash pepper
1 can (16 ounces) stewed
   tomatoes, undrained
1 can (16 ounces) sliced
   carrots, undrained
1 can (17 ounces) early garden
   sweet peas, undrained

½ cup dry white wine (optional)

1. Sprinkle 3 tablespoons chicken broth over turkey pieces; set aside.
2. Sauté garlic and onion in butter in large kettle or Dutch oven.
3. Blend in flour, seasoned salt, rosemary and pepper. Add remaining broth.
4. Cook over low heat, stirring constantly until mixture boils and thickens.
5. Add turkey, tomatoes, carrots and peas. Reduce heat and simmer 20 minutes.
6. Add wine, if desired; boil 1 minute.

Turkey Vegetable Soup

Serves 6

1½ quarts turkey stock
1 cup crushed canned tomatoes
½ cup diced, peeled potatoes
½ cup diced celery
½ cup sliced zucchini
½ cup chopped carrots
½ cup sliced green beans, fresh
   or frozen

¼ cup chopped onion
1 teaspoon salt
¼ teaspoon poultry seasoning
3 tablespoons original Worcestershire
   sauce
1 cup diced, cooked turkey
¼ cup frozen peas
1 tablespoon chopped fresh parsley

1. Heat turkey stock, tomatoes, potatoes, celery, zucchini, carrots, green beans, onion,
   salt, poultry seasoning and Worcestershire together in large saucepan.
2. Simmer, covered, until vegetables are tender, about 20 minutes.
3. Add turkey, peas and parsley. Heat until hot.

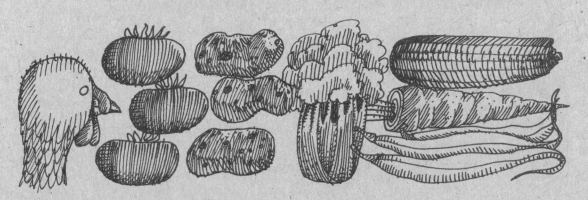

Sopa de Legumbres
(Mexican Vegetable Soup)

Serves 8

4 cups beef broth

4 cups water

1 can (8 ounces) tomato sauce

¼ cup instant minced onion

1¼ teaspoons thyme leaves, crushed

1¼ teaspoons instant minced garlic

1 teaspoon salt

½ teaspoon whole black pepper

4 whole cloves

1½ cups peeled potatoes, cut in ½-inch cubes

4 cups peeled acorn squash, cut in ½-inch cubes

½ pound boneless beef shoulder or chuck, cut in ½-inch cubes

4 cups coarsely sliced cabbage

¾ cup sliced carrot

¾ cup sliced celery

2 ears corn, cut in 1-inch lengths

1. Combine beef broth, water, tomato sauce, onion, thyme, garlic and salt in a large saucepot.
2. Add black pepper and cloves (tied in cheesecloth, if desired). Bring to a boil.
3. Reduce heat and simmer, covered, for 30 minutes.
4. Add potatoes and squash. Simmer, covered, 10 minutes.
5. Add beef, cabbage, carrot, celery and corn. Simmer, covered, until meat and vegetables are tender, about 10 minutes.

Worcestered Beef & Vegetable Soup

Serves 6

1½ pounds boneless beef chuck, cut in ½-inch cubes

2 tablespoons flour

1 teaspoon salt

1 teaspoon paprika

2 tablespoons corn oil

1½ quarts beef stock or water

1½ quarts canned tomatoes, chopped

½ cup original Worcestershire sauce

⅓ cup chopped onion

½ teaspoon minced garlic

½ cup sliced carrots

½ cup chopped celery

½ cup diced, peeled potatoes

1. Dredge meat with flour that has been mixed with salt and paprika; shake off excess.
2. Heat oil in large saucepan until hot. Brown meat in hot oil on all sides. Drain off excess fat.
3. Add beef stock, tomatoes, Worcestershire, onion and garlic. Bring to a boil.
4. Reduce heat and simmer, covered, until meat is almost tender, about 1½ hours.
5. Add carrots, celery and potatoes; mix gently.
6. Simmer, covered, until vegetables are tender, 20 minutes.

Steak Soup, Kansas Style

Serves 12 to 14

1 pound round steak, minced
1 cup butter or margarine
1 cup all-purpose flour
1 medium onion, chopped
1 large carrot, chopped
3 stalks celery, chopped
1 can (1 pound 13 ounces) tomatoes, chopped

3 quarts beef stock (page 95) or consommé
1 tablespoon original Worcestershire sauce
salt to taste
pepper to taste
1½ cups light cream or half-and-half

1. Brown meat in butter; stir in flour until smooth.
2. Add onion, carrot and celery; cook 10 minutes, stirring often.
3. Add remaining ingredients except cream; bring to a boil.
4. Simmer 1 to 3 hours. (The longer the soup cooks, the better it is.)
5. Add cream during last 5 minutes of cooking.

NOTE: *Soup can be frozen for future use.*

Hearty Vegetable Soup

Serves 12

2 lean meaty soup bones (preferably beef shank)
1 cup each of any 5 vegetables: sliced carrots, diced celery, sliced zucchini, sliced green beans, sliced leeks, sliced parsnips, chopped cabbage, peeled and cubed potato

3 quarts water
1 can (1 pound 12 ounces) tomatoes, cut up
1½ teaspoons seasoned salt
½ teaspoon seasoned pepper
1 cup barley
1 cup sliced fresh mushrooms

1. Brown soup bones either in skillet over high heat or in 400° F. oven.
2. Combine all ingredients except barley and mushrooms in large soup kettle; bring to a boil.
3. Reduce heat and simmer, covered, 2 hours.
4. Add barley; simmer 1 hour longer.
5. Add mushrooms; simmer 10 minutes.
6. Remove soup bones from kettle; let cool slightly.
7. Remove meat from bone; cut meat into pieces and return to soup.
8. Refrigerate overnight.
9. Skim any fat from surface; reheat soup and adjust seasonings before serving.

Lamb Barley Soup

Serves 8

2 tablespoons butter	2 bay leaves
1½ pounds ground lamb	½ cup barley
1 cup onions, chopped	1½ quarts water
1 cup celery, chopped	¼ cup lemon juice
1 cup sliced carrots	½ teaspoon salt
1½ cups peas, fresh or frozen	¼ teaspoon pepper

¼ cup chopped parsley

1. Melt butter in large pan; add lamb, onions and celery and cook until lamb is lightly browned, stirring often.
2. Pour off most of the fat; add carrots, peas, bay leaves, barley, water, lemon juice, salt and pepper.
3. Cover and cook over low heat 45 minutes, or until vegetables are tender, stirring often.
4. Add parsley; serve piping hot.

Mom's Hearty Vegetable Soup

Serves 12

4 stalks celery	¼ teaspoon ground pepper
1½ pounds beef with bone	2 stalks celery, chopped
8 cups water	6 medium potatoes
4 teaspoons salt	8 small carrots
2 teaspoons parsley	2 medium onions

2 cans (1 pound 4 ounces each) tomatoes

1. Wash celery stalks and leaves; cut stalks in pieces.
2. Cut meat off bone and cut meat into 1½-inch pieces; place meat and meat bone in saucepan.
3. Add water, salt, parsley, pepper and celery; cook gently 2 hours, or until meat is tender.
4. Meanwhile, peel and dice potatoes, scrape carrots and cut in ½-inch pieces, and peel and thinly slice onions.
5. Add vegetables to soup; continue to cook 1 hour longer, or until vegetables are tender.
6. Add tomatoes; cook soup 10 minutes longer.
7. Taste to correct seasonings and serve.

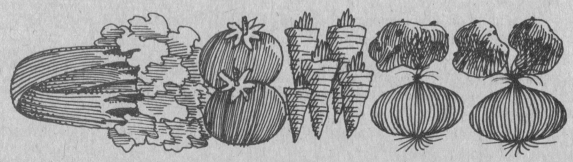

French-Canadian Pea Soup

Serves 4 to 6

1 pound salt pork
dry mustard
1 pound yellow peas
1 onion, peeled and halved
3 cloves
salt to taste

pepper to taste
1 large clove garlic, pressed
1 small carrot, peeled and sliced
cold water
thick dark bread
butter or sharp Cheddar cheese

1. Brush salt pork with mustard; cover and refrigerate overnight.
2. Wash and drain yellow peas. Cover with water and soak overnight (or at least 12 hours).
3. Put salt pork in large stockpot with drained peas.
4. Stick cloves into onion halves; add to pork-pea mixture.
5. Add salt, pepper, garlic, carrot and cold water to cover; bring to a boil.
6. Reduce heat and simmer; skim off foam.
7. Cover and simmer 3 to 4 hours, or until peas are very tender, skimming foam several times while soup simmers.
8. When soup is done, remove salt pork. Cut into bite-size pieces and return to pot.
9. Serve with thick slices of dark bread spread with butter or sharp Cheddar cheese.

NOTE: Makes an inexpensive meal.

Southern Corn-Okra Soup

Serves 6 to 8

2 tablespoons bacon drippings
   or 1 slice bacon, minced
2 tablespoons minced onion
3 pounds chicken, cut into
   serving pieces
½ cup flour

1 teaspoon salt
½ teaspoon black pepper
2 cups corn, fresh or canned
1 cup sliced okra, fresh or
   frozen
1 large fresh tomato, chopped

5 to 6 cups water

1. Heat bacon drippings or fry minced bacon in large soup pot.
2. Add onions; stir until heated through.
3. Mix flour with salt and pepper; dredge chicken pieces with seasoned flour.
4. Add chicken pieces to soup pot, one at a time, browning on all sides.
5. Add corn and okra; stir.
6. Lower heat to simmer, cover, and steam ingredients about 8 minutes, stirring often.
7. Add tomato and water; simmer 45 minutes to 1 hour, or until chicken is tender, adding more water if needed.
8. Spoon into large soup bowls with a piece of chicken for each serving.

Wheat Germ Pork Ball Soup

Serves 4

2 cans (10¾ ounces) condensed
  chicken broth
1 soup can water
2 ounces thin spaghetti
1 medium clove garlic, minced or
  pressed
1 teaspoon ginger root, grated,
  or ½ teaspoon ground ginger

1 cup carrots, cut in julienne strips
1 cup broccoli, thinly sliced
  (about ¼ pound)
Wheat Germ Pork Balls
1 cup fresh pea pods or
  1 package (6 ounces) frozen pea pods
1 cup chopped fresh spinach, romaine
  or chard, packed

1. Heat chicken broth and water to a boil.
2. Add spaghetti, garlic and ginger.
3. Return mixture to boiling; cover and simmer 6 minutes.
4. Add carrots and broccoli.
5. Continue to simmer, covered, 2 to 3 minutes longer or until vegetables are tender-crisp.
6. Add wheat germ pork balls, pea pods and spinach. Heat through.

Wheat Germ Pork Balls

½ pound ground pork
¾ cup vacuum-packed
  wheat germ
½ cup water chestnuts, chopped
2 tablespoons soy sauce

2 tablespoons water
1½ teaspoons fresh ginger root, grated,
  or ½ teaspoon ground ginger
⅛ teaspoon ground black pepper

1. Combine all ingredients. Form into 24 balls.
2. Place on baking sheet. Bake in preheated 400° F. oven 8 minutes, or until lightly browned.
3. Remove from oven, cover, and keep warm.

NOTE: For an interesting variation, follow recipe as given using ½ pound bulk pork sausage, 1 tablespoon soy sauce and 3 tablespoons water.

Lima Bean Cheese Soup Pronto

Serves 4

1 cup chopped onion
½ cup chopped green pepper
2 tablespoons butter
2 cans (11 ounces each) condensed
    Cheddar cheese soup
1½ soup cans water
1 cup frozen cut green beans

1 jar (2½ ounces) dried beef,
    rinsed and torn in shreds
1 package (10 ounces) frozen
    lima beans
1 cup diced potato
1 teaspoon prepared horseradish
1 teaspoon prepared yellow mustard

1. Cook onion and green pepper in butter until tender.
2. Add remaining ingredients. Bring to a boil.
3. Reduce heat and simmer 20 minutes, or until potato is done.

Quick Beef-Vegetable Soup

Serves 4

½ pound lean ground beef
1 can (10½ ounces) condensed
    minestrone soup
1 can (11 ounces) condensed tomato
    bisque soup

2 soup cans water
½ cup uncooked small bow noodles
½ teaspoon Italian seasoning, crushed
⅛ teaspoon freshly ground black pepper
2 cups frozen peas

grated Parmesan or Romano cheese

1. Brown meat in teflon-lined pan; stir to separate meat.
2. Pour off and discard fat.
3. Add remaining ingredients except peas and cheese. Bring to a boil.
4. Reduce heat and simmer 15 minutes.
5. Add peas; simmer 10 minutes longer, stirring often.
6. Serve with Parmesan cheese.

Borscht

Serves 5 to 6

2 cups shredded fresh beets
1 tablespoon butter or margarine
1 tablespoon vinegar or lemon juice
2 cans (10½ ounces each)
    condensed consommé

1 can (10¾ ounces) condensed onion
    soup
1 soup can water
1 cup tomato juice (more if desired)
2 cups shredded cabbage

¼ to ½ cup dairy sour cream

1. Cook beets in butter over low heat for a few minutes.
2. Add vinegar; cover and simmer 20 minutes.
3. Add soups, water, tomato juice, and cabbage. Cover and cook 10 minutes longer.
4. Serve hot; or chilled with sour cream as a garnish or stirred in just before serving.

Bloody Mary Soup

Serves 6

¼ cup butter
½ pound mushrooms, sliced
2 cans (16 ounces each) clamato juice
1½ tablespoons original Worcestershire sauce

1 teaspoon seasoned salt
½ cup vodka or gin
1 cup dairy sour cream (for garnish)
1 package (.56 ounces) toasted
 onion dip (for garnish)

1. Melt butter in large saucepan; sauté mushrooms until tender.
2. Stir in clamato juice, Worcestershire and seasoned salt; heat to serving temperature.
3. Turn into chafing dish.
4. Heat vodka, flame, and pour over soup.
5. Combine sour cream and onion dip; use as garnish for soup.

NOTE: *Three cups tomato juice and 1 cup clam juice may be substituted for clamato juice. Three tablespoons onion soup mix plus 1 tablespoon milk may be substituted for sour cream-onion dip.*

Cheesy Soup

Serves 6

½ cup minced carrots
½ cup diced celery
½ cup diced onion
½ cup diced green or
 red pepper
¼ cup butter or margarine

¼ cup flour
1 quart chicken broth
3 cups shredded Cheddar cheese
2 cups evaporated milk
¼ teaspoon salt
freshly ground black pepper

dry sherry

1. Sauté carrots, celery, onion and green pepper in butter 5 minutes.
2. Stir in flour until pasty.
3. Add chicken broth; simmer 5 minutes.
4. Add cheese slowly, stirring until melted.
5. Add evaporated milk and salt. Season to taste with pepper.
6. Add small amount of sherry just before serving.

Consommé Burgundy

Serves 4 to 6

4 cups clear rich beef broth,
 (page 95)
½ cup boiling water

1 small carrot, julienne
1 small onion, thinly sliced
¼ cup dry burgundy

1. Simmer all ingredients together in saucepan except burgundy about 3 to 5 minutes, or until vegetables are tender.
2. Add burgundy; heat but do not boil. Serve at once.

Gourmet Cheese Soup

Serves 4 to 5

3 slices bacon, cut up
½ cup chopped green onions
2 tablespoons flour
1 can (10½ ounces) cream of
   chicken soup

2 cups (8 ounces) shredded Cheddar
   cheese
1½ cups (12-ounce can) beer
1 cup milk
melba toast rounds

1. Cook bacon until crisp.
2. Add onion; sauté until tender, 1 to 2 minutes.
3. Remove from heat; stir in flour.
4. Stir in soup and heat to boiling.
5. Stir in cheese until melted.
6. Stir in beer and milk until foam disappears and soup is hot. (Do not boil.)
7. Serve topped with melba toast rounds.

NOTE: To make toast rounds, cut 2-inch circles from sandwich bread. Brush both sides with melted butter and place on baking sheet. Toast in preheated 400° F. oven 5 minutes; turn and toast an additional 5 minutes.

Chinese Hot & Sour Soup

Serves 4

4 small Chinese dried black
   mushrooms (optional)
½ cup canned bamboo shoots,
   drained and slivered
¼ pound boneless pork, slivered
1 tablespoon soy sauce
½ teaspoon salt
4 cups basic chicken stock (page 95)
   or canned chicken broth

1 cup slivered bean curd, fresh or
   canned
1 teaspoon ground white pepper
3 tablespoons red wine vinegar
2 tablespoons cornstarch mixed with
   2 tablespoons cold water
1 egg, beaten
1 tablespoon sesame oil
1 green onion, minced (for garnish)

1. Soak mushrooms in boiling water to cover for 30 minutes.
2. Drain; remove stems and shred caps.
3. Combine mushrooms, bamboo shoots, pork, soy sauce, salt and chicken stock in large stockpot. Bring to a boil.
4. Reduce heat and simmer 3 minutes.
5. Add bean curd, pepper and vinegar; bring to a boil again.
6. Add cornstarch-water mixture, stirring until soup thickens.
7. Gradually stir in egg.
8. Remove from heat and ladle into soup plates. Garnish with chopped green onion.

NOTE: This is a basic soup that can become a family favorite. It's a fine way to use leftover chicken or roast. Some Chinese cooks add chopped fresh tomatoes to soup to give the stock a nice tang!

Quick Manhattan Clam Chowder

Serves 6

½ cup onion flakes
½ teaspoon instant minced garlic
¼ cup water
2 tablespoons butter or margarine
1 can (1 pound 12 ounces) tomatoes, broken up
1 can (1 pound) whole potatoes, drained and diced

1 can (10½ ounces) minced clams
1 bottle (8 ounces) clam juice
1 bay leaf
1 teaspoon thyme leaves
¼ teaspoon salt
⅛ teaspoon ground black pepper
1½ tablespoons parsley flakes

1. Rehydrate onion flakes and minced garlic in water for 10 minutes.
2. Melt butter in large saucepan.
3. Add onion and garlic; sauté 5 minutes.
4. Add tomatoes, potatoes, clams, clam juice, bay leaf, thyme, salt and black pepper. Bring to a boil.
5. Reduce heat, cover, and simmer 20 minutes.
6. Sprinkle with parsley flakes just before serving.

Quick 'n' Hearty Corn & Fish Soup

Serves 4

1 can (1 pound) stewed tomatoes, broken up
1 bottle (8 fluid ounces) clam juice
1 package (12 ounces) frozen fish fillets, thawed and chunked

1 package (10 ounces) frozen succotash, thawed
1 tablespoon original Worcestershire sauce
¼ teaspoon salt

1. Combine all ingredients in saucepan.
2. Simmer, uncovered, until fish flakes when tested with a fork, about 15 minutes.

Ham & Rice Soup, Microwaved

Serves 4

¼ cup minced ham
¼ cup instant rice
¼ cup butter

2 teaspoons dried parsley flakes
4 teaspoons chicken bouillon granules
4 cups water

1. Combine ham, rice, butter, parsley and bouillon in 1½-quart casserole dish.
2. Cook on HIGH for 2 to 3 minutes.
3. Stir in water; cook on HIGH for 6 to 8 minutes, or until bubbling hot.

Creamed Corn Soup

Serves 10

4 slices bacon
¼ cup chopped onion
1 can (1 pound 1 ounce) cream-
style corn
1 can (10¾ ounces) condensed
cream of chicken soup
2 cups milk

½ cup water
1 envelope (.19 ounces) chicken-
flavored broth mix
1 tablespoon original Worcestershire
sauce
½ teaspoon salt
¼ cup chopped parsley

1. Fry bacon in large saucepan until crisp. Drain on paper towels, crumble, and set aside.
2. Sauté onion in pan drippings 2 minutes.
3. Stir in corn, soup, milk, water, chicken broth mix, Worcestershire and salt. Bring to a boil.
4. Reduce heat and simmer, uncovered, 2 minutes longer.
5. Stir in parsley and reserved bacon.

Spanish Garlic Soup

Serves 4

4 large cloves fresh garlic,
peeled
2 cans (10½ ounces each)
condensed beef broth

2 cups water
1 cup dry sherry
4 small slices French bread
¼ cup butter, softened

2 tablespoons grated Parmesan cheese

1. Add garlic to beef broth. Cover and simmer 15 minutes, or until garlic is soft.
2. Remove garlic and set aside.
3. Add water and sherry to broth. Heat to serving temperature.
4. Toast bread on one side under broiler.
5. Remove and spread untoasted sides with butter.
6. Mash garlic; spread over bread and sprinkle with cheese.
7. Broil until brown and bubbly, about ½ minute.
8. Place toasted bread slice in each of 4 serving bowls. Ladle hot soup over it and serve at once.

Seafood Bisque Pronto

Serves 6

1 can (10½ ounces) condensed
   green pea soup
1 can (10½ ounces) condensed
   tomato soup
1 cup light cream

1 pound crab meat, frozen or fresh,
   or 1 pound cooked, shelled and
   deveined shrimp, cut in quarters
1 tablespoon brown sugar
2 tablespoons rum

2 tablespoons chopped chives (for garnish)

1. Combine pea and tomato soups with cream in saucepan; heat, 15 minutes, stirring often. (Do not boil.)
2. Add crab meat or shrimp; simmer 10 minutes (Do not boil.)
3. Remove from heat; stir in brown sugar and rum.
4. Serve in consommé cups; garnish with chives.

Chinese Beef & Cabbage Soup

Serves 6

1 tablespoon soy sauce
1 teaspoon sesame oil (Chinese grocery)
½ pound boneless sirloin steak,
   thinly sliced
1 dried tangerine peel (Chinese
   grocery), cut up

4 cans (14 ounces) beef broth
½ pound Chinese cabbage, cut in
   2-inch slices
3 dried Chinese mushrooms, soaked
   and quartered
½ teaspoon sugar

1. In bowl, combine soy sauce and oil; add beef and tangerine peel; tossing to coat.
2. Set mixture aside for 30 minutes; stirring now and then.
3. In a kettle, bring broth to a boil; add cabbage, mushrooms and sugar and cook over low heat 10 minutes.
4. Add beef mixture; cook 5 minutes (longer, if desired, or until done). Serve at once.

NOTE: A beautiful soup to look at; delicate to taste.

Lettie's Liver Soup

Serves 4 to 6

3 slices bacon
1 tablespoon butter
2 tablespoons chopped onion
1 tablespoon chopped parsley
3 carrots, minced

3 celery stalks, finely chopped
1 pound beef liver
2 cans (10¾ ounces each) beef bouillon
2 soup cans water
1½ teaspoons Angostura bitters

3 egg yolks, well beaten

1. Cook bacon until crisp; remove from pan.
2. Add butter to bacon fat; slowly sauté onion, parsley, carrots, celery and liver until meat is tender and vegetables are golden, about 15 minutes.
3. Put entire mixture (liver, bacon and vegetables) through food chopper or blend in electric blender.
4. Put bouillon diluted with water into soup pot; add meat mixture and Angostura. Simmer 5 minutes, stirring constantly.
5. Just before serving, slowly and gradually mix in egg yolks.

Pork Vegetable Soup, Southern Style

Serves 4

1 pound boneless pork shoulder
1 tablespoon flour
1 teaspoon salt
½ teaspoon freshly grated black pepper
1 tablespoon corn oil
1 medium potato, peeled and cut in ½-inch cubes
1 can (12 ounces) whole kernel corn, drained

1 small onion, sliced
2 tablespoons catsup
1 tablespoon honey
1 tablespoon fresh lemon juice or vinegar
1 clove garlic, pressed
3½ cups water
1 package (10 ounces) frozen okra, sliced
2 tablespoons diced green pepper

1. Cut pork into 1¼-inch cubes.
2. Combine flour, salt and pepper.
3. Dredge pork in seasoned flour; brown in hot oil until brown on all sides.
4. Add potato, corn, onion, catsup, honey, lemon juice, garlic and water. Cover and simmer 1 hour.
5. Add okra and green pepper. Cover and simmer 30 minutes longer, or until pork and vegetables are fork-tender.
6. Taste to correct seasonings. Serve piping hot.

Minestrone Pronto

Serves 8 to 10

¼ cup olive or corn oil
1 cup minced onion
½ cup chopped celery
6 cups beef broth or clam juice
2 medium zucchini, cut into ¼-inch
  cubes
1 can (1 pound) Italian tomatoes

1 can (1 pound) cannelini beans
  or other white beans
1 cup uncooked macaroni
1 cup finely chopped cabbage
½ cup chopped parsley
1 clove fresh garlic, minced
1 teaspoon salt

½ teaspoon freshly ground black pepper

1. Heat oil in medium saucepan.
2. Add onion and celery, cook until crisp-tender, 12 to 15 minutes.
3. Add broth, zucchini, tomatoes, beans, macaroni, cabbage, parsley and garlic. Simmer, uncovered, 30 minutes.
4. Season to taste with salt and pepper. Serve with hunks of crusty Italian bread.

Summer Squash Soup

Serves 4

2 cans (13¾ ounces each) beef
  broth (3⅓ cups)
2 medium-size yellow squashes,
  sliced
2 medium onions, sliced (1 cup)

pinch pepper
¼ cup plain yogurt
fresh alfalfa sprouts or
  shredded carrots
  (optional garnish)

1. Simmer broth in large stockpot.
2. Add squash and onions; simmer until tender, about 15 minutes.
3. Season with pepper.
4. In container of electric blender, combine broth, vegetables and yogurt. Blend until smooth.
5. Serve hot or cold. Garnish with fresh alfalfa sprouts or shredded carrots, if desired.

NOTE: Choose either crookneck or straightneck squash for this soup.

Tangy Appetizer Soup

Serves 4

2 cans (10½ ounces each) beef
  broth
2 soup cans water

1 tablespoon prepared horseradish
2 to 4 drops of fresh lime or
  lemon juice

½ teaspoon dill weed

1. Mix all ingredients in saucepan; heat, stirring occasionally.
2. Serve in mugs or bowls.

Clear Mushroom Soup & Cheese Brambles

Serves 6

¼ cup margarine
4 cups (about ¾ pound) sliced
   fresh mushrooms
1 cup sliced onion

2 tablespoons chopped parsley
2 tablespoons flour
¼ teaspoon pepper
5 cups chicken broth

1. Melt margarine in large saucepan.
2. Sauté mushrooms, onion and parsley until tender.
3. Stir in flour and pepper. Remove from heat.
4. Gradually stir in chicken broth. Bring to a boil, stirring constantly.
5. Reduce heat; simmer 5 minutes.

Cheese Brambles

Makes about 20 pastries

½ cup margarine, softened
1 package (3 ounces) cream cheese
1 cup unsifted flour

¼ teaspoon original Worcestershire
   sauce
dash cayenne pepper

about ¼ pound Cheddar cheese, cut into ½-inch cubes

1. Cream margarine and cream cheese together until smooth.
2. Blend in flour, Worcestershire sauce and cayenne.
3. Gather dough into a ball; wrap and chill 1 hour.
4. Roll out pastry on a floured board to ⅛-inch thickness. Cut into 3-inch squares.
5. Place a cheese cube in center of each square. Fold in half to form triangles; seal edges well.
6. Reroll scraps; repeat.
7. Place on baking sheets. Bake in preheated 450° F. oven 10 minutes, or until golden brown. Serve warm.

NOTE: A nice variation on soup and sandwiches for lunch!

Spinach-Lime Soup

Serves 2

1 can (10¾ ounces) condensed
   cream of chicken soup
1 soup can milk
1 cup spinach leaves, torn
   in small pieces

1 teaspoon lime juice
toasted coconut (for garnish)
chopped macadamia nuts
lime slices or wedges

1. Combine soup, milk, spinach and lime juice in blender; blend until smooth.
2. Heat mixture in saucepan, stirring occasionally.
3. Garnish with coconut.
4. Serve with nuts and lime wedges.

Japanese Bean Curd Soup

Serves 6

4 dried mushrooms, soaked
  in cold water 30 minutes
2 cans (10¾ ounces each)
  condensed chicken broth
2 soup cans water

2 tablespoons cornstarch
2 tablespoons soy sauce
2 tablespoons sweet sherry
2 thin slices ginger root
2 cups bean curd, diced

1. Drain mushrooms; slice.
2. In saucepan, combine all ingredients except bean curd; bring to a boil, stirring constantly.
3. Reduce heat, cover, and cook over low heat 15 minutes.
4. Add bean curd; cook 5 minutes more, stirring occasionally.
5. Remove ginger and serve.

NOTE: Japanese bean curd (tofu) is available fresh or canned in supermarkets or health food stores.

Chicken Cup Oriental

Serves 6 to 8

½ cup green pepper, chopped
⅛ teaspoon ground ginger
2 tablespoons butter or margarine
3 cans (10¾ ounces each) condensed cream of chicken soup

2 soup cans water
1 soup can milk
1 can (13¾ ounces) crushed
  pineapple, drained
toasted coconut (for garnish)

1. Cook pepper with ginger in butter in saucepan until tender.
2. Stir in remaining ingredients except coconut; heat, stirring occasionally.
3. Garnish with toasted coconut.

Dieter's Egg Drop Soup

Serves 4

2 cans chicken broth
1 small can (4 ounces) sliced mushrooms
  or ½ cup fresh mushrooms, sliced

1 scallion with tops, finely chopped
1 egg, slightly beaten
soy sauce to taste

1. Bring chicken broth to a boil.
2. Add mushrooms and scallion.
3. Pour in egg while stirring slowly so eggs form shreds.
4. Add soy sauce to taste.

Sour Cream Mushroom Soup

Serves 4 to 6

¼ cup butter
1 teaspoon garlic salt
4 cups mushrooms, sliced
½ cup chopped onion

2 cups double-strength beef bouillon
1 tablespoon soy sauce
¼ teaspoon fines herbes
⅛ teaspoon white pepper

½ cup dairy sour cream

1. Melt butter in large skillet; stir in garlic salt.
2. Add mushrooms; sauté until tender.
3. Add chopped onion; cook until soft.
4. Stir in bouillon, soy sauce, fines herbes and pepper. Cover and simmer 5 minutes.
5. Remove from heat; thoroughly blend in sour cream. Serve immediately.

Okra Soup Supreme

Serves 6

3 large onions, chopped
½ stick sweet butter
1 pound tomatoes, peeled, seeded
   and chopped

½ pound fresh okra, cut in 1-inch pieces
1½ quarts chicken stock (page 95)
salt to taste
white pepper to taste

3 tablespoons cooked rice

1. Sauté onions in butter until limp.
2. Add tomatoes and okra; sauté, stirring 2 to 3 minutes.
3. Add chicken stock; heat until simmering.
4. Season to taste with salt and pepper. Add rice just before serving.

NOTE: For an unusual touch, add ¼ cup cream-style corn in lieu of rice to this very southern soup.

Sunny Black Magic Sipper

Serves 2 to 3

1 can (11 ounces) condensed black
   bean soup
1 can (10½ ounces) condensed
   beef broth

1 soup can water
½ cup dairy sour cream
½ teaspoon dry mustard
5 drops yellow food coloring

toasted sunflower seeds, lightly salted

1. Combine bean soup and beef broth in saucepan. Heat and stir.
2. Gradually stir in water; heat thoroughly.
3. Blend together sour cream, mustard and food coloring.
4. Spoon soup into soup plates.
5. Garnish with sour cream mixture; sprinkle with sunflower seeds.

Tomato Beef Bouillon

Serves 3 to 4

1 can (10½ ounces) beef bouillon
1 can (8 ounces) tomato juice
¼ teaspoon onion salt
⅛ teaspoon celery salt
pinch of marjoram

1. Combine all ingredients in saucepan.
2. Simmer several minutes to blend flavors.
3. Serve hot or cold.

Tomato Bouillon

Serves 4 to 6

3 cups strained tomato juice
¼ small bay leaf
¼ cup celery, cut up with leaves
2 tablespoons chopped fennel
2 whole cloves
½ teaspoon fresh herbs: oregano, basil or dill

1 small skinned, chopped onion, sautéed in 1 tablespoon butter
1 tablespoon butter
½ teaspoon salt
few grains pepper
few grains celery salt
dairy sour cream

1. Combine tomato juice, bay leaf, celery, fennel, cloves, fresh herbs and sautéed onion in saucepan. Bring to a boil.
2. Simmer 5 minutes; strain.
3. Add butter, salt, and pepper and celery salt to taste. Heat, stirring.
4. Serve bouillon hot or cold in cups topped with a dollop of sour cream.

Quick Clam Tomato Soup

Serves 3 to 4

1 can (about 8 ounces) minced clams
¼ cup chopped onion
¼ cup chopped leeks
2 tablespoons chopped shallots
2 tablespoons olive oil

¼ teaspoon ground coriander
¼ teaspoon fennel seed
1 can (11 ounces) condensed tomato bisque soup
½ cup water
croutons (optional garnish)

1. Drain clams, reserving juice; set aside.
2. Cook onion, leeks and shallots in olive oil with coriander and fennel in saucepan until tender.
3. Add soup, reserved clam juice and water.
4. Pour into blender; blend until smooth.
5. Return mixture to saucepan; add minced clams and heat, stirring occasionally.
6. Garnish with croutons, if desired.

Cary's Sausage Vegetable Soup

Makes about 2 quarts (6 to 8 servings)

4 cups beef stock or broth
2 cups water
1 cup chopped onion
2 cloves garlic, mashed
1½ teaspoons dried oregano
  leaves, crumbled

3 carrots, sliced
1½ pounds Italian sweet
  sausage, sliced
1 pound fresh mushrooms, sliced
1 pound fresh spinach, washed,
  trimmed and chopped

1. Bring beef stock and water to a boil in large kettle; add onion, garlic and oregano.
2. Reduce heat and simmer 15 minutes.
3. Add carrots; cook 15 minutes longer, or until carrots are tender.
4. Sauté sausage in skillet; remove and drain on paper towels.
5. Add sausage and mushrooms to kettle; bring to a boil.
6. Add spinach; cook 1 minute.
7. Serve at once.

Food Processor Fresh Tomato Soup

Serves 4

1 pound fresh ripe tomatoes
1 medium onion, quartered
1 clove garlic, peeled and
  crushed
½ teaspoon seasoned salt
2 teaspoons sugar (optional)
¼ teaspoon paprika

¼ teaspoon basil
¼ teaspoon thyme
2 teaspoons cornstarch
1 tablespoon butter
1 cup tomato juice
Croutons
¼ cup half-and-half (optional)

1. Peel tomatoes by plunging into boiling water 1 minute, then into cold water. (Skins will slip off easily.)
2. Cut tomatoes into quarters.
3. Put metal blade in place in processor; process tomatoes, onion, garlic, seasonings and cornstarch until mixture is puréed.
4. Melt butter in medium-size saucepan; add tomato mixture and juice.
5. Cook, stirring constantly, until soup comes to a boil; simmer 5 minutes.
6. Top with croutons to serve.
7. For Cream of Tomato Soup, add half-and-half just before serving.

Croutons

sliced stale whole grain
  bread

sweet butter
grated Parmesan cheese

1. Spread bread very lightly with butter; sprinkle with Parmesan cheese.
2. Arrange bread slices on baking sheet; bake in preheated 300° F. oven 15 minutes.
3. Break or cut bread into pieces. (Croutons will keep well in tightly sealed container.)

167

Gooseberry Soup

Serves 4

1 pound fresh gooseberries
rind and juice of ½ lemon
3-inch piece stick cinnamon

1 quart water
½ cup sugar
2 tablespoons cornstarch

½ cup dry white wine (optional)

1. Wash gooseberries; put berries into saucepan with thinly pared lemon rind, cinnamon stick and water. Simmer until gooseberries soften.
2. Remove cinnamon stick and lemon.
3. Put mixture through a fine-hair sieve.
4. Return mixture to rinsed saucepan; add sugar and cornstarch blended together. Boil 10 minutes, stirring.
5. Add wine and lemon juice; reheat. Serve hot.

NOTE: *Great dessert! Nice and tart-flavored!*

Grape Dessert Soup

Serves 8

1½ cups water
⅓ cup sugar
1 stick cinnamon
2 cups white grape juice
3 tablespoons quick-cooking tapioca

1 can (18 ounces) pineapple juice
1½ teaspoons grated lemon peel
2 cups red or white seedless
grapes
½ cup rosé wine

1. Combine water, sugar, cinnamon and grape juice. Bring to a boil.
2. Add tapioca and cook 5 minutes, stirring often.
3. Remove from heat; add pineapple juice and lemon peel. Chill.
4. Remove cinnamon stick before serving. Stir in grapes and wine.

NOTE: *If desired, use red grape juice and red wine for deep color. An unusual dessert soup!*

Blackberry Soup

Serves 3 to 4

1 quart fresh blackberries
4 teaspoons lemon juice
6 tablespoons sugar
2 teaspoons cornstarch

dash salt
¾ cup water
lemon slices (for garnish)
mint leaves (for garnish)

1. Wash blackberries; crush and put through sieve or press in electric blender.
2. Stir in lemon juice; set berry mixture aside.
3. Combine sugar, cornstarch and salt in saucepan; blend in water and bring to a boil.
4. Cook 1 minute, or until mixture clears.
5. Remove from heat; stir in blackberry purée.
6. Cover and chill for several hours.
7. Serve in chilled bouillon cups; garnish with fresh lemon slices and mint leaves.

Huckleberry Soup

Serves 6 to 8

2 quarts water
scant cup sugar
¼ lemon rind, thinly sliced
4½ cups cleaned huckleberries
    or blueberries

2 tablespoons cold water
1 tablespoon cornstarch
dash salt
whipped cream or yogurt
    (optional)

1. Combine water, sugar, yellow part of lemon rind and huckleberries. Bring to a boil in large saucepan.
2. Cook until berries soften, stirring occasionally.
3. Blend cold water with cornstarch. Stir in small amount of berry mixture, then return to remaining berry liquid with salt, stirring until smooth.
4. Cook until slightly thickened, stirring.
5. Serve hot or cold. Serve with whipped cream or yogurt, if desired.

Orange Fruit Soup

Serves 8

2 tablespoons quick-cooking
    tapioca
2½ cups Florida orange juice
2 tablespoons sugar
dash of salt
2 cinnamon sticks

1½ cups cut-up Florida
    orange sections with juice
1 package (12 ounces) frozen
    sliced peaches, thawed, and cut
    in pieces
1 banana, sliced

sour cream (optional)

1. Mix tapioca, orange juice, sugar and salt in saucepan. Let stand 5 minutes.
2. Add cinnamon sticks. Bring to a boil over medium heat.
3. Remove from heat; cool 20 minutes.
4. Remove cinnamon sticks.
5. Add oranges, peaches, and bananas; heat.
6. If desired, serve with sour cream and additional orange sections.

Cold Raspberry Soup

Serves 6

1 package (10 ounces) frozen raspberries,
    thawed
1 can (11 ounces) mandarin oranges,
    undrained
½ cup fresh orange juice

¼ cup dry red wine
¼ cup lemon juice
1 cup dry white wine
1 tablespoon kirsch
finely chopped fresh mint

mint sprigs (for garnish)

1. Combine all ingredients except mint in glass bowl or jar.
2. Taste, adjusting flavor with additional lemon juice, sugar and white wine; chill well.
3. To serve, sprinkle with minced mint; garnish with mint sprigs.

NOTE: *Works as a delightful finish to a summer meal or as a punch.*

Apple Curry Soup

Serves 4 to 5

½ cup chopped onion
4 medium tart apples, peeled and cut in pieces
2½ teaspoons curry powder
3 tablespoons butter
1 can (10¾ ounces) condensed cream of chicken soup

1 can (10¾ ounces) condensed chicken broth
2 teaspoons lemon juice
3 teaspoons sugar
dash cayenne pepper
1 cup light cream

1. Cook onion, apple and curry powder in butter in saucepan until tender.
2. Add soup, broth, lemon juice, sugar and pepper.
3. Pour mixture into blender; blend until smooth.
4. Return mixture to saucepan; gradually stir in cream and heat, stirring occasionally.
5. Chill 6 hours before serving.

NOTE: Great as dessert to seal a meal!

Swedish Fruit Soup

Makes 2 quarts

2 cups mixed dried fruits: apricots, peaches, pears and pitted prunes
½ cup seedless raisins
2 quarts water
1 cup sugar

3-inch piece stick cinnamon
3 tablespoons tapioca
2 teaspoons Angostura aromatic bitters
few drops red food coloring
whipped or dairy sour cream

1. Place dried fruits in large kettle with tight-fitting cover. Pour cold water over fruits and let stand 1 hour.
2. Add sugar and cinnamon; cook slowly, covered, 1 hour.
3. Soften tapioca in ½ cup cold water 5 minutes.
4. Add Angostura; pour into soup.
5. Cook until soup is clear, about 10 minutes.
6. Remove from heat and add food coloring.
7. Cool, then chill thoroughly in refrigerator.
8. Serve in soup bowls with dollop of sweet whipped or sour cream.

NOTE: Fantastic dessert in hot or cold weather!

Soup Service & Garnishes

Soup Service: *How* the soup is presented has a great deal to do with your enjoyment of this delightful dish. Think beyond the traditional shallow soup plate or cream soup bowls. Ladle soup from a deep-covered casserole or bean pot — it's pretty to look at and keeps the soup piping hot too! Or sip soup from attractive mugs or spoon jellied consommé into frosty sherbet glasses.

Soup Garnishes: Add color and a bit of flavor too. A perfect example is a bowl of bright red tomato soup topped off with pungent chopped fresh parsley or chives. Some other garnishes include:

>**freshly grated Parmesan or Romano cheese**
>**lemon slices**
>**grated orange or lemon rind**
>**butter-fried croutons**
>**paprika**
>**crisp potato chips**
>**sliced pimiento-stuffed olives**
>**whipped cream or sour cream**
>**popcorn**
>**ground nutmeg**
>**toasted rounds of French bread**

Curry Cheese Muffins

½ cup Cheddar cheese, shredded
2 tablespoons mayonnaise

scant ½ teaspoon curry powder
2 English muffins, split

1. Combine cheese and mayonnaise.
2. Add curry powder to taste.
3. Spread on split English muffins; run under broiler.
4. Serve with cream of pea soup, or cut into tiny wedges for hot hors d'oeuvres.

Helen's Pepper Cornbread

1 box cornbread mix
1 fresh green pepper, diced
1 fresh red pepper, diced, or
 ½ teaspoon crushed red pepper

1 can (8 ounces) corn kernels,
 drained
chopped pimiento (optional)

1. Mix cornbread mix according to package directions.
2. Add diced green and red pepper, corn kernels, and chopped pimiento, if desired.
3. Pour into greased pan and bake until golden brown. Phenomenal with bean or ham soup!

Biscuit Salt Sticks

Serves 8

1 package prepared biscuits   caraway seeds
2 tablespoons butter, melted   coarse salt

1. Wrap a 3 x 5-inch strip of aluminum foil around the handle of a wooden spoon.
2. Roll each biscuit between your hands, stretching to a rope 10 inches long.
3. Wrap dough around the aluminum foil.
4. Slip foil off spoon handle onto a baking sheet.
5. Repeat for each biscuit.
6. Brush biscuits with butter; sprinkle with caraway seeds and salt.
7. Bake in preheated 450° F. oven 12 minutes, or until browned.
8. Twist ends of aluminum foil in opposite directions; carefully slip biscuits from foil.

California Wheat Germ Buns

Serves 6

1 package (13¾ ounces) hot roll mix
1½ cups finely shredded cabbage
1 cup minced onion
2 tablespoons water
½ pound bulk pork sausage
⅔ cup vacuum-packed toasted wheat germ

⅓ cup minced fresh parsley
1 teaspoon salt
½ teaspoon thyme leaves, crushed
4 teaspoons original Worcestershire sauce
1 egg, beaten

1. Prepare hot roll dough according to package directions; cover and let rise in warm place while preparing filling.
2. To prepare filling:
   a. Place cabbage, onion and water in skillet. Cover and bring to a boil.
   b. Steam over medium heat 5 minutes.
   c. Remove from skillet; set aside.
   d. Brown sausage in same skillet over medium-high heat. Drain off and discard all but 1 teaspoon fat.
   e. Add wheat germ to sausage and stir 1 minute.
   f. Remove from heat; add cabbage mixture, parsley, salt, thyme and Worcestershire.
3. Turn dough onto lightly floured surface.
4. Divide into 6 equal parts. Roll each part into 6-inch round.
5. Spoon filling into center of rounds.
6. Gather edges of dough up over filling to meet in center. Pinch together to seal.
7. Carefully lift with spatula to greased baking sheet.
8. Brush with beaten egg.
9. Let rise 30 to 45 minutes in warm place.
10. Bake in preheated 400° F. oven 20 to 25 minutes, or until golden.

Poppy Seed Biscuit Twists

Serves 6 to 8

1 package biscuits   2 tablespoons butter, melted
                          poppy seeds

1. Roll each biscuit between hands, stretching to 8 inches long.
2. Shape dough into a loop; pull one end of dough partly through center.
3. Place on greased baking sheet.
4. Brush biscuits lightly with butter. Sprinkle with poppy seeds.
5. Bake in preheated 450° F. oven 12 minutes, or until golden brown. Serve piping hot with corn chowder.

Fancy Bread Fingers

Makes 24 fingers

6 frankfurter buns   ¼ cup butter or margarine
¼ cup garlic spread   ¼ cup grated Parmesan cheese
                 poppy seeds or sesame seeds

1. Cut buns in half lengthwise; then cut again lengthwise to make bread fingers.
2. Melt garlic spread and butter together and brush onto cut sides of bread.
3. Sprinkle with grated cheese and poppy seeds.
4. Place on cookie sheet.
5. Toast in preheated 450° F. oven 8 minutes.
6. Serve piping hot with your favorite soup. Excellent with green salads and Italian-type casseroles.

Knaidlach

Makes 18 matzo balls

⅓ cup peanut oil   ⅛ teaspoon pepper
½ cup minced onion   2 tablespoons minced parsley
2 eggs, separated   ⅔ cup matzo meal
⅓ cup cold water   boiling chicken stock (page 95)
1 teaspoon salt   or salted water

1. Heat peanut oil in saucepan; cook onion in hot oil until tender.
2. Remove from heat.
3. Beat together egg yolks, cold water, salt and pepper.
4. Gradually beat in onions until completely blended.
5. Stir in parsley and matzo meal.
6. Beat egg whites until stiff peaks form; gradually fold into matzo meal mixture.
7. Cover and chill in refrigerator 1 hour.
8. Using 2 teaspoons, measure rounded teaspoons of matzo meal mixture, shape into balls, and drop into boiling chicken soup or salted water. Serve with hot soup.

Kasha Kreplach

Makes 2 dozen

¼ cup peanut oil
1⅓ cups cooked kasha
½ cup grated onion
1½ teaspoons salt

¼ teaspoon pepper
3 eggs
1½ cups unsifted
   all-purpose flour

2 teaspoons cold water

1. Heat peanut oil in large skillet.
2. Add kasha, onion, 1 teaspoon salt and pepper; sauté mixture 5 minutes.
3. Remove pan from heat; allow to cool 15 minutes.
4. Stir in 1 egg.
5. Sift flour and remaining salt into large mixing bowl or onto wooden board. Make a well in center and add remaining eggs and water.
6. Using hands, work into a dough; knead until smooth and elastic, about 8 to 10 minutes.
7. Divide dough in half. Roll each half into a 9 x 12-inch rectangle. Between rolling strokes, carefully stretch dough with hands from the center outward.
8. Cut into 3-inch squares; fill each square with 1 tablespoon kasha.
9. Moisten 2 adjacent edges with water; fold unmoistened edges over to form triangles. Seal edges tightly.
10. Cook in boiling salted water 2 to 3 minutes, or until kreplach rise to surface of water. Drain. (If desired, kreplach may be sautéed in peanut oil until golden.)

Potato Knishes

Makes 3½ dozen

3 cups mashed potatoes
¾ minced onion
6 tablespoons peanut oil
1⅝ teaspoons salt

⅛ teaspoon pepper
1¼ cups unsifted flour
1 tablespoon sugar
3 tablespoons lukewarm water

1 egg, beaten

1. Combine mashed potatoes, onion, 2 tablespoons peanut oil, 1½ teaspoons salt and pepper. Set aside.
2. Mix together flour, sugar and ⅛ teaspoon salt. Stir in remaining peanut oil, water and egg.
3. Knead dough on lightly floured board until smooth and elastic, about 3 to 5 minutes.
4. Roll dough into a 21 x 9-inch rectangle. Cut into three 21 x 3-inch strips.
5. Place a layer of potato filling ¾-inch high and ¾-inch wide down center of each strip.
6. Lift flap of dough over filling and roll over the remaining dough. Seal well.
7. Cut into 1½-inch knishes.
8. Place on baking sheets, cut side up, and flatten slightly with palm of hand.
9. Brush lightly with peanut oil.
10. Bake in preheated 350° F. oven 30 minutes, or until lightly browned.

Salads

Introduction

Few dishes appeal more than salads, especially to Americans looking for something colorful, tasteful and low in calories. Salads are excellent sources of vitamins, minerals and cellulose. Protein additions — cheese, eggs, nuts, fish, poultry, meat or legumes — can turn the versatile salad into a meal itself.

Envision the glorious salad! It's more than just another dish. It requires a creative act to become an improvisation. The key to making any successful salad is in the selection and preparation of the ingredients, be it a bowl filled with sassy, crisp assorted greens dressed with a tangy dressing, a colorful array of mouth-watering fruits-in-season with a creamy-curry dressing, or a heartier combination of cooked pasta tossed with morsels of cooked seafood or julienne strips of cooked chicken or ham.

The salad must taste as good as it looks! All it takes is imagination and time to balance colors, textures and flavors. When selecting the salad, consider carefully the rest of the menu. The salad could provide a simple prelude to the main course, a serve-along dish to roast or fowl, or as a dessert to "cleanse the palate," when served after the entrée.

The time of year affects both the availability of salad materials and the cost of creating your culinary masterpiece. Spring and summer especially provide a host of fresh garden produce ranging from the first tender spring lettuce to watercress to the dandelions of late summer. Fortunately, the salad season is year-round, thanks to the miracle of modern transportation and technology.

Treat greens with tender loving care – they deserve it! Shake off excess moisture after careful washing. Chill one to two hours in hydrator or seal in plastic bags until ready to use.

Just a word about the salad dressing. Choose oils and vinegars as carefully as you do the greens. In fact, it's often the oils and vinegars that make the difference between an ordinary and a great salad. An increasing number of oils and vinegars are available in supermarkets, health food and specialty food stores. Don't drown the salad by using too much dressing!

Fortunately, there's a variety of excellent commercial salad dressings available on the market, ranging from rich and highly caloric to diet versions. And just a word of advice to folks who refrain from adding mayonnaise to meat salads during hot summer months. A recent study done at the University of Wisconsin, reported in the February, 1982, issue of "Journal of Food Protection," helps disprove the old belief that mayonnaise-meat salads spoil more readily than others. The study, in fact, proves that addition of commercial mayonnaise to meat salads actually helps reduce spoilage, probably due to its high acidity (lemon juice or vinegar), by retarding the growth of harmful bacteria. The study advises, however, that "addition of mayonnaise should not be considered a substitute for refrigeration for preserving meat salads from a growth of food-borne pathogens."

Lastly, the salad can provide a memorable ending to the meal, be it fresh fruit cut-up and served on a plate with crisp greens or marinated with fresh mint, compote-style, or encased in sparkling jewel-toned, fruit-flavored gelatins. Bon appetit!

J.B.

Caesar Salad

Serves 4

2 heads romaine lettuce
1 clove garlic
⅔ cup olive oil
¼ cup fresh lemon juice
2 tablespoons red wine vinegar

2 cans anchovy fillets, drained
⅓ cup crisp croutons
½ cup Parmesan cheese, freshly grated
2 eggs
freshly ground black pepper

1. Wash greens and tear into bite-size pieces. Chill.
2. Using huge wooden bowl, rub with garlic clove; discard clove.
3. Add greens; add oil, vinegar and lemon juice.
4. Snip anchovy fillets into bowl; toss lightly to coat leaves.
5. Add croutons and half of cheese.
6. Beat eggs in small bowl with wire whisk until creamy; add to salad and toss lightly.
7. Sprinkle with remaining cheese before serving.
8. Grind fresh black pepper over to taste. (Anchovies are salty enough, so no additional salt is needed.)

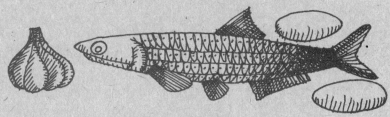

Little Caesar Salad

Serves 6

1 head western iceberg lettuce
4 cloves fresh garlic
1½ cups salad oil
½ cup tarragon flavor wine vinegar
1 tablespoon prepared yellow mustard
2 teaspoons sugar
2 teaspoons seasoned salt
2 teaspoons original Worcestershire
  sauce

½ teaspoon herb pepper seasoning
1/16 teaspoon Tabasco sauce
¼ cup sliced green onions
¼ crumbled blue cheese
2 tablespoons finely chopped parsley
½ cup chow mein noodles
⅓ cup salami, cut in julienne strips
¼ cup small toast rounds or
  croutons

1. Core, rinse and thoroughly drain lettuce; chill in disposable plastic bag or crisper.
2. Squeeze garlic using a garlic press to measure 2 teaspoons.
3. Combine garlic with oil, vinegar, mustard, sugar, salt, Worcestershire sauce, herb pepper seasoning and Tabasco in a screw-top pint jar.
4. Cover, shake well to blend. Chill.
5. At serving time, shred lettuce to measure 2 quarts; toss with onions, blue cheese and parsley.
6. Shake dressing again; pour ½ cup over salad and toss lightly.
7. Top with noodles, salami and toast rounds.
8. Serve at once. Pass additional dressing.

NOTE: Dressing recipe makes 2 cups. Store extra dressing in refrigerator for future use.

Dutch Hot Cabbage

Serves 4 to 6

2 slices bacon
1 small head cabbage
1 stalk celery

pepper
Slaw Dressing

1. Dice and fry bacon.
2. Shred cabbage and dice celery.
3. Add cabbage and celery to bacon; cook just enough to absorb the fat but not to brown, turning frequently.
4. Add pepper as desired. Pour Slaw Dressing over cabbage and toss.

Slaw Dressing

1 egg
¼ cup vinegar
1 cup water

2 tablespoons flour
½ cup sugar
½ teaspoon salt

1. Beat egg well, add vinegar and water.
2. Combine flour, sugar and salt; slowly blend into egg mixture to avoid lumps. Beat until smooth.
3. Cook over low heat, stirring until mixture coats spoon.

Orange & Red Onion Salad
with Vinaigrette Dressing

Serves 6

2 bunches fresh spinach, washed and
   drained
4 oranges, peeled and sectioned

2 red onions, peeled and thinly
   sliced in rings
Vinaigrette Dressing

1. Toss chilled salad ingredients in a large bowl.
2. Pour dressing over all and serve.

Vinaigrette Dressing

Makes about 1 cup

¼ teaspoon paprika
¼ teaspoon dry mustard
4 to 5 tablespoons lemon juice
   or red wine vinegar

¼ teaspoon celery seed
¼ teaspoon seasoned salt
¼ teaspoon garlic salt
¾ cup fine-grade olive or
   corn oil

1. Combine all ingredients, except oil, blending thoroughly.
2. Mix in oil. (For best flavor, refrigerate several hours before serving.)

Deviled Red Cabbage Salad

Serves 4 to 6

2 cups red cabbage, shredded
¼ cup green pepper strips
½ cup celery, thinly sliced

1 tablespoon onion, minced
3 tablespoons corn oil
¼ cup vinegar
½ teaspoon salt

1. Combine cabbage, green pepper, celery and onion; mix lightly.
2. Blend oil, vinegar and salt; pour over vegetables and toss to blend.

Buffet Garden Salad

Serves 12

1 head lettuce, torn in small pieces
3 cups shredded curly endive
1 cup red onion, thinly sliced
1 medium cucumber, scored and sliced
1 can (15 ounces) artichoke hearts,
  drained and quartered

1 large tomato, cut into wedges
¾ cup peanut oil
¼ cup white vinegar
½ teaspoon sugar
½ teaspoon salt
⅛ teaspoon pepper

1. Combine lettuce, curly endive, red onion, cucumber, artichokes and tomato wedges in a large salad bowl. Chill until ready to serve.
2. Combine peanut oil, vinegar, sugar, salt and pepper. Shake or mix together until thoroughly blended.
3. Pour ½ cup dressing over salad mixture; toss well.
4. Store remaining dressing in refrigerator for future use.

Escarole Salad

Serves 4

¾ cup corn oil
¼ cup red wine vinegar
1 teaspoon dry mustard
½ teaspoon salt
½ teaspoon dried tarragon
  leaves

¼ teaspoon pepper
1 clove garlic, split
6 cups torn escarole leaves
1 cup cooked red kidney beans
1 cup zucchini strips
¼ cup sliced red onion

1. In a 1-pint jar with tight fitting lid place corn oil, vinegar, mustard, salt, tarragon, pepper and garlic. Cover and shake well.
2. Refrigerate for several hours.
3. Remove garlic.
4. In large bowl toss together escarole, beans, zucchini and onion. Serve with dressing.

Ever-Green Salad with Herbed French Dressing

Serves 12

½ pound tender escarole leaves
½ pound tender chicory leaves
½ pound spinach leaves, stems
  removed
½ pound Chinese cabbage, cut in
  1-inch pieces

2 endives, sliced lengthwise
1 ripe avocado, peeled and cut
  into thin slices
½ cup cooked green peas
½ cup green pepper, chopped
Herbed French Dressing

1. Wash greens well; pat-dry. Tear or cut into small pieces.
2. Place ingredients in large salad bowl.
3. Just before serving, pour Herbed French Dressing over greens; toss lightly.

Herbed French Dressing

Makes 1 cup

¾ cup corn oil
¼ cup wine vinegar
1 clove garlic, split
1 tablespoon sugar
1 teaspoon salt

1 teaspoon paprika
1 teaspoon dry mustard
½ teaspoon dried tarragon leaves
½ teaspoon dried thyme leaves
½ teaspoon dried oregano

¼ teaspoon pepper

1. Place oil, vinegar, garlic, sugar, salt, paprika, mustard, tarragon, thyme, oregano and pepper into bottle or jar. Cover tightly and shake well.
2. Chill several hours.
3. Remove garlic.

Garden Chicory & Onion Salad

Serves 4

1 large bunch chicory
1 small red onion, peeled and
  cut into rings
6 tablespoons corn oil
6 tablespoons fresh lemon juice

½ teaspoon salt
⅛ teaspoon pepper
2 tablespoons snipped fresh tarragon or
  1 tablespoon dried tarragon
1 orange, peeled and sliced

additional freshly ground pepper

1. Wash chicory, drain thoroughly, and tear into bite-size pieces.
2. Combine with onion rings in a bowl. Chill well.
3. Mix together oil, lemon juice, salt, ⅛ teaspoon pepper and tarragon; beat until blended.
4. Add orange slices and dressing to salad; toss.
5. Grind pepper over salad just before serving.

Garden Salad
with Blue Cheese Vinaigrette

Serves 10

6 cups iceberg lettuce, finely chopped
2 cups tomatoes, seeded and chopped
1 cup broccoli, finely chopped
⅓ cup zucchini, chopped

2 hard-cooked eggs, chopped
freshly ground black pepper
Blue Cheese Vinaigrette

1. Spread chopped lettuce evenly over bottom of a large, shallow bowl.
2. Arrange remaining ingredients except pepper and Blue Cheese Vinaigrette in rows over lettuce, with tomato in center and broccoli and onion on one side, zucchini and egg on other side.
3. Cover salad with damp paper towel and plastic wrap; refrigerate.
4. To serve, grind pepper over salad; add Blue Cheese Vinaigrette and toss.

Blue Cheese Vinaigrette

Makes 1½ cups

1 cup corn oil
3 tablespoons white vinegar
¼ teaspoon dry mustard

½ teaspoon basil leaves, crumbled
2 ounces blue cheese, crumbled

1. Combine oil, vinegar, mustard, basil and blue cheese in blender container.
2. Blend until smooth.

Chinese Spinach Salad

Serves 2

¼ pound fresh spinach
10 whole fresh mushrooms,
   thinly sliced
2 tablespoons soy sauce

2 tablespoons rice vinegar
1 tablespoon salad oil
2 tablespoons water
½ teaspoon fresh ginger, minced

bulgur — cracked wheat (optional)

1. Wash spinach; break off tough stems. Drain well.
2. Place on two salad plates. Top with sliced mushrooms.
3. Combine soy sauce, vinegar, oil and water; whisk.
4. Mince ginger; add to dressing. Use some of dressing for salad and pour some on bulgur, if desired.

NOTE: Bulgur is a kind of cracked wheat popular in Turkey and the Middle East as a substitute for rice.

Spinach & Mushroom Salad

Serves 6 to 8

1 pound fresh spinach, washed and
  drained
½ head romaine lettuce, washed and
  drained
3 canned pimientos, drained and cut
  in thin slivers
¼ pound fresh mushrooms, sliced

6 slices crisp bacon, crumbled
pinch of sugar
salt to taste
pepper to taste
⅓ cup oil
3 tablespoons vinegar
1 cup cheese and garlic croutons

1. Mix together spinach leaves and lettuce leaves that have been torn into generous bite-size pieces.
2. Add all the other ingredients except croutons; toss well.
3. Just before serving, add croutons; toss lightly.

Tossed Greens Salad

Serves 6 to 8

3 cups leaf lettuce, torn
2 cups curly endive, torn
1 cup kale, torn

1 cup raw mushrooms, sliced
½ cup radishes, sliced
⅓ cup dill pickle, coarsely chopped

1. Place lettuce, endive and kale in salad bowl.
2. Arrange mushrooms, radishes and dill pickle over leafy greens.
3. Serve with Blue Cheese Dressing or Low-Cal Tomato Dressing.

Blue Cheese Dressing

Makes 1½ cups

1 cup dairy sour cream
¼ cup mayonnaise
¼ cup blue cheese, crumbled

2 tablespoons green onion, thinly
  sliced
1 teaspoon fresh lemon juice

Combine all ingredients; chill.

Low-Cal Tomato Dressing

Makes 1 cup

1 can (8 ounces) tomato sauce
2 tablespoons wine vinegar
1 teaspoon onion, grated
. 1 teaspoon original Worcestershire sauce

½ teaspoon dried salad herb leaves,
  crushed
¼ teaspoon salt

Combine all ingredients in jar; cover and shake well before serving.

182

Western Way Salad

Serves 6 to 8

3 cups romaine, torn
2 cups escarole, torn
1 cup spinach, torn

1 cup cherry tomatoes, halved
½ cup celery, thinly sliced
Western Way Dressing

1. Place romaine, escarole and spinach in salad bowl.
2. Arrange cherry tomatoes and celery over leafy greens.
3. Serve with Western Way Dressing.

Western Way Dressing

Makes 2 cups

¾ cup mayonnaise
¾ cup dairy sour cream
1 cup parsley, finely chopped
2 hard-cooked eggs, chopped

1 can (2 ounces) anchovies, drained
  and chopped
1 clove garlic, minced
¼ teaspoon coarsely ground black pepper

Combine all ingredients; chill.

NOTE: Western Way Dressing is also excellent as a dip for raw vegetables!

Salad de Castel Novel

Serves 6 to 8

1 teaspoon dry mustard
1 teaspoon seasoned salt
1 teaspoon seasoned pepper
1 teaspoon pinch of herbs
¼ teaspoon garlic powder
  with parsley
⅓ cup red wine vinegar
1 cup olive oil
1 head Romaine lettuce

2 heads Bibb lettuce, torn into
  bite-size pieces
¾ cup walnuts, quartered
¼ pound thick-sliced bacon, cut
  into ⅜ x ⅜-inch pieces and
  cooked (optional)
½ cup coarsely grated Gruyere
  cheese
1½ cups croutons

1. Combine seasonings and vinegar in tight-sealing container; shake well.
2. Add olive oil; shake again for about 30 seconds.
3. Refrigerate several hours for best flavor.
4. Toss together remaining ingredients in large salad bowl; add dressing and toss again.
   Serve immediately.

California Walking Salad

Serves 6 to 8

1 pound seedless grapes, pulled from stems
1 red apple, cored and cubed
½ cup seedless raisins

¼ cup roasted peanuts, chopped
1 head iceberg lettuce, cored, rinsed, drained and chilled

1. Mix grapes, apple, raisins and peanuts in bowl.
2. Carefully remove lettuce leaves from head, one at a time.
3. Put ½ cup of fruit mixture in each lettuce cup. Serve out of hand.

Cherry Ambrosia Salad
with Honey-Orange Dressing

Serves 8

2 cups fresh sweet cherries
3 oranges
1 cup seedless green grapes

½ cup flaked coconut
Honey Orange Dressing

1. Wash cherries; pit if desired.
2. Peel oranges, removing all white membrane; slice.
3. Layer fruits in salad bowl, sprinkling each layer with coconut.
4. Serve with Honey-Orange Dressing.

Honey-Orange Dressing

Makes 1¼ cups

1 package softened cream cheese
2 tablespoons honey
2 teaspoons grated orange peel
1 teaspoon salt

⅛ teaspoon paprika
dash of cayenne
¼ cup fresh orange juice
2 tablespoons fresh lemon juice

1. Combine cream cheese, honey, orange peel, salt, paprika and cayenne; blend thoroughly.
2. Gradually add orange and lemon juices; stir until smooth.

Fresh Fruit Salad

Serves 6 to 8

1 egg, well beaten
¼ cup honey
1 tablespoon fresh lime juice
½ cup heavy cream, whipped

8 cups cut-up fresh fruit: cantaloupe,
   strawberries, grapes, bananas, apples
   and oranges
½ cup peanuts, coarsely chopped
crisp salad greens

1. Combine egg, honey and lime juice in a saucepan.
2. Cook over medium heat, stirring constantly, until thickened.
3. Remove from heat; cool 30 minutes.
4. Fold in whipped cream; chill until ready to serve.
5. Just before serving, blend fruits and peanuts. Arrange on crisp salad greens. Garnish with egg-honey dressing.

NOTE: For a festive touch, serve fruit salad in scooped-out melon halves.

Fruit & Celery Salad

Serves 4

1 can (11 ounces) mandarin oranges
½ cup raisins

2 apples
2 stalks of celery
French dressing or mayonnaise

1. Drain orange sections; reserve liquid.
2. Soak raisins in the liquid 20 minutes.
3. Quarter apples, leaving skin on. Cut out cores and soak apple pieces in salted water 5 minutes to prevent discoloring. Slice apple pieces.
4. Chop celery coarsely.
5. Drain raisins.
6. Combine all ingredients, toss with French dressing or mayonnaise.

Fresh Orange Waldorf Salad

Serves 4 to 6

grated peel of ½ fresh orange
4 oranges, peeled and cut in bite-size
  pieces
1 medium red apple, unpeeled and cut
  in bite-size pieces

1 cup miniature marshmallows
½ cup sliced celery
½ cup mayonnaise
⅓ cup chopped walnuts
⅛ teaspoon ground cinnamon
salad greens (optional)

1. Combine all ingredients; chill well.
2. Serve on salad greens, if desired.

Orange & Avocado Salad

Serves 6

¾ cup mayonnaise
¼ cup fresh orange juice
½ teaspoon paprika
½ teaspoon salt

2 California avocados, peeled, seeded, and sliced
3 fresh oranges, peeled and sliced
iceberg lettuce

1. Combine mayonnaise, orange juice, paprika and salt.
2. Alternate slices of avocado and orange on lettuce leaves. Drizzle with mayonnaise orange dressing.

Orange Fall Fruit Combo

Serves 6

3 oranges, peeled and cut in half-cartwheels
2 pears, unpeeled and cut in bite-size pieces
2 bananas, sliced
1 cup grapes, cut in half and seeded

⅓ cup Curacao or other orange-flavored liqueur
½ cup heavy cream
¼ cup confectioners' sugar
grated peel of ½ fresh orange
⅛ teaspoon ground cinnamon

1. Combine fruits and Curacao in bowl; chill.
2. Whip heavy cream with confectioners' sugar.
3. Stir in orange peel and cinnamon. Serve over fruit.

Fruit Peanut Salad

Serves 6

¼ cup honey
2 tablespoons creamy peanut butter
½ cup plain yogurt
2 medium cantaloupes
1½ cups orange sections, halved
1½ cups apple, unpared and cubed

1 can (1 pound 4½ ounces) pineapple chunks, well drained
1 large banana, sliced
½ cup peanuts
shredded lettuce
maraschino cherries

1. Blend together honey and peanut butter.
2. Gradually stir in yogurt. Mix until well blended; chill.
3. Pare melons. Cut each into 3 crosswise slices with jagged edges. Remove seeds; chill.
4. Combine orange sections, apple, pineapple, banana and peanuts in a large bowl.
5. Toss gently with half the prepared dressing mixture just until fruit is coated.
6. Place melon slices in center of luncheon plates; surround with shredded lettuce.
7. Fill center of each melon slice with 1 cup fruit mixture. Serve garnished with cherries. Serve remaining honey-peanut butter mixture separately.

Polynesian Fruit Platter

Serves 4

1 pineapple
2 kiwi fruit, peeled and sliced
1 cup papaya balls

¼ cup almonds, toasted
1 teaspoon shredded ginger root
bottled French dressing

1. Cut pineapple in half lengthwise, through the crown.
2. Remove fruit, leaving shells intact.
3. Core fruit and cut into chunks.
4. Combine pineapple chunks with kiwi, papaya, nuts, ginger root and enough dressing to moisten; mix lightly.
5. Spoon fruit mixture into pineapple shells.

Parsley-Pear Bowl

Serves 10

4 large fresh California
  Bartlett pears, halved, cored and
  sliced (about 5 cups)
⅓ cup fresh lemon juice
1 bunch parsley

½ teaspoon celery salt
½ teaspoon caraway seeds
¼ teaspoon seasoned salt
⅛ teaspoon pepper
1 tablespoon salad oil

1. Toss sliced pears with lemon juice in salad bowl.
2. Mince parsley to get 1 cup lightly packed.
3. Add parsley along with all remaining ingredients to pears; toss well.
4. Serve with grilled German sausages or barbecued steak.

Picture-Pretty Waldorfs

Serves 4 to 6

2 or 3 unpeeled red apples, cored
2 teaspoons fresh lemon juice
¼ teaspoon salt
1 cup celery, diced

½ cup chopped California walnuts
lettuce leaves
mayonnaise
walnut quarters (for garnish)

1. Cut large slices from 2 apples; sprinkle with lemon juice to keep bright.
2. Dice remaining apple.
3. Drain lemon juice from slices and pour over diced apples; add salt, celery, walnuts and enough mayonnaise to moisten. Toss well.
4. Starting with one apple slice on lettuce leaf, reassemble apple slices.
5. Garnish each reassembled apple with diced apple-mayonnaise mixture; top with walnut quarter.

Pineapple Banana Peanut Salad

Serves 6

1 can (1 pound 4 ounces) pineapple
   chunks
3 medium bananas, diced

½ cup peanuts
½ cup mayonnaise
lettuce leaves (optional)

1. Drain pineapple chunks, saving 2 tablespoons syrup.
2. Combine pineapple, bananas and peanuts in a bowl.
3. Blend mayonnaise and reserved pineapple syrup for dressing.
4. Add dressing to fruit mixture; toss gently.
5. Serve on lettuce leaves, if desired.

Pear Salad Mozambique
with Spicy Dressing

Serves 6

½ teaspoon ground cardamon
½ teaspoon ground coriander
1 teaspoon pumpkin pie spice
¼ teaspoon salt
¼ teaspoon cayenne pepper
2 teaspoons sugar

1 tablespoon fresh lemon juice
½ cup Sauterne or Chablis wine
6 fresh California Bartlett pears
   (with stems on)
western iceberg lettuce
Spicy Dressing

1. Combine spices, salt, cayenne, sugar, lemon juice and wine in saucepan; heat.
2. Meanwhile, pare and core pears from blossom end, leaving stems on.
3. Arrange pears, upright, in pan with spiced liquid. Cover and cook gently until barely tender, 10 to 15 minutes, basting now and then with liquid.
4. Lift pears from pan with slotted spoon and chill.
5. Measure pan liquid. If more than ¼ cup, cook down to this measure; if less, add additional wine to this measure. Set this liquid aside to use in making Spicy Dressing.
6. When ready to serve, arrange pears on crisp lettuce. Spoon on Spicy Dressing.

Spicy Dressing

Makes about ¾ cup

¼ cup reserved liquid from
   poaching pears
2 tablespoons onion, minced
¼ teaspoon garlic powder

½ teaspoon salt
1 tablespoon parsley, chopped
¼ cup tomato, diced
⅓ cup salad oil

Combine ingredients and mix well.

Walnut Fruit Salad Plate

Serves 6

3 oranges, cut in sections
2 grapefruits, cut in sections
1 medium avocado
salt
fresh lemon juice
3 bananas

mayonnaise
½ cup chopped California walnuts
1 medium head lettuce
6 small clusters of grapes
1 pint orange sherbet
fruit salad dressing

1. Chill orange and grapefruit sections.
2. Peel avocado; cut in wedges and sprinkle generously with salt and lemon juice; chill.
3. At serving time, peel bananas, dip in lemon juice and cut in half lengthwise. Coat cut surface of banana with mayonnaise and sprinkle with walnuts.
4. For each serving, arrange banana half on shredded lettuce. Alternate citrus fruits with avocado. Add a cluster of grapes and a scoop of sherbet in small lettuce cup.
5. Serve with your favorite fruit salad dressing, as a luncheon salad, with hot bread.

Winter Fruit Compote

Serves 6 to 8

1 can (15¼ ounces) pineapple chunks
  in its own juice, chilled
2 oranges
2 apples

2 bananas
½ cup mayonnaise
½ cup dairy sour cream
2 tablespoons honey

1. Drain pineapple, reserving juice.
2. Pare oranges; slice thinly.
3. Slice apples into thin wedges.
4. Slice bananas.
5. Dip apples and bananas in reserved pineapple juice to prevent browning.
6. Arrange fruits in compôte.
7. Combine 2 tablespoons reserved pineapple juice, mayonnaise, sour cream and honey. Mix well; serve over fruit.

Apple Salad à la Moutarde

Serves 4

2 Granny Smith apples, cored
   and sliced
1 cup sliced celery
½ cup seedless red grapes
¼ cup dairy sour cream

1½ teaspoons Dijon-style or
   prepared mustard
2 teaspoons chopped chives
¼ teaspoon salt
crisp salad greens

1. Combine all ingredients except salad greens in medium-size bowl; toss lightly.
2. Cover and chill.
3. Serve on bed of salad greens.

Pineapple Tuna Slaw

Serves 6 to 8

1 can (15¼ ounces) pineapple
   tidbits in own juice
5 cups finely shredded cabbage
1 carrot, shredded
1 can (7 ounces) water-packed
   tuna, drained and flaked

½ cup mayonnaise
½ cup dairy sour cream
1 tablespoon sugar
1 teaspoon poppy seeds
½ teaspoon instant minced
   onion

1. Drain pineapple, reserving 1 tablespoon juice.
2. Combine cabbage, carrot, tuna and pineapple.
3. Blend together mayonnaise, sour cream, sugar, reserved pineapple juice, poppy seeds and onion.
4. Toss vegetable-tuna mixture lightly with dressing.

Fresh Fruit Elegance

Serves 4 to 6

1 fresh pineapple, chilled
2 bananas, sliced
1 cup strawberries, chilled

⅓ cup blueberries, chilled
½ cup lime sherbet
½ cup mayonnaise

1. Keeping crown intact, carefully cut pineapple to resemble a basket with a handle.
2. Scoop out fruit; discard core and cut pineapple into cubes.
3. Combine pineapple, bananas and strawberries; place in pineapple basket shell.
4. Just before serving, sprinkle with blueberries.
5. Combine sherbet and mayonnaise; chill. Serve over fruit salad.

Waldorf Salad with Pineapple

Serves 6

2 cups diced apples	1 cup cubed fresh pineapple
1 tablespoon sugar	1 cup chopped celery
½ teaspoon lemon juice	½ cup chopped walnuts
dash salt	¼ cup mayonnaise
	lettuce

1. Sprinkle apples with sugar, lemon juice and salt; mix with pineapple.
2. Add celery and nuts; add mayonnaise and mix lightly.
3. Chill. Serve in lettuce cups or lettuce-lined bowl.

Sun Island Mold

Serves 10

1 can (15¼ ounces) pineapple tidbits in own juice	2 packages (3 ounces each) orange-flavored gelatin
3 cups water	1 package (8 ounces) cream cheese, softened
2 tablespoons lemon juice	1 can (8 ounces) mandarin orange sections, drained (optional garnish)
10 whole cloves	
2 cinnamon sticks, about 3 inches each	

1. Drain pineapple, reserving juice.
2. Combine reserved pineapple juice, water, lemon juice, cloves and cinnamon in saucepan; bring to a boil.
3. Reduce heat and simmer, covered, 5 minutes.
4. Remove from heat; add gelatin, stirring until completely dissolved.
5. Remove spices. Reserve ⅓ cup gelatin mixture.
6. Pour remaining gelatin mixture slowly into bowl, being careful not to allow any sediment from spices to go into bowl; chill until partially set.
7. Fold in pineapple.
8. Pour into 6-cup mold; chill until firm.
9. Whip cream cheese with reserved gelatin; spread over mold. Chill until firm.
10. Garnish with mandarin oranges, if desired.

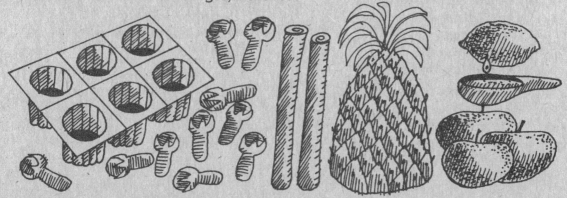

Celeriac & Carrot Salad

Serves 6

4 cups celeriac, shredded	¼ cup capers, drained
4 cups carrots, shredded	¾ cup mayonnaise
⅓ cup parsley, minced	2 tablespoons Dijon-style mustard
⅓ cup chives, snipped	2 tablespoons fresh lemon juice
¼ cup dill pickle, chopped	¼ teaspoon white pepper

lettuce leaves

1. Toss together celeriac, carrots, parsley, chives, dill pickle and capers in large bowl.
2. Combine mayonnaise, mustard, lemon juice and white pepper.
3. Pour dressing over vegetables, tossing to coat. Chill.
4. Spoon into lettuce-lined bowl.

Corn Patch Salad, Microwaved

Serves 6

2 cups fresh corn kernels (3 to 4 ears)	½ teaspoon salt
1 cup cabbage, shredded	¾ cup white vinegar
2 stalks celery, chopped	¾ cup sugar
1 small onion, chopped	⅓ cup water
1 medium red pepper, chopped	1 teaspoon powdered mustard
½ medium green pepper, chopped	½ teaspoon turmeric
	1 tablespoon cornstarch

1. Combine vegetables and salt in 2-quart glass measuring cup, tossing to blend well.
2. Cover and cook on HIGH for 6 to 8 minutes; stirring once.
3. Combine remaining ingredients in 1-quart glass measuring cup; cook on HIGH 3 to 4 minutes, stirring twice. (Mixture should thicken slightly.)
4. Pour over vegetables and toss to coat. Chill 2 hours, or until serving time.

Dilled Sour Cream-Cucumber Salad

Serves 6

4 medium cucumbers	½ teaspoon salt
¾ cup sour cream	¼ teaspoon pepper
1½ tablespoons vinegar	3 tablespoons fresh minced dill or parsley
2 tablespoons oil	
¼ teaspoon sugar	

1. Peel cucumbers and cut in thin slices.
2. Combine sour cream, vinegar, oil, sugar, salt and pepper. Pour over cucumbers.
3. Cover and chill 1 hour or longer.
4. Sprinkle with dill before serving.

Fall Salad Platter

Serves 6

1 small head chicory
1 small head Boston or Bibb lettuce
6 scallions, sliced
3 carrots, pared and thinly sliced
3 tomatoes, cut in wedges
3 raw zucchini, sliced

¼ pound raw mushrooms, cleaned and sliced
1 medium turnip, peeled and shredded
1 can (16 ounces) whole baby beets, drained
1¼ cups bottled vinaigrette dressing

1. Wash and pat-dry chicory and lettuce leaves.
2. Line a large, shallow salad bowl or tray with leaves.
3. Arrange scallions, carrots, tomatoes, zucchini, mushrooms, shredded turnip and whole beets on plate in rows.
4. Cover salad tightly with plastic wrap and chill 30 minutes.
5. At serving time, pour dressing over evenly.

Fatoush
(Mixed Vegetable Salad)

Serves 6

1½ cups croutons
6 tablespoons olive or salad oil
3 cups cherry tomatoes, halved
3 cups cucumbers, peeled and diced
½ cup radishes, sliced

1 tablespoon mint flakes, crumbled
1 tablespoon dried chives
1½ teaspoons salt
⅛ teaspoon ground black pepper
1½ teaspoons fresh lemon juice

1. Combine croutons with oil; toss until well coated. Set aside.
2. Combine remaining ingredients in salad bowl.
3. Add croutons; toss gently. Serve with lamb or beef.

Fennel, Tomato & Chicory Salad

Serves 4

1 head fennel
1 small head chicory
2 large firm tomatoes
1 clove garlic

salt to taste
freshly ground pepper to taste
2 tablespoons olive oil
2 teaspoons vinegar

1. Remove outer leaves from fennel and chicory; wash carefully.
2. Cut fennel into thin slices; cut chicory into 2-inch pieces. Wash thoroughly again; drain well on paper towels.
3. Peel and quarter tomatoes.
4. Rub salad bowl with garlic. Add fennel, chicory, tomatoes, salt and pepper to salad bowl.
5. Blend oil and vinegar separately; pour over salad. Toss to mix thoroughly.
6. Chill in refrigerator 5 minutes before serving.

Italian Salad with Croutons

Serves 4 to 6

2 cups Italian bread cubes
1 bottle (8 ounces) Italian dressing
2 quarts torn assorted greens

2 cups caulifloweret slices
2 cups broccoli flowerets
1½ cups zucchini slices

1. Toss bread cubes with ¼ cup dressing.
2. Bake on cookie sheet in preheated 350° F. oven 20 minutes, turning occasionally.
3. Combine in a salad bowl assorted greens, cauliflower, broccoli, zucchini and bread cubes with ⅓ cup dressing. Toss lightly. Serve with additional dressing, if desired.

Marinated Brussels Sprouts Salad

Serves 6 to 8

2 packages (10 ounces each) frozen
   Brussels sprouts, cooked and drained
1 pound yellow squash, sliced and blanched
½ pound fresh raw mushrooms, sliced

1 large red onion, peeled and thinly
   sliced
¾ cup bottled Italian dressing
¼ teaspoon thyme leaves

1. Arrange vegetables in large, shallow dish.
2. Mix dressing and thyme leaves; pour over vegetables.
3. Cover and chill 2 or more hours.
4. To serve, arrange vegetables in rows on large platter; drizzle any remaining dressing over top of salad.

NOTE: To blanch squash, pour boiling water over squash in colander and allow to drain.

Marinated Greek Salad

Serves 6

3 tomatoes, diced
1 cucumber, peeled, seeded and diced
1 green pepper, seeded and diced
1 small onion, peeled and cut into
   julienne strips
1 tablespoon fresh lemon juice

1 tablespoon vinegar
1 tablespoon oregano
2 tablespoons parsley, minced
1 teaspoon salt
¼ teaspoon pepper
½ cup olive oil

1. Combine tomatoes, cucumber, green pepper, and onion in a salad bowl.
2. Whisk lemon juice, vinegar, oregano, parsley, salt and pepper until salt is dissolved.
3. Whisk in oil, 1 tablespoon at a time.
4. Pour over vegetables; stir to coat.
5. Cover and chill several hours.

Minted Mixed Vegetable Salad

Serves 6

1½ cups croutons
6 tablespoons olive oil
3 cups cherry tomatoes, halved
3 cups diced, peeled cucumbers
½ cup sliced radishes
1 tablespoon mint flakes, crumbled

1 tablespoon dried chives
1½ teaspoons salt
⅛ teaspoon freshly ground
   black pepper
1½ teaspoons lemon juice
½ teaspoon finely grated lemon rind

1. Combine croutons with oil; toss until well coated. Set aside.
2. Combine remaining ingredients in salad bowl.
3. Add croutons; toss gently. Serve with lamb or beef.

Pepper & Onions Vinaigrette

Serves 8

6 green peppers
1 or 2 red or sweet white onions
2 cloves garlic, finely chopped
6 tablespoons olive or salad oil

2 tablespoons wine vinegar
1 teaspoon dried basil
½ teaspoon salt
freshly ground pepper

1. Seed peppers; thinly slice into rings.
2. Peel onions; thinly slice and separate into rings.
3. Combine peppers, onions, and garlic in bowl.
4. Whisk together oil, vinegar, basil, salt and pepper; pour over peppers and onions.
5. Toss well and let stand 1 hour before serving.

Picnic Cole Slaw

Serves 12

¾ cup mayonnaise
¼ cup cider vinegar
½ green pepper, finely chopped

1 teaspoon salt substitute or
   fresh lemon juice to taste
freshly ground pepper

1 head (3 to 4 pounds) cabbage

1. Mix mayonnaise, vinegar, green pepper, salt substitute and pepper to taste.
2. Shred cabbage; toss with mayonnaise mixture until well coated.
3. Cover and chill until serving time.

Sliced Cucumbers & Onions
with Yogurt Dressing

Serves 4

1 large cucumber, thinly sliced
4 green onions and tops, thinly sliced
juice of 1 lemon
1 cup plain yogurt

1 teaspoon salt
⅛ teaspoon freshly ground pepper
chopped parsley and paprika
(for garnish)

1. Mix sliced cucumber and onion slices with lemon juice; let stand 1 hour.
2. Drain well, then mix with yogurt and seasonings. Chill.
3. Sprinkle with parsley and paprika before serving.

Sweet Potato Salad
with Honey Vinaigrette Dressing

Serves 6 to 8

3½ pounds fresh sweet potatoes
salted water
1 medium onion, cut into thin rings

1 green pepper, cut into thin strips
Honey Vinaigrette Dressing

1. Wash sweet potatoes.
2. Heat enough salted water to boiling to cover sweet potatoes.
3. Add sweet potatoes in jackets; bring back to a boil. Cover and cook 20 to 30 minutes, or until sweet potatoes are fork-tender.
4. Cool; halve potatoes lengthwise, then cut into ¼-inch slices.
5. Combine sweet potato, onion and green pepper in large bowl.
6. Pour Honey Vinaigrette Dressing over it, tossing lightly to coat vegetables.
7. Cover and refrigerate 3 to 6 hours, or overnight.
8. Served chilled or at room temperature.

Honey Vinaigrette Dressing

1 cup tarragon vinegar
½ cup vegetable oil
1 tablespoon honey
2 bay leaves, crumbled

½ teaspoon salt
¼ teaspoon pepper
¼ teaspoon oregano, crumbled
¼ teaspoon thyme, crumbled

2 cloves garlic, minced or pressed

1. Combine all ingredients in jar with tight-fitting lid.
2. Shake vigorously until well mixed.

Zucchini-Carrot Salad with Blue Cheese Dressing

Serves 6

2 zucchini, cut julienne
1 red pepper, chopped or
   cut in short strips

2 carrots, cut julienne
Blue Cheese Dressing
lettuce

1. Combine zucchini, red pepper and carrots in bowl.
2. Chill, covered, until ready to serve.
3. Just before serving, toss with Blue Cheese Dressing. Serve on lettuce.

Blue Cheese Dressing

1 cup plain yogurt
1 clove garlic, crushed
¼ teaspoon dry mustard
1½ teaspoons wine vinegar

¼ cup crumbled blue cheese (optional)
1 teaspoon sugar
¼ teaspoon salt
1 tablespoon minced parsley

1. Combine yogurt, garlic, mustard, vinegar, blue cheese, sugar, salt and parsley.
2. Stir well; chill.

Four-Bean Salad

Serves 6 to 8

1 package (10 ounces) frozen
   green beans, thawed
1 package (10 ounces) frozen
   wax beans, thawed
1 can (20 ounces) ceci beans,
   drained
1 can (16 ounces) red kidney beans,
   drained

1 cup coarsely chopped onion
¾ cup corn oil
¾ cup cider vinegar
¼ cup sugar
1½ teaspoons salt
½ teaspoon pepper

1. In large bowl, toss together beans and onion.
2. In small bowl, stir together corn oil, vinegar, sugar, salt and pepper until well blended;
   pour over bean mixture, tossing to coat well.
3. Cover and refrigerate several hours, or overnight, stirring occasionally.

Chicken-Walnut Sandwich Salads

Serves 6

6 soft-crust French rolls
1½ cups cooked chicken or
turkey, diced
1 cup celery, sliced
¾ cup coarsely chopped California
walnuts, toasted

¼ cup sweet pickles
¼ cup stuffed olives
¼ cup mayonnaise
2 teaspoons fresh lemon juice
salt to taste
pepper to taste

melted butter or margarine

1. Cut top from rolls and hollow out, leaving crusts about ½-inch thick. Reserve insides.
2. Add remaining ingredients, except butter, to 1 cup crumbs from rolls; toss lightly.
3. Fill rolls with mixture; replace tops and brush with butter.
4. Wrap in foil and bake in preheated 425° F. oven 25 minutes, or until heated through.

Hawaiian Fresh Pineapple Chicken Salad with Ginger Dressing

Serves 2

1 whole skinned chicken breast,
cooked and chilled
lettuce
1 can (8 ounces) sliced pineapple,
cut in halves, or ½ pineapple,
peeled, cored and sliced about
½ inch thick
⅓ cup cottage cheese

⅛ teaspoon dry mustard
1 teaspoon chopped capers
salt to taste
pepper to taste
melba toast
paprika (optional)
radish roses
Ginger Dressing

1. Slice chicken crosswise about ½ inch thick. Arrange chicken on a bed of lettuce on 2 large plates, alternating with slices of pineapple.
2. Cover and chill.
3. Combine cottage cheese, mustard and capers.
4. Season to taste with salt and pepper.
5. Spread on melba toast. Sprinkle with paprika.
6. Surround chicken salad with melba toast and garnish with radish roses. Serve with Ginger Dressing.

Ginger Dressing

Makes ½ cup

¼ cup mayonnaise
2 tablespoons dairy sour cream
2 to 3 teaspoons minced crystal-
lized ginger

dash ground ginger
1 tablespoon minced chutney
½ teaspoon grated lemon or lime peel

1. Combine all ingredients. Mix well.
2. Chill until serving time.

Cobb Salad Supreme with French Dressing

Serves 6

½ head iceberg lettuce
½ bunch watercress
1 small bunch chicory endive
½ head romaine
2 tablespoons minced chives
2 medium tomatoes
6 strips bacon, cooked

1 boneless chicken breast,
  cooked and skinned
1 avocado, peeled
3 hard-cooked eggs
½ cup Roquefort cheese, crumbled
French Dressing

1. Chop lettuce, watercress, endive and romaine into very fine pieces, using knife or food processor.
2. Mix together in a large wide bowl, or individual wide shallow bowls.
3. Add chives.
4. Peel, seed, and dice tomatoes.
5. Dice bacon, chicken breasts, avocado and eggs.
6. Arrange chopped ingredients in narrow strips or wedges across top of greens. Sprinkle with cheese; chill.
7. To serve, toss with ½ cup French Dressing.

French Dressing

Makes 1½ cups

¼ cup water
¼ cup red wine vinegar
¼ teaspoon sugar
1½ teaspoons fresh lemon juice
½ teaspoon salt
½ teaspoon pepper

½ teaspoon original Worcestershire
  sauce
¾ teaspoon dry mustard
½ clove garlic, minced
¼ cup olive oil
¾ cup oil

1. Combine water, vinegar, sugar, lemon juice, salt, pepper, Worcestershire, mustard, garlic and oils.
2. Chill. Shake well before using.

Festive Chicken Salad

Serves 4 to 6

2 cups cooked chicken, chopped
1 cup fresh or canned pineapple chunks
½ cup celery, sliced
½ cup mayonnaise or salad dressing
½ teaspoon salt

½ teaspoon curry powder (optional)
1 tablespoon pineapple juice or milk
¾ cup 100% natural cereal
pineapple shells or lettuce leaves
orange slices (optional garnish)

strawberries (optional garnish)

1. Combine all ingredients except cereal and garnish in large bowl; mix well. Chill.
2. Just before serving, stir in cereal.
3. Serve in pineapple boats or on lettuce leaves.
4. Sprinkle with additional cereal and garnish with orange slices and strawberries, if desired.

Oriental Cherry Chicken Salad

Serves 4

2 cups pitted Northwest fresh sweet
   cherries
1 can (11 ounces) mandarin orange
   segments, drained
1½ cups cooked chicken, diced
½ cup celery, chopped

⅓ cup toasted slivered almonds
½ cup mayonnaise
1 teaspoon soy sauce
1 tablespoon fresh lemon juice
⅛ teaspoon ground ginger
crisp lettuce

1. Combine cherries, orange segments, chicken, celery and almonds.
2. Blend mayonnaise, soy sauce, lemon juice and ginger; toss with cherry mixture.
3. Serve on individual lettuce-lined salad plates.

California Summer Turkey & Fruit Salad

Serves 4

2 cups cut-up cooked turkey
1 cup fresh pineapple chunks or
   1 can (8 ounces) pineapple chunks,
   drained
1 cup seedless grapes, halved
1 cup cantaloupe chunks

½ cup chopped walnuts
⅓ cup whipping cream
¼ cup finely chopped chutney
3 tablespoons mayonnaise
dash of salt
lettuce leaves

1. Combine turkey, pineapple, grapes, cantaloupe and walnuts in a large bowl.
2. Whip cream in a medium bowl; fold in chutney, mayonnaise and salt.
3. Add whipped cream to turkey mixture; toss to combine.
4. Refrigerate several hours before serving. Serve on lettuce leaves.

Pineapple-Turkey Salad with Lime Dressing

Serves 4

1 small pineapple
lettuce leaves
1½ cups cooked turkey, chicken or
  ham, diced

½ cup celery, chopped
¼ cup green olives, chopped
1 cup toasted blanched almonds
Lime Dressing

1. Cut pineapple in half; scoop out pulp and dice.
2. Combine diced pineapple, lettuce, turkey, celery, olives and almonds. Toss with enough creamy Lime Dressing to moisten.
3. Pile back into shells. Serve with additional dressing.

Lime Dressing

Makes about 1 cup

1 cup sour cream or yogurt
2 tablespoons honey

2 tablespoons lime juice
dash salt

1 teaspoon grated lime peel

Blend all ingredients together thoroughly.

Turkey Salad Continental

Serves 6

2 cups crisp torn lettuce
1 cup diced cooked turkey
1 cup diced red apple
1 cup chopped celery
¼ cup chopped red onion

¼ cup chopped walnuts
⅓ cup mayonnaise
1 tablespoon fresh lemon or lime juice
½ teaspoon sage
¼ teaspoon salt

croissants (optional)

1. Combine lettuce, turkey, apple, celery, onion and walnuts in large mixing bowl.
2. In separate bowl, combine mayonnaise, lemon juice, sage and salt until smooth.
3. Add mayonnaise mixture to turkey mixture; toss to coat ingredients.
4. Serve at once. Great with croissants.

NOTE: A fine way to use leftover turkey or chicken.

201

Hot Turkey-Broccoli Salad

Serves 4 to 6

2 cups cooked turkey, diced
¼ cup onion, minced
½ cup chicken broth
¾ cup mayonnaise
¼ cup dairy sour cream

2 teaspoons Dijon-style mustard
1 cup Cheddar cheese, shredded
1½ cups broccoli flowerettes, blanched
2 egg whites
¼ cup toasted sliced almonds

1. Combine turkey, onion, chicken broth, mayonnaise, sour cream and mustard in large bowl. Mix thoroughly.
2. Mix in cheese and half the broccoli.
3. Beat egg whites until stiff. Fold gently into turkey mixture.
4. Spoon mixture into 4 to 6 ramekins or small baking dishes. Arrange remaining broccoli around edges.
5. Bake in preheated 375° F. oven 25 to 30 minutes, or until golden. Sprinkle with toasted almonds.

Turkey 'n' Spaghetti Summer Salad

Serves 6 to 8

10 ounces spaghetti
1 medium zucchini, thinly sliced
2 cups cut-up cooked turkey
1 can (8 ounces) cut green beans, drained
2 medium green onions, chopped
⅓ cup sliced ripe olives
18 cherry tomatoes, halved

1 teaspoon salt
¼ teaspoon grated Parmesan cheese
¼ cup white wine vinegar
⅔ cup olive oil
2 tablespoons water
1 packet (.6 ounce) Italian salad dressing mix

1. Cook spaghetti according to package directions; drain and rinse with cold water.
2. Meanwhile, cook zucchini in small amount of water just until tender. Rinse in cold water; drain.
3. Place spaghetti, zucchini, turkey, green beans, onions, olives, tomatoes, salt and Parmesan cheese in a large bowl.
4. Beat together vinegar, oil, water and salad dressing mix in a small bowl. Pour over spaghetti mixture and toss lightly. Refrigerate several hours or overnight to blend flavors.

Crab-Noodle Salad

Serves 6 to 8

2 cups cooked crab meat, diced
½ cup onion, finely chopped
½ cup celery, finely chopped
½ cup parsley, finely chopped

½ cup peeled and seeded tomatoes, finely chopped
2 cups cold cooked egg noodles
Dressing

1. Combine crab, onion, celery, parsley and tomatoes.
2. Toss crab mixture with noodles and Dressing until thoroughly mixed.
3. Chill at least 1 hour before serving.

Dressing

½ cup olive oil
2 tablespoons red wine vinegar

1 teaspoon salt
1 teaspoon Dijon mustard

1 tablespoon basil, finely chopped

Mix together all ingredients. Blend well.

Rock Lobster Green Noodle Salad

Serves 8

24 ounces frozen South African rock lobster tails
1 package (8 ounces) spinach egg noodles
2 cups chicken broth
2 tablespoons fresh lemon juice

freshly ground black pepper
2 stalks celery, cut in ½-inch pieces
1 cucumber, sliced
1 large onion, sliced
1 cup mayonnaise

1 teaspoon curry powder

1. Drop frozen rock lobster tails into boiling salted water. When water reboils, cook 3 minutes.
2. Drain immediately; drench with cold water.
3. Cut away underside membrane, remove meat in one piece, and slice into medallions. Set aside.
4. Cook and drain noodles according to package directions.
5. Combine noodles in a large bowl with 1½ cups hot chicken broth, lemon juice and pepper to taste. Cool.
6. At serving time, top noodles with rock lobster medallions, celery, cucumber, and onion.
7. Mix mayonnaise with remaining chicken broth and curry powder until smooth. Pour over top of salad.

Crab-Corn Vinaigrette Salad

Serves 8

1½ pounds crab legs in shell, thawed
2 cups cooked corn kernels
1 green pepper, chopped
1 red pepper, chopped
2 carrots, shredded
2 green onions, finely chopped
2 tomatoes, seeded and chopped

¼ cup peanut oil
2 tablespoons fresh lemon juice
2 tablespoons fresh lime juice
1½ teaspoons sugar
½ teaspoon salt
¼ teaspoon white pepper
curly lettuce leaves

1. Use poultry or kitchen shears to cut shells; remove meat and break into small pieces.
2. Combine corn, red and green peppers, carrots, onions and tomatoes in large bowl. Add crab meat.
3. Mix together oil, lemon juice, lime juice and sugar in small bowl.
4. Pour oil-juice mixture over crab mixture; toss to coat.
5. Taste and add salt and white pepper.
6. Refrigerate until ready to serve.
7. Place curly lettuce leaves on individual salad plates; spoon crab salad into plates.

Surfers' Salad

Serves 6 to 8

4 or 5 fresh nectarines
3 cups iceberg lettuce, shredded
2 cans (7½ ounces each) crab meat, drained and flaked, or 1 pound cooked crab meat
3 or 4 hard-cooked eggs, sliced
1½ cups bread croutons

1 ripe California avocado, sliced
¼ cup green onion, chopped
½ cup dairy sour cream
¼ cup catsup
1 teaspoon original Worcestershire sauce
1 teaspoon prepared horseradish

1. Slice nectarines to yield 2½ cups. Set aside a few slices for garnish; place remainder in large salad bowl.
2. Add to bowl lettuce, crab meat, eggs, croutons, avocado and onion.
3. Toss salad lightly and garnish with nectarine slices. Chill.
4. Blend sour cream, catsup, Worcestershire and horseradish in small dish; pass dressing along with salad.

Rock Lobster & Bean Salad

Serves 8

8 (2 ounces each) South African rock
  lobster tails, frozen
1 can (1 pound 4 ounces) chick peas,
  drained
1 can (15½ ounces) kidney
  beans, drained
1 cup celery, chopped
1 can (7 ounces) sweet red pimientos,
  drained and chopped

2 medium-size dill pickles, diced
1 green pepper, chopped
½ cup scallions, sliced
⅔ cup sour cream
⅔ cup mayonnaise
2 tablespoons prepared horseradish
1 tablespoon prepared mustard
3 tablespoons catsup
shredded green cabbage

1. Drop lobster tails into boiling salted water. When water reboils, boil for 3 minutes.
2. Drain immediately; drench with cold water.
3. With scissors, remove underside membrane and pull out lobster meat in one piece. Cut each tail in half lengthwise.
4. Combine chick peas, kidney beans, celery, pimientos, pickles, pepper and scallions. Chill thoroughly.
5. Combine sour cream, mayonnaise, horseradish, mustard and catsup. Mix well.
6. For each serving, place 1 cup of bean mixture and 2 halves of rock lobster meat on top of shredded cabbage in serving dish. Top with sauce.

Rock Lobster Salad, Hot or Cold

Serves 6

12 ounces frozen South African rock
  lobster tails
1 can (20 ounces) chick peas, drained
1 can (15¼ ounces) kidney beans,
  drained
1 cup celery, sliced

½ cup green pepper, diced
¼ cup onion, chopped
½ cup dairy sour cream
½ cup mayonnaise
1 tablespoon horseradish
salt to taste

1 tablespoon prepared yellow mustard

1. Drop frozen rock lobster into boiling salted water. When water reboils, boil 3 minutes. (Larger 4-ounce tails require 5 minutes boiling time.)
2. Drain immediately; drench with cold water.
3. With scissors, remove underside membrane. Pull out meat and dice.
4. Place lobster meat in mixing bowl. Stir in all remaining ingredients.
5. Chill to serve cold.
6. To serve hot, place mixture in a greased 1½-quart ovenproof casserole. Bake in a pre-heated 350° F. oven 30 to 35 minutes, or until piping hot.

Marinated Oyster Salad

Serves 2

1 can (8 ounces) whole oysters
1 can (8 ounces) water chestnuts, drained
1 medium tomato, seeded and chopped
¼ cup onion, diced
¼ cup parsley, chopped

1 small cucumber, thinly sliced
1 clove garlic, pressed
½ cup vegetable oil
¼ cup red wine vinegar
½ teaspoon oregano, crumbled
½ teaspoon salt

crisp salad greens

1. Drain oysters; slice water chestnuts.
2. Toss together oysters, chestnuts, tomatoes, onion and parsley.
3. Spoon into 1-quart shallow glass casserole. Arrange cucumber on top.
4. Combine garlic, oil, vinegar, oregano and salt in a screw-top jar. Shake well.
5. Pour over oyster mixture and cucumber.
6. Cover and refrigerate 1 hour.
7. Drain marinade and reserve.
8. Spoon oyster mixture and cucumber onto 2 plates lined with crisp salad greens. Pour marinade over salad, if desired.

Canned Salmon, Tuna & Pea Salad

Serves 6

1 can (1 pound) salmon
1 can (13 ounces) water-packed tuna fish
¾ cup prepared French dressing
2 cups cabbage, shredded

1 cup canned or cooked peas
2 tablespoons mayonnaise
lettuce
2 shelled, hard-cooked eggs (for garnish)

1. Break up salmon and tuna into large pieces.
2. Pour ½ cup French dressing over salmon and tuna. Chill.
3. To serve, arrange tuna-salmon mixture in center of platter.
4. Toss together cabbage, peas, ¼ cup French dressing and mayonnaise.
5. Arrange in 6 lettuce cups around fish. Garnish with hard-cooked eggs.

Salmon Flower Salad

Serves 4

1 can salmon
1 large tomato
1 jar (6 ounces) marinated
   artichoke hearts
½ head lettuce

½ large green pepper, thinly sliced
2 hard-cooked eggs, thinly sliced
½ cup dairy sour cream
1 teaspoon horseradish
freshly ground pepper

1. Drain salmon; remove bones and skin. Separate into bite-size chunks.
2. Cut tomato into 12 wedges.
3. Drain artichoke hearts, reserving 2 tablespoons marinade.
4. Tear lettuce into large pieces; arrange on four individual serving plates.
5. In a circular pattern, arrange tomato wedges alternately with green pepper strips, artichoke hearts and egg slices on each plate.
6. Place salmon in centers.
7. Mix together sour cream, horseradish and reserved artichoke marinade. Spoon decoratively over salad.
8. Sprinkle ground pepper over dressing.

Shrimp Avocado Boats

Serves 12

3 cups green shrimp, peeled
   and halved lengthwise
salt
2 tablespoons fresh lemon juice
dash original Worcestershire sauce
2 tablespoons butter or margarine
2 cups dry white wine
½ cup corn oil
¼ cup white vinegar

1 tablespoon sugar
1½ tablespoons brandy
1½ green apples, peeled, quartered
   and thinly sliced
1½ cucumbers, peeled, seeded
   and thinly sliced
6 whole ripe California avocados,
   halved
pepper (optional)

1. Marinate shrimp with salt, lemon juice and Worcestershire sauce.
2. Poach quickly in butter and white wine. Do not overcook. (Shrimp are done when they begin to turn pink.)
3. Remove from heat; cool.
4. Mix together oil, vinegar, sugar and brandy.
5. Add shrimp and poaching juice to oil-vinegar mixture.
6. Add apples and cucumbers; marinate 20 minutes or longer.
7. Scrape three-fourths of the avocado flesh out of skins; mash into a purée.
8. Mix puréed avocado with shrimp at the last minute. Taste to correct seasoning, adding more salt and some pepper, if necessary.
9. Spoon mixture into avocado shells. Serve as first or main course.

NOTE: *Salad is unusual but tasty. Can be made in advance. Serve with biscuits or bread sticks for a summer meal-in-one.*

Salmon-Macaroni Salad

Serves 6

1 package (7 ounces) macaroni
shells, cooked, rinsed and drained
3 hard-cooked eggs, chopped
1 can (7¾ ounces) salmon,
drained and flaked
1 cup mayonnaise
1 cup celery, finely chopped

¼ cup green pepper, chopped
2 tablespoons chopped pimiento
2 tablespoons fresh lemon juice
2 tablespoons sweet pickle relish
4 teaspoons instant chicken bouillon
lettuce leaves
tomato wedges (optional garnish)

sliced hard-cooked egg (optional garnish)

1. Combine all ingredients except lettuce, tomatoes and hard-cooked egg slices in a bowl; mix well.
2. Cover and chill thoroughly.
3. Stir before serving.
4. Serve in lettuce-lined bowl, garnished with tomato wedges and hard-cooked egg slices, if desired.

Salmon Pasta Salad

Serves 6

1 can (16 ounces) salmon
4 cups cooked large shell macaroni
1 cup celery, sliced
½ cup carrots, diced
½ cup cooked peas
½ cup parsley, chopped
¼ cup green onion, chopped

½ cup oil
4 tablespoons fresh lemon juice
2 tablespoons vinegar
1 teaspoon dill weed, crumbled
1 teaspoon celery seeds
½ teaspoon salt
lettuce leaves (optional)

1. Drain salmon.
2. Combine macaroni, celery, carrots, peas, parsley and onion.
3. Combine oil, lemon juice, vinegar, dill weed, celery seeds and salt in jar. Cover tightly and shake well to blend.
4. Pour dressing over macaroni mixture; toss well.
5. Refrigerate ½ hour. Toss again.
6. Break salmon into large pieces; fold into macaroni mixture.
7. Spoon salad into bowl lined with lettuce leaves, if desired.

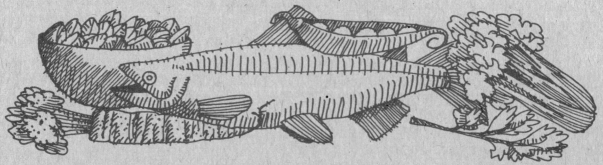

Mushroom-Shrimp & Dill Salad

Serves 4

½ pound cooked fresh shrimp
2 cups fresh mushrooms, sliced
12 cherry tomatoes, halved
2 tablespoons green onions, sliced
½ cup dairy sour cream

1 teaspoon fresh lemon juice
½ teaspoon horseradish
½ teaspoon dill weed, crumbled
½ teaspoon seasoned salt
crisp salad greens

1 avocado, peeled, seeded and sliced

1. Combine shrimp, mushrooms, tomatoes and onions in medium bowl.
2. Combine sour cream, lemon juice, horseradish, dill weed and seasoned salt for dressing.
3. Spoon shrimp mixture on salad plates lined with crisp salad greens.
4. Arrange avocado around shrimp mixture. Serve with dressing.

Seafood Salad with Avocado Hollandaise Dressing

Serves 6

lettuce leaves
1 package (10 ounces) frozen asparagus spears, cooked, or canned white asparagus, drained
1 pound large shrimp, cooked, shelled and deveined

½ pound scallops or cubed white fish, cooked in butter
2 hard-cooked eggs, sliced
⅓ cup ripe olives
Avocado Hollandaise Dressing

1. On large platter, arrange lettuce leaves and top with asparagus, shrimp, scallops, and hard-cooked eggs, arranged in any fashion desired.
2. Garnish with olives.
3. Serve with Avocado Hollandaise Dressing.

Avocado Hollandaise Dressing

Makes 1¼ cups

2 eggs
¼ cup fresh lemon juice
½ cup butter or margarine, melted

1 ripe avocado, peeled and seeded
2 teaspoons salt
onion salt

dash cayenne

1. Blend eggs with lemon juice in blender until lemon colored.
2. Slowly add bubbly hot butter on low speed.
3. Cut up avocado and blend into egg-butter mixture until smooth.
4. Add salt, onion salt to taste and cayenne.
5. Chill 30 minutes.

209

Walnut-Shrimp Salad

Serves 4 to 6

½ cup California walnuts, coarsely chopped, toasted and seasoned with garlic salt
1 pound shrimp, cooked and cleaned

1 cup celery, sliced
3 large oranges, pared and segmented
½ cup prepared French dressing
lettuce leaves
watercress (for garnish)

1. Marinate walnuts, shrimp, celery and oranges in French dressing ½ hour before serving; chill.
2. Arrange on lettuce leaves for salad plates.
3. Sprinkle with additional garlic salt, if desired. Garnish with watercress.

Avocado Half-Shells with Seafood

Serves 6

½ cup chili sauce
½ cup mayonnaise
1 teaspoon capers
fresh lemon juice
1 tablespoon original Worcestershire sauce
dash Tabasco
1 teaspoon salt

¼ teaspoon pepper
1 pound shrimp, shelled and cooked
1 can (7¾ ounces) crab meat, drained and flaked
1 can (5 ounces) lobster, drained and flaked
6 ripe California avocados
lemon or lime wedges (for garnish)

1. Combine chili sauce, mayonnaise, capers, lemon juice, Worcestershire sauce, Tabasco, salt and pepper.
2. Toss chili mixture with seafood; chill.
3. Halve avocados lengthwise, twisting gently to separate halves. Whack a sharp knife directly into seeds and twist to lift out.
4. Brush avocado with lemon juice; fill with seafood salad and garnish with lemon wedges.

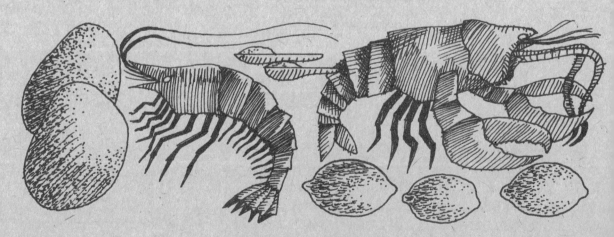

Seafood-Stuffed Tomatoes

Serves 6

1 package (7 ounces) frozen shrimp, cooked, or 1 cup cooked shrimp
1 package (6 ounces) frozen crab meat, thawed and well drained
1 cup carrots, grated
1 hard-cooked egg, chopped
2 tablespoons green onions, sliced

1 cup dairy sour cream
3 tablespoons parsley, chopped
1 teaspoon lemon rind
2 tablespoons fresh lemon juice
1 teaspoon prepared mustard
1 teaspoon salt
⅛ teaspoon pepper

6 large tomatoes

1. Cut shrimp into small pieces; flake crab meat.
2. Combine shrimp, crab meat, carrots, egg and onion in a bowl; chill.
3. Combine sour cream, parsley, lemon rind and juice, mustard, salt and pepper in a small bowl; chill.
4. Lightly toss dressing with seafood mixture. Chill.
5. Remove a slice from the stem and blossom ends of tomatoes. Make 3 cuts into each tomato, going about two-thirds down into it, but not all the way through. Spread apart carefully and place ¼ cup seafood mixture between each sliced section.

Avocado Salad Niçoise

Serves 6

1 head iceberg lettuce
1 head butter lettuce
1 large sweet red onion, cut in slices
3 ripe California avocados, halved and peeled
fresh lemon juice
1 can (12½ ounces) white chunk tuna, chilled and drained
6 flat anchovy fillets, drained

1 can (1 pound) whole green beans, chilled and drained
2 cans (14½ ounces each) whole boiled potatoes, chilled and drained
2 hard-cooked eggs, peeled and halved (for garnish)
giant pitted ripe olives (for garnish)
bottled oil and red wine vinegar salad dressing
freshly snipped parsley (optional)

2 lemons, cut into wedges (optional)

1. Cut iceberg lettuce into six ½-inch-thick rafts; lay side by side across center of large tray.
2. Arrange row of butter lettuce along sides of tray on each side of iceberg lettuce.
3. Top each lettuce "raft" with onion slice.
4. Sprinkle avocado half-shells with lemon juice; place cut side up on onion slices.
5. Fill half-shells with tuna; top each with an anchovy fillet.
6. Surround with an arrangement of green beans and potatoes.
7. Garnish with hard-cooked eggs and ripe olives.
8. At serving time, drizzle salad dressing over tray.
9. If desired, sprinkle salad with parsley and pass plate of lemon wedges.

Ripe Olive Tuna Salad Sandwich

Serves 4 to 6

1 cup canned pitted California
  ripe olives
1 cup celery, diced
2 cans (7 ounces each) tuna, drained
4 hard-cooked eggs, diced
⅓ cup mayonnaise

¼ cup dairy sour cream
1 tablespoon fresh lemon juice
½ teaspoon salt
½ teaspoon dill weed
1 teaspoon prepared mustard
⅛ teaspoon pepper

6 slices white or whole wheat bread

1. Cut ripe olives into large wedges.
2. Combine olives with celery, tuna and eggs.
3. Blend all remaining ingredients except bread.
4. Mix lightly with olive-tuna mixture.
5. Serve on bread slices.

Tuna Tabboulch

Serves 4

1 cup bulgur (cracked wheat)
2 cups water
2 chicken or vegetable bouillon
  cubes
1 bunch scallions, sliced
½ cup minced parsley
2 tablespoons chopped mint
¼ cup fresh lemon juice
3 tablespoons corn oil

1 teaspoon salt
¼ teaspoon pepper
2 cans (7 ounces each) tuna,
  packed in vegetable oil
2 tomatoes, cut in wedges
2 cucumbers, sliced
pitted ripe olives
romaine leaves
Yogurt Dressing

1. Place bulgur in medium-size bowl.
2. Heat water and bouillon cubes to boiling.
3. Pour bouillon over bulgur. Let stand 1 to 2 hours, until liquid is absorbed.
4. Stir in scallions, parsley, mint, lemon juice, oil, salt, pepper and tuna. Cover and chill for several hours.
5. To serve, pile tuna mixture on platter; surround with tomato wedges, cucumber and black olives.
6. Serve with romaine leaves and Yogurt Dressing.

Yogurt Dressing

1 cup plain yogurt
1 tablespoon chopped fresh mint

¼ teaspoon salt

1. Mix all ingredients in small bowl.
2. Chill until serving time.

Walnut-Tuna Stuffed Tomato

Serves 4 to 6

4 large or 6 medium tomatoes
salt, light sprinkle
pepper, light sprinkle
1 can (6½ or 7 ounces) tuna
2 hard-cooked eggs, diced
2 green onions, thinly sliced
1 cup celery, sliced
2 tablespoons pickle, chopped

1 tablespoon pimiento or green
   pepper, chopped
1 tablespoon capers
2 teaspoons fresh lemon juice
1 teaspoon prepared mustard
¼ teaspoon salt
¼ cup mayonnaise
¾ cup chopped California walnuts

1. Peel tomatoes and sprinkle lightly with salt and pepper; chill 2 hours.
2. Mix tuna with eggs, onions, celery, pickle, pimiento, capers, lemon juice, mustard and ¼ teaspoon salt; chill.
3. At serving time, add ¼ cup mayonnaise and ½ cup of the walnuts; toss until blended.
4. Turn tomatoes, stem end down. Cut each one not quite through into 6 to 8 sections; spread apart.
5. Fill with salad mixture; top with additional mayonnaise and remaining walnuts.

Zesty Seafood Vegetable Salad

Serves 4 to 6

For the Fish Marinade

2 cups water
juice of 3 fresh lemons
1 pound frozen cod, haddock
   or sole

1 cup corn oil
1 teaspoon salt
1 teaspoon celery seed
¼ teaspoon cayenne pepper

1. Combine water and ⅓ lemon juice in 10-inch skillet; bring to a boil.
2. Add frozen fish; simmer, covered, 20 minutes, or until fish flakes easily with fork.
3. Remove fish; cut into bite-size pieces. Discard poaching liquid.
4. Combine oil, remaining lemon juice, salt, celery seed and cayenne pepper in mixing bowl; add fish and chill well.

For the Salad

1 small head cabbage (1 pound),
   cut into bite-size pieces
2 medium tomatoes, cut in
   wedges

1 medium cucumber, scored and
   sliced
1 small green pepper, cut in
   thin strips

1. Combine ingredients in salad bowl; chill well.
2. To serve, toss fish and marinade with salad ingredients.

Avocado, Spinach & Bacon Salad

Serves 6

½ cup bottled French dressing
1 clove garlic, minced
1 pound crisp young spinach, washed and drained

½ ripe California avocado
fresh lemon juice
3 hard-cooked eggs, shelled and chopped
6 slices crisp-cooked bacon, crumbled

1. Combine French dressing and garlic; cover and refrigerate.
2. Tear spinach in pieces in salad bowl; refrigerate.
3. At serving time, peel avocado, cut into slices, and sprinkle with lemon juice.
4. Add avocado slices to spinach along with chopped egg and crumbled bacon. Pour over salad dressing; toss gently.

Artichoke Chef's Salad with Curry Dressing

Serves 6 to 8

2 jars (6 ounces each) marinated artichoke hearts
1 head iceberg lettuce
1 apple

1 pear
⅔ cup ham or turkey strips
½ cup Monterey Jack cheese strips
Curry Dressing

1. Drain artichoke hearts, reserving marinade for dressing.
2. Line chilled salad bowl with outer lettuce leaves. Shred remainder of lettuce and mound in bowl.
3. Core and cut apple and pear into slices; arrange on lettuce with ham, cheese and artichoke hearts. Serve with Curry Dressing.

Curry Dressing

Makes ⅞ cup

1 package (3 ounces) cream cheese
3 tablespoons reserved artichoke marinade
¼ cup mayonnaise

1 teaspoon onion powder
½ teaspoon basil, crumbled
¼ teaspoon salt
⅛ teaspoon curry powder

1 tablespoon chopped pimiento

1. Soften cream cheese.
2. Blend in artichoke marinade, beating until smooth.
3. Stir in mayonnaise, onion powder, basil, salt and curry powder. Mix well.
4. Add pimiento and blend.

Artichokes with Hot Corn Salad

Serves 8

8 slices bacon, diced
⅓ cup butter
1 cup green pepper, chopped
1 tablespoon chopped onion
2 packages (10 ounces each) frozen
    whole kernel corn, cooked

salt to taste
pepper to taste
8 medium artichokes, prepared
    according to basic directions*
melted butter

1. In large skillet, sauté bacon until crisp.
2. Remove bacon, reserving ¼ cup of drippings; drain on paper towels.
3. Add ⅓ cup butter to drippings and heat.
4. Add green pepper and onion; sauté until just tender.
5. Stir in corn, salt and pepper to taste. Heat through.
6. Fill hot artichokes with mixture; top with crumbled bacon.
7. Serve with melted butter.

*NOTE: Wash artichokes, cut off stems at base, and remove small bottom leaves. Stand artichokes upright in deep saucepan, add 1½ teaspoons salt and 2 to 3 inches boiling water. Cover and boil gently 30 to 45 minutes. Drain, spread leaves, and remove thistle. Drain again.

Italian-Style Antipasto Spaghetti Salad

Serves 6 to 8

⅓ cup olive oil
¼ cup wine vinegar
1 tablespoon chopped capers
1½ teaspoons oregano leaves,
    crushed
½ teaspoon salt
¼ teaspoon garlic powder
⅛ teaspoon freshly ground black pepper
8 ounces spaghetti
1 can (16 ounces) red kidney beans,
    drained and rinsed

1 can (10½ ounces) chick peas,
    drained and rinsed
¼ cup green salad olives, chopped
2 tablespoons parsley, chopped
¼ pound sliced boiled ham, cut
    in strips
¼ pound sliced provolone cheese,
    cut in strips
¼ pound sliced hard salami, cut in
    strips
¼ cup sweet roasted peppers,
    cut in strips

1. Combine oil, vinegar, capers, oregano, salt, garlic powder and pepper; set aside.
2. Cook spaghetti according to package directions. Rinse and drain. Place in a large serving bowl.
3. Add kidney beans, chick peas, salad olives, parsley and reserved oil-vinegar dressing.
4. Add half each of ham, cheese, salami and roasted pepper strips; toss well.
5. Cover and refrigerate until chilled, about 1 hour.
6. Top with remaining ham, cheese, salami and roasted pepper strips.

Picnic Bean Salad

Serves 4

1 can (16 ounces) pork and beans in tomato sauce
1 cup celery, sliced

1 cup green pepper, coarsely chopped
1 tablespoon molasses
¼ cup bottled Italian dressing

1. Combine beans, celery, green pepper, molasses and dressing in a large bowl. Toss to blend thoroughly.
2. Chill before serving.

Buffet Green Bean Salad

Serves 10 to 12

1 can (2 ounces) anchovy fillets, drained and chopped
1 cup mayonnaise
1 cup dairy sour cream
⅛ cup tarragon vinegar
3 green onions, finely chopped

salt to taste
pepper to taste
4 cans (16 ounces each) whole green beans
sieved hard-cooked egg yolks (for garnish)
chopped hard-cooked egg whites (for garnish)
cherry tomatoes (for garnish)

1. Mix together anchovies, mayonnaise, sour cream, vinegar and onions.
2. Season to taste with salt and pepper.
3. Drain green beans well.
4. Toss with dressing and let stand, covered, in refrigerator at least 4 hours.
5. Serve garnished with egg yolks and whites and cherry tomatoes.

Dig Deep Salad

Serves 12 to 14

1 head lettuce, shredded
2 medium red onions, sliced
1 to 2 green peppers, sliced
1 can (8 ounces) water chestnuts, sliced
1 package (10 ounces) frozen green peas, uncooked

3 to 4 ribs celery, chopped
2 cups mayonnaise
Romano cheese
3 tablespoons sugar
3 hard-cooked eggs, sliced (for garnish)
4 strips bacon, crumbled (for garnish)
1 to 2 tomatoes, sliced (for garnish)

1. Layer lettuce, onions, green peppers, water chestnuts, green peas and celery in a 9 x 13-inch pan.
2. Spread mayonnaise over top layer.
3. Sprinkle with Romano cheese and sugar. Do not stir.
4. Cover and refrigerate 24 hours.
5. Remove from refrigerator 45 minutes before serving. Garnish with sliced eggs, bacon and tomatoes.

Mediterranean Meatball Salad

Serves 6

¼ cup corn oil
2 tablespoons water
1 tablespoon fresh lemon juice
1 teaspoon dried mint leaves
1 pound lean ground beef
¼ cup finely grated onion
½ cup soft whole wheat bread crumbs
3 tablespoons chopped parsley

½ teaspoon salt
¼ teaspoon pepper
1½ cups diagonally sliced carrots, cooked and drained
1 cup cubed green pepper
3 cups lightly packed torn salad greens
1 large tomato, cut in wedges

1. In small jar with tight-fitting lid, place 2 tablespoons corn oil, water, lemon juice and mint.
2. Cover and shake well.
3. Refrigerate at least 1 hour.
4. In large bowl, mix beef, onion, bread crumbs, parsley, salt and pepper until well blended.
5. Shape into 1-inch meatballs.
6. Heat remaining 2 tablespoons corn oil in large skillet.
7. Add ½ of meatballs; cook, shaking pan often, 10 minutes, or until brown on all sides and cooked.
8. Remove and drain well on paper towels.
9. Brown remaining meatballs.
10. Toss together meatballs, carrots and green pepper in large bowl.
11 Cover and refrigerate 1 hour.
12. To serve, toss meatball mixture with dressing. Arrange on platter with salad greens and tomato.

LOW-CALORIE VERSION: Follow recipe for Mediterranean Meatball Salad. Omit bread crumbs and remaining 2 tablespoons corn oil for browning meatballs. In bowl, mix beef, onion, parsley, 1 tablespoon prepared mustard, salt and pepper. Shape into 1-inch balls. Place on 15½ x 10½ x 1-inch jelly roll pan. Bake in preheated 450° F. oven 8 to 10 minutes, turning once, or until cooked and browned on all sides. Continue as in basic recipe.

Layered Chef Salad

Serves 6 to 8

½ cup quick-cooking pearled
  barley
1½ cups boiling salted water
4 cups torn lettuce
2 cups cooked ham or chicken, cubed
1 cup diced green pepper

1 cup sliced celery
1¼ cups mayonnaise
2 tablespoons prepared yellow mustard
1 tablespoon sugar
1 teaspoon dill weed
1 cup shredded sharp Cheddar cheese

⅓ cup sliced green onion

1. Cook barley in boiling salted water, covered, 10 to 12 minutes, or until tender, stirring occasionally.
2. Drain and cool.
3. Arrange layer of lettuce, ham, green pepper, barley and celery in 3-quart salad bowl.
4. Combine mayonnaise, mustard, sugar and dill weed; mix well.
5. Spoon mayonnaise-dill mixture on top of lettuce layer, spreading to edges of bowl.
6. Sprinkle cheese and green onion over mayonnaise.
7. Cover with plastic wrap and refrigerate several hours, or overnight.
8. Toss salad just before serving. Great for buffet or Sunday night supper!

Ripe Olive Pizza Salad

Serves 6

1 cup pitted California
  ripe olives
romaine lettuce
30 thin slices Mozzarella cheese,
  about 12 ounces

30 thin slices salami (about 6 ounces)
Pizza Dressing
grated Parmesan cheese

1. Cut ripe olives into halves.
2. Line individual salad plates with romaine.
3. Cover with alternating layers of cheese, ripe olives and salami, using 5 slices cheese and salami for each layer. Top with more ripe olive halves.
4. Sprinkle with Pizza Dressing and Parmesan cheese.

Pizza Dressing

Makes ½ cup

¼ cup salad oil
2 tablespoons garlic wine vinegar
½ teaspoon salt

¼ teaspoon crumbled oregano
2 tablespoons catsup
2 tablespoons grated Parmesan cheese

1. Combine oil, vinegar, salt, oregano, catsup and Parmesan cheese.
2. Cover and shake until well blended.

Hot Dutch Potato Salad

Serves 8 to 10

4 slices bacon
½ cup onion, chopped
½ cup green pepper, chopped
¼ cup vinegar
1 teaspoon salt

⅛ teaspoon pepper
1 teaspoon sugar
1 egg
1 quart hot cooked potatoes, cubed
¼ cup raw carrot, grated

3 hard-cooked eggs

1. Dice bacon and pan-fry.
2. Add chopped onion and green pepper. Cook 3 minutes.
3. Add vinegar, salt, pepper, sugar and beaten egg. Cook slightly.
4. Add cubed potatoes, grated carrot and diced hard-cooked eggs. Blend slightly and serve hot.

Monterey Baked Salad

Serves 6

1 pound lean ground beef
1 teaspoon garlic powder
1 teaspoon onion powder
1½ teaspoons salt
¼ teaspoon Tabasco sauce
1 tablespoon lemon juice

½ cup mayonnaise
3 cups cooked rice
1 cup celery, sliced
½ cup green pepper, chopped
2 medium tomatoes, cut in eighths
1 cup corn chips, crushed

1. Sauté meat with garlic and onion powders in a lightly greased skillet about 10 minutes, or until done.
2. Blend salt, Tabasco, lemon juice and mayonnaise.
3. Add this mixture and remaining ingredients, except corn chips, to ground beef.
4. Turn mixture into a greased 1-quart casserole. Top with corn chips.
5. Bake in preheated 375° F. oven 25 to 30 minutes.

NOTE: Great with tostados!

Tostada Salad

Serves 6 to 8

1 pound lean ground beef
1 package (1¼ ounces) taco seasoning mix
¾ cup water
¾ teaspoon seasoned salt
1 can (14 ounces) red kidney beans, drained

4 tomatoes, cut into wedges
1 ripe avocado, cut in thin slices
1 package (6¼ ounces) tortilla chips
1 head lettuce, torn into small pieces
4 ounces Cheddar cheese, grated
1 cup onion, chopped

1. Brown ground beef in skillet; drain fat.
2. Add taco seasoning mix, water, seasoned salt and beans. Cover and simmer for 10 minutes.
3. Reserve some of tomato wedges, avocado slices and tortilla chips for garnish. Combine the rest with remaining ingredients in a large salad bowl.
4. Add ground beef mixture; toss lightly.
5. Garnish with reserved tomatoes, avocado and tortilla chips. Serve at once.

NOTE: Hearty enough for main-dish fare.

California Salami Salad with Tarragon Dressing

Serves 4

1 head romaine, washed and chilled
2 oranges, thinly sliced
12 thin slices Italian salami, cut in halves
1 small red onion, peeled and sliced

1 jar (6 ounces) marinated artichoke hearts
⅓ cup toasted almonds, slivered
Tarragon Dressing

1. Tear romaine into bite-size pieces; place in salad bowl.
2. Arrange orange slices in a circle on top; cover with salami slices.
3. Scatter onion slices over salami.
4. Cut artichokes in halves; reserve dressing. Place artichokes in center of salad.
5. Scatter almonds over top.
6. At table, pour Tarragon Dressing and mix lightly to serve. Terrific with hot garlic Italian bread.

Tarragon Dressing

artichoke dressing, from marinated artichoke hearts
2 tablespoons fine-grade olive oil
1 tablespoon dry white wine vinegar

1 teaspoon orange peel, grated
¼ teaspoon dried tarragon, crumbled
1 clove garlic, peeled and minced
½ teaspoon Dijon-style mustard

Combine all ingredients; blend well.

Yam 'n' Ham Salad

Serves 6

4 medium yams
1 pound boiled ham
1 cup green seedless grapes, halved
1 pear, cored and cubed
¼ cup honey
¾ cup dairy sour cream

3 tablespoons fresh lemon juice
½ teaspoon salt
¼ teaspoon pepper
¼ teaspoon cinnamon
¼ teaspoon dry mustard
lettuce leaves

1. Bake yams in preheated 350° F. oven 40 minutes, or boil, covered, in lightly salted water for 20 minutes, or until just tender.
2. Cool. Remove peel.
3. Cut yams and ham into ½-inch cubes.
4. Combine cubes in large bowl with grapes and pear.
5. Refrigerate until thoroughly chilled.
6. Combine remaining ingredients in small bowl; pour over yam mixture just before serving. Toss lightly.
7. Arrange on platter lined with lettuce leaves.

Tropical Pork Salad

Serves 4 to 6

1½ to 2 cups cooked pork, cubed
2 cups chilled cooked rice
½ cup green pepper, chopped
½ cup celery, sliced
1 can (8 ounces) pineapple chunks
   in juice

½ cup prepared salad dressing
¼ teaspoon ginger
¼ teaspoon salt
crisp salad greens
mint or watercress
   (optional garnish)

1. Combine pork, rice, green pepper and celery in bowl.
2. Drain pineapple chunks; reserve 2 tablespoons juice.
3. Add pineapple chunks to salad ingredients.
4. Combine and mix salad dressing, 2 tablespoons pineapple juice, ginger and salt; mix well.
5. Pour over salad ingredients; toss lightly to coat evenly.
6. Cover and chill well. Serve on chilled greens. Garnish with mint or watercress, if desired.

Frying Pan Salad of Spinach & Nectarines

Serves 4 to 6

3 to 4 cups fresh spinach leaves
2 medium-size fresh nectarines
2 or 3 tablespoons green onions,
thinly sliced

4 slices bacon
¼ cup cider vinegar
½ teaspoon salt
1 tablespoon brown sugar

1. Wash and tear spinach leaves from stems. Tear large leaves into pieces and pack down in cup to measure. Pat with paper towels to remove excess moisture.
2. Coarsely chop nectarines to yield 1 cup.
3. Combine spinach, nectarines and onions in a bowl or plastic bag.
4. Cut bacon into ½-inch pieces and fry until crisp in large skillet. Drain crisp bits and add to spinach combination.
5. Pour all but 2 tablespoons of bacon drippings from pan.
6. Add to remaining drippings vinegar, salt and brown sugar. Heat just to simmering.
7. Remove from heat and add spinach combination; toss well. Serve at once while slightly warm.

Oriental Pepper Steak Salad Cups

Serves 2

¼ cup bottled low-calorie Russian
dressing
2 teaspoons soy sauce
dash ground ginger
½ cup cooked beef strips
(about 3 ounces)

¾ cup fresh mushrooms, sliced
½ cup fresh bean sprouts
½ cup fresh broccoli flowerets
2 medium green peppers, tops removed
and scooped out

1. Blend together dressing, soy sauce and ginger in medium-size shallow baking dish.
2. Add beef, mushrooms, bean sprouts and broccoli.
3. Cover and marinate in refrigerator, turning occasionally, 4 hours or overnight.
4. Spoon beef mixture into pepper cups; wrap and chill.

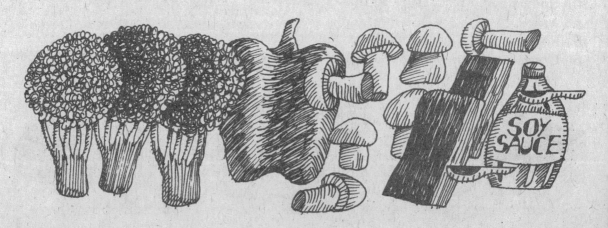

Pineapple Rice Salad

Serves 8

½ cup chopped onion
1 cup long grain white rice
2 tablespoons butter
2 cups chicken broth
1 can (20 ounces) pineapple
   tidbits in own juice
¼ cup mayonnaise

¼ cup dairy sour cream
2 tablespoons soy sauce
¼ teaspoon garlic powder
1 cup julienne ham
¼ cup sliced green onion
½ green pepper, cut into
   1-inch strips

1. Sauté onion and rice in butter until onion is soft.
2. Add chicken broth; bring to a boil.
3. Cover and simmer 20 minutes. Chill.
4. Drain pineapple, reserving 1 tablespoon juice.
5. Combine mayonnaise, sour cream, soy sauce, garlic powder and reserved juice; mix thoroughly with rice.
6. Fold in pineapple, ham, green onion and green pepper; chill.

Golden West Platter

Serves 8

1 fresh pineapple
8 thin slices cooked ham
1 package (6 ounces) sliced
   salami
lettuce or crisp salad greens
1 avocado
8 green onions

2 medium tomatoes, sliced
1 package (6 ounces) sliced
   Swiss cheese, cut into 1½-inch
   strips
½ cup mayonnaise
⅓ cup dairy sour cream
¼ cup milk

3 ounces blue cheese, crumbled

1. Peel pineapple; cut into 16 spears. Remove core and discard.
2. Roll ham slices; roll salami slices. Secure with toothpicks.
3. Peel avocado; cut into 8 wedges.
4. On lettuce-lined serving dish, arrange pineapple, ham, salami, avocado, green onions, tomatoes, and cheese; chill until ready to serve.
5. Combine mayonnaise, sour cream and milk; mix until well blended.
6. Fold in blue cheese; chill. Serve with salad.

American Macaroni Salad

Serves 6 to 8

1 cup salad macaroni (4 ounces)
1 cup real mayonnaise
3 tablespoons milk
1½ teaspoons prepared mustard
½ teaspoon salt
⅛ teaspoon pepper

1 cup cubed bologna (4 ounces)
½ cup cubed processed American cheese (2 ounces)
¼ cup chopped onion
¼ cup diced bread-and-butter pickles

1. Cook macaroni according to package directions; rinse in cold water and drain.
2. Combine mayonnaise, milk, mustard, salt and pepper in large bowl.
3. Add macaroni, bologna, cheese, onion and pickles; toss to coat well.
4. Cover and refrigerate at least 2 hours before serving.

Italian Macaroni Salad

Serves 8

2 cups macaroni shells (8 ounces)
1 cup real mayonnaise
1 can (7¾ ounces) marinara sauce
¼ cup milk

½ teaspoon salt
½ teaspoon dried oregano leaves
4 ounces pepperoni, sliced or cut in strips

1 cup chopped celery

1. Cook shells according to package instructions; rinse in cold water and drain.
2. Stir together mayonnaise, marinara sauce, milk, salt and oregano in large bowl.
3. Add macaroni, pepperoni and celery; toss to coat well.
4. Cover and refrigerate at least 2 hours.

Patio Macaroni Salad

Serves 6 to 8

1 cup salad macaroni (4 ounces)
1 cup real mayonnaise
2 tablespoons milk
1 tablespoon lemon juice
1 tablespoon horseradish
½ teaspoon salt
⅛ teaspoon pepper

½ package (10 ounces) frozen peas, cooked and drained (1 cup)
4 ounces cooked ham, cut in julienne strips (1 cup)
4 ounces Swiss cheese, cut in julienne strips (1 cup)
½ cup chopped green onions

1. Cook macaroni according to package directions; rinse in cold water, and drain.
2. Combine mayonnaise, milk, lemon juice, horseradish, salt and pepper.
3. Add macaroni, peas, ham, cheese and onions; toss to coat well.
4. Cover and refrigerate at least 2 hours before serving.

Autumn Salad

Serves 4 to 6

2 cans (1 pound each) whole kernel
   corn, drained
1 cup celery, sliced
1 cup tomatoes, diced
¼ cup green pepper, chopped
1 sprig fresh dill, minced or
   ½ teaspoon dried dill
¾ cup corn oil

¼ cup vinegar
1 teaspoon sugar
½ teaspoon salt
½ teaspoon paprika
½ teaspoon dry mustard
¼ teaspoon Tabasco sauce
salad greens
onion rings (for garnish)

1. Combine corn, celery, tomatoes, green pepper and dill in a large bowl.
2. Blend remaining ingredients except greens and onion rings together with an egg beater.
3. Pour dressing over vegetables in bowl. Marinate 1 hour before serving.
4. Place in large serving bowl lined with salad greens. Garnish with onion rings.

Avocado Accordion Salad with Pineapple-Honey Dressing

Serves 4

2 ripe California avocados
4 slices canned pineapple, with juice
lemon juice, or juice from canned
   pineapple

salad greens
1 pint cottage cheese
Pineapple-Honey Dressing

1. Cut avocados lengthwise into halves; remove seeds and skin. Cut each half crosswise into 4 pieces.
2. Sprinkle avocados with enough lemon juice or pineapple juice to coat.
3. Cut pineapple slices into halves.
4. Line four salad plates with greens.
5. Spoon cottage cheese over greens to make "beds" for accordions.
6. Reassemble one avocado half over each serving of cottage cheese, alternating avocado pieces with pineapple halves.
7. Serve with Pineapple-Honey Dressing.

Pineapple-Honey Dressing

¼ cup syrup from canned pineapple
¼ cup honey

¼ cup lemon juice
chopped fresh mint (optional)

Combine ingredients. Mix well.

Avocado Salad Mexicano

Serves 6 to 8

½ cup western tomato, diced
½ cup cooked vegetable: green beans or peas
¼ cup green pepper, chopped
¼ cup celery, chopped
3 tablespoons green onion, chopped
¼ cup ripe olives, sliced

1 to 2 tablespoons blue cheese, crumbled
¼ cup prepared French dressing
salt to taste
pepper to taste
3 or 4 California avocados
lime or lemon juice
salad greens

whole ripe olives

1. Gently mix tomato, beans or peas, green pepper, celery, onion, olives, cheese and French dressing.
2. Season to taste with salt and pepper; chill.
3. Just before serving, cut avocados lengthwise into halves; remove seeds and skin. Sprinkle with lime juice.
4. Arrange avocados on salad greens.
5. Heap marinated vegetable mixture into avocados. Top each serving with whole olive.

California Avocado-Mushroom Salad

Serves 6

⅓ cup olive oil
1 tablespoon wine vinegar
1 tablespoon parsley, chopped
1 clove garlic, halved
1 teaspoon salt

freshly ground black pepper
juice of 1 lemon
2 ripe California avocados
½ pound mushrooms, thinly sliced
crisp lettuce leaves

parsley (optional garnish)

1. Combine oil, vinegar, parsley, garlic, salt, pepper and lemon juice; chill well.
2. Halve avocados lengthwise, twisting gently to separate halves. Whack a sharp knife directly into seeds and twist to lift out. Peel.
3. Place avocados, cavity-side down, on cutting surface, and slice very thin.
4. Layer sliced avocados and mushrooms on platter.
5. Marinate in dressing 1 hour before serving.
6. Drain and serve on lettuce leaves.
7. Garnish with parsley, if desired.

Beans 'n' Rice Salad

Serves 6

2 cups quick-cooking rice
1⅓ cups water
¾ teaspoon salt
1 tablespoon butter
1 cup canned kidney beans, drained
1 cup canned garbanzo beans, drained

1 tomato, diced
½ cup celery, sliced
½ cup green pepper, chopped
¼ cup red onion, chopped
½ teaspoon chili powder
3 tablespoons vinegar

5 tablespoons oil

1. Combine rice, water, ½ teaspoon salt and butter in medium saucepan.
2. Bring to a boil; cover and simmer until all water is absorbed, about 5 minutes.
3. Place rice in bowl and refrigerate.
4. When chilled, add beans, tomato, celery, green pepper and onion to rice.
5. In jar, combine remaining ¼ teaspoon salt, chili powder and vinegar.
6. Add oil; cover and shake vigorously.
7. Pour over rice mixture and toss gently.

Cabbage Slaw

Serves 6 to 8

4 cups green or red cabbage, shredded
½ cup wheat germ
¼ cup scallions, chopped
⅓ cup fresh parsley, chopped
½ cup almonds, chopped

1 cup plain yogurt
½ teaspoon dill weed
¼ teaspoon dry mustard
salt to taste
carrot curls and black olives (for garnish)

1. Combine cabbage, wheat germ, scallions, parsley and almonds. Set aside.
2. Mix together yogurt, dill, mustard and salt.
3. Pour yogurt mixture over cabbage mixture; toss to mix.
4. Pack into a 1-quart mold and refrigerate.
5. Unmold onto serving plate. Garnish with carrot curls and black olives.

Carousel Rice Salad

Serves 6 to 8

3 cups cold cooked rice
1 cup carrots, grated
1 cup celery, sliced
⅓ cup sweet pickle, diced

1 teaspoon salt
dash of pepper
½ teaspoon sweet basil
1 cup dairy sour cream

salad greens

1. Combine rice, carrots, celery, sweet pickle, salt and pepper. Toss lightly, then chill.
2. Blend basil into sour cream.
3. Serve chilled rice mixture on salad greens. Top with seasoned sour cream.

Bean Sprout-Sunflower Salad

Serves 2 to 3

2 cups fresh bean sprouts
¼ cup sunflower seeds (raw and shelled)
¼ cup julienned white meat of chicken
⅓ cup julienned Oriental barbecued pork, or left-over pork roast
¼ medium canned Jalapeño pepper, thinly sliced
½ teaspoon Dijon-style mustard

⅓ cup safflower oil
¼ cup julienned green onion
⅓ cup red wine vinegar
juice of ½ lemon
salt to taste
cracked black pepper to taste
garnish: watercress; tomato wedges; hard-cooked eggs, quartered; and pitted black olives

1. Blanch bean sprouts in boiling water 1½ to 2 minutes. Drain and cool.
2. Simmer sunflower seeds in water 10 minutes. Drain and chill.
3. Mix remaining ingredients except sunflower seeds and garnish together.
4. Place mixture in lettuce cups on plates.
5. Sprinkle sunflower seeds over salad.
6. Decorate plates with watercress, tomato wedges, eggs and black olives.

Bulgur Salad

Serves 4 to 6

¾ cup bulgur
¾ cup Sauterne
¾ cup water
1½ teaspoons salt
½ cup red onion, sliced
1 cup fresh parsley, chopped
⅓ cup oil

3 tablespoons fresh lemon juice
1 teaspoon dried mint, crumbled, or 1 teaspoon minced fresh mint
⅛ teaspoon oregano, crumbled
⅛ teaspoon pepper
cherry tomatoes
pita bread, cut in small wedges

mint sprigs (for garnish)

1. Combine bulgur, Sauterne, water and ¾ teaspoon salt. Heat to boiling.
2. Cover and let stand until cold.
3. Add onion and parsley.
4. Combine remaining salt with oil, lemon juice, mint, oregano and pepper in small jar. Cover and shake well.
5. Pour over salad mixture and toss lightly.
6. Chill, covered, until serving time.
7. To assemble, heap bulgur in center of platter and surround alternately with cherry tomatoes and pita bread. Garnish with mint sprigs.

NOTE: Makes a meal-in-one.

Celestial Carrot Salad

Serves 4

½ pound carrots, grated
1 tablespoon fresh lemon juice
dash of salt
¼ cup miniature marshmallows
1 can (8½ ounces) pineapple tidbits
  or mandarin oranges, drained

1 tablespoon honey
¼ teaspoon mace
½ cup plain yogurt
crisp lettuce leaves (optional)

1. Combine carrots, lemon juice and salt.
2. Add marshmallows and fruit.
3. Blend honey with mace and yogurt. Chill well.
4. Serve on lettuce leaves, if desired.

NOTE: *A wonderful side dish for cold chicken!*

Chilean Grape Salad with Herbed Dressing

Serves 4

2 cups halved seedless green or
  red Chilean grapes, or
  combination of both
½ cup thin slices sweet red onion
½ cup thin strips red or green
  sweet pepper

½ cup thin half-slices cucumber
1 quart small lettuce leaves, or
  coarsely shredded lettuce
1 large firm, ripe banana
Herbed Dressing

1. Rinse and stem grapes; seed red grapes if used. Leave grapes whole or cut in half, as desired. Chill.
2. Prepare vegetables in slices or strips and chill.
3. When ready to serve, turn lettuce into chilled salad bowl.
4. Peel and slice banana.
5. Arrange grapes, banana and vegetables on lettuce.
6. Toss with Herbed Dressing when served.

NOTE: *Use 1 cup julienne strips of cooked chicken or ham for a heartier salad.*

Herbed Dressing

Makes about ½ cup

¼ cup garlic flavored
  wine vinegar
⅓ cup salad oil
3 drops Tabasco sauce

1 teaspoon sugar
½ teaspoon seasoned salt
⅛ teaspoon finely crumbled oregano

1. Beat together wine vinegar, oil, sugar, seasoned salt, oregano and Tabasco.
2. Mix before serving.

Cold Pasta Salad for 25

4 boxes (16 ounces each) macaroni
shells
2 packages (10 ounces each) frozen
chopped spinach, cooked and drained
6 tablespoons dried basil
18 cloves garlic, chopped

1½ cups Parmesan cheese, grated
2 cups olive oil
¼ cup red wine vinegar
2 teaspoons salt, or more to taste
1 teaspoon pepper
cherry tomatoes (for garnish)

1. Cook macaroni to package directions.
2. Drain; refrigerate, covered, until cool.
3. Combine remaining ingredients, except tomatoes, in medium bowl. Toss with chilled macaroni.
4. Refrigerate salad, covered, at least 2 hours.
5. Serve cold. Garnish with cherry tomatoes.

NOTE: *Great for a crowd!*

French Brie Salad

Serves 6

½ pound Brie cheese, rind removed and
softened at room temperature
6 granola cookies, processed into
fine crumbs

1 can (16 ounces) mandarin oranges,
drained
1 cup seedless green grapes, cut in half
lengthwise

3 to 4 small heads Bibb lettuce, thoroughly washed and dried

1. Mold softened Brie into small squares, rectangles or rounds.
2. Roll in cookie crumbs to coat completely.
3. Refrigerate on plate until serving time.
4. When ready to serve, arrange Brie shapes, oranges and grapes on lettuce leaves in individual salad dishes or on a serving platter. Serve without dressing.

Golden Apple-Spinach Salad

Serves 4

1 pound fresh spinach
1 Red or Golden Delicious apple
½ cup sunflower seeds
4 green onions, sliced

2 tablespoons fresh lemon juice
3 tablespoons olive oil
½ teaspoon salt
freshly ground pepper

1. Wash and drain spinach. Coarsely tear into salad bowl.
2. Thinly slice unpeeled apple; add to bowl with sunflower seeds and green onions.
3. Blend lemon juice, olive oil and salt; toss with salad.
4. Sprinkle with freshly ground pepper.

Feta Greek Salad

Serves 4 to 6

Salad

1 head romaine lettuce, torn into
  bite-size pieces
3 tomatoes, cut up
1 onion, thinly sliced
1 green pepper, seeded and chopped
  (optional)

1 cucumber, peeled and sliced
1 cup black olives, preferably Greek
½ pound feta cheese, sliced or cut
  into chunks
1 can (2 ounces) anchovies, drained
  (optional)

Dressing

¼ cup olive oil
2 tablespoons vinegar

generous pinch oregano
salt and pepper to taste

1. Chill all vegetables, olives, cheese and anchovies.
2. Combine Dressing ingredients.
3. When ready to serve, toss all vegetables and olives. Top with cheese and anchovies, if desired. Serve with Dressing.

Fresh Fruit Salad with Poppy Seed Dressing

Serves 6

¾ cup corn oil
¼ cup honey
⅓ cup white vinegar
1 tablespoon poppy seeds
1 teaspoon dry mustard

½ teaspoon salt
lettuce leaves
1 pineapple, cut in chunks (3 cups)
1 pint strawberries, halved (2 cups)
1 cup cantaloupe balls

12 ounces cottage cheese

1. In blender container, place corn oil, honey, vinegar, poppy seeds, mustard and salt.
2. Cover and blend on medium speed 20 seconds, or until well mixed.
3. Pour into jar with tight-fitting lid. Cover and refrigerate.
4. On six lettuce-lined plates, arrange fruit and cottage cheese.
5. Serve with dressing. (Store any remaining dressing tightly covered in refrigerator.)

Macaroni Olive Salad

Serves 6

2 cups (8 ounces) elbow macaroni
1 tablespoon salt
3 quarts boiling water
½ cup dairy sour cream
½ cup mayonnaise
⅓ cup milk
½ teaspoon dry mustard
1 teaspoon basil leaves, crushed

1 tablespoon fresh lemon juice
⅓ cup onion, chopped
1 cup raw carrots, thinly sliced
¾ cup cucumber, peeled, seeded and diced
½ cup red radishes, sliced
¾ cup pimiento-stuffed olives, sliced
salt to taste
pepper to taste ·

1. Gradually add macaroni and salt to rapidly boiling water so water continues to boil.
   Cook, uncovered, stirring occasionally, until tender.
2. Drain in colander, rinse with cold water, and drain again.
3. Blend together sour cream, mayonnaise, milk, dry mustard, basil leaves, and lemon
   juice in large bowl.
4. Add macaroni, vegetables and olive slices. Toss until combined.
5. Season to taste with salt and pepper.
6. Cover and chill for several hours.

Piña Frijole Salad

Serves 8 to 10

1 can (20 ounces) pineapple slices
   in their own juice
⅓ cup olive oil
⅓ cup red wine vinegar
2 tablespoons green onion, chopped
2 tablespoons dill pickles, chopped

2 teaspoons sugar
½ teaspoon chili powder
dash Tabasco sauce
1 can (16 ounces) kidney beans, drained
1 cup celery, sliced
6 cups torn lettuce

cherry tomatoes (for garnish)

1. Drain pineapple, reserving ½ cup juice for dressing. (Reserve remaining juice for other
   uses.)
2. Chill pineapple until ready to use.
3. Combine reserved ½ cup juice, olive oil, vinegar, onion, pickles, sugar, chili powder,
   Tabasco, kidney beans and celery. Marinate overnight.
4. Just before serving, place lettuce in salad bowl. Line sides with pineapple slices. Pour
   kidney bean mixture in center. Garnish with cherry tomatoes.
5. Toss before serving.

"Dilled" Potato Salad

Serves 6 to 8

1 cup dairy sour cream
½ cup salad dressing
3 tablespoons vinegar
1½ teaspoons salt
¼ teaspoon pepper
1 teaspoon dill weed
6 cups cooked potatoes, sliced

1 cup celery, thinly sliced
¾ cup onion, minced
½ cup cucumber, peeled, diced and
   well drained
½ cup green pepper, chopped
½ cup radishes, sliced
chilled salad greens

3 hard-cooked eggs, sliced (for garnish)

1. Mix sour cream with salad dressing, vinegar, salt, pepper and dill weed.
2. Toss together in large bowl cooked potatoes, celery, onion, cucumber, green pepper, radishes and all but 3 or 4 egg slices (save for garnish).
3. Mix gently with dressing; chill to blend flavors.
4. Serve on crisp greens on individual plates; garnish with sliced eggs.

Tossed Taco Salad with Spicy Dressing

Serves 4 to 6

4 corn tortillas
oil for deep frying
Spicy Dressing
1 can (15¼ ounces) red kidney beans,
   drained and rinsed
1 small red onion, cut in thin rings

1 small cucumber, peeled, seeded and
   chopped
2 medium tomatoes, peeled, chopped
   and drained
1 small green pepper, chopped
2 cups shredded lettuce

1. Cut tortillas in half, then cut in ½-inch strips.
2. Fry in deep oil until crisp.
3. Drain on paper towels; set aside.
4. Prepare Spicy Dressing and chill.
5. Combine kidney beans, onion, cucumber, tomatoes, green pepper and lettuce. Toss with Spicy Dressing and serve topped with tortilla strips.

Spicy Dressing

Makes 2 cups

½ avocado, cut into chunks
¼ cup dairy sour cream
¼ cup canned enchilada sauce

1 small clove garlic, minced
2 teaspoons fresh lemon juice
¼ teaspoon salt

freshly ground pepper to taste

1. Place avocado and sour cream in blender container; blend until puréed.
2. Add enchilada sauce, garlic, lemon juice, salt and pepper to taste.
3. Blend until dressing is smooth and creamy.

233

Tomato Rice Supper Salad

Serves 4

1 cup uncooked rice
2 medium tomatoes, diced
1 tablespoon parsley, chopped
¼ cup green onions, chopped
2 tablespoons ripe olives, sliced
⅓ cup celery, chopped
2 teaspoons oil
1 tablespoon vinegar

⅛ teaspoon dry mustard
⅛ teaspoon paprika
dash garlic powder
dash cayenne
salt to taste
crisp lettuce cups
peach halves
assorted cold cuts

parsley sprigs (for garnish)

1. Cook rice according to package directions. Chill.
2. Combine rice with tomatoes, parsley, onions, olives and celery.
3. Blend together oil, vinegar, mustard, paprika, garlic powder and cayenne.
4. Pour dressing over salad and toss lightly.
5. Season to taste with salt. Chill.
6. Just before serving, spoon into lettuce cups for individual servings.
7. Serve with peach halves and cold cuts.
8. Garnish with parsley.

Vegetable Salad Surprise

Serves 4

4 medium tomatoes
2 medium green peppers
8 hard-cooked eggs
⅔ cup mayonnaise
¼ cup sweet pickles, diced

1 teaspoon salt
¼ teaspoon pepper
½ teaspoon paprika
1 tablespoon chopped chives
lettuce leaves

1. Wash tomatoes and green peppers.
2. Cut top ⅓ off tomatoes. (Save for sandwiches or salads.) Scoop out pulp from rest of each tomato.
3. Cut off top ½ inch of peppers and discard. Remove seeds.
4. Carefully slice two 1-inch rings from each pepper. (Save remaining pepper for other use.)
5. Place rings of peppers on top of tomato shells.
6. Shell eggs and mash.
7. Add mayonnaise, sweet pickles, salt, pepper, paprika and chives; mix.
8. Stuff shells with egg mixture.
9. Serve on lettuce leaves.

Macaroni Ambrosia Salad

Serves 6 to 8

1 cup salad macaroni (4 ounces)
1 cup real mayonnaise
¾ cup flaked coconut
1 tablespoon honey

1 tablespoon milk
¼ teaspoon ground cinnamon
1 can (17 ounces) fruit cocktail, well drained

½ cup toasted slivered almonds (for garnish)

1. Cook macaroni according to package directions; rinse in cold water and drain.
2. Stir together mayonnaise, coconut, honey, milk and cinnamon in bowl.
3. Add macaroni and fruit cocktail; toss to coat well.
4. Cover and refrigerate at least 2 hours; garnish with almonds.

Creamy Italian Bean Salad

Serves 6 to 8

1 package (0.87 ounces) sour cream onion salad dressing mix
1 cup milk
1 cup mayonnaise

1 cup cooked Italian green beans
8 cherry tomatoes, halved
3 medium new potatoes, cooked, peeled and cubed

1. Prepare salad dressing mix according to package directions; use ½ cup dressing for recipe. (Refrigerate remaining 1½ cups dressing for later use.)
2. Combine dressing, beans, tomatoes and potatoes; toss lightly but thoroughly to coat.
3. Chill before serving.

Wilted Spinach Salad

Serves 4 to 6

6 slices bacon
1 can (1 pound 4 ounces) chunk pineapple in syrup
1 bunch fresh spinach
2 teaspoons cornstarch
3 tablespoons cider vinegar

½ teaspoon original Worcester-shire sauce
¼ teaspoon dry mustard
1 can (3 ounces) French fried onions
freshly ground pepper

1. Chop bacon; fry in wok or skillet until crisp.
2. Drain and reserve bacon, discarding all but 2 tablespoons pan drippings.
3. Drain pineapple, reserving syrup.
4. Wash spinach; dry and remove stems. Set aside.
5. Mix cornstarch, vinegar, Worcestershire sauce, mustard and pineapple syrup; stir into hot bacon drippings. Cook, stirring, about 2 minutes, or until sauce thickens slightly.
6. Add pineapple chunks; heat through.
7. Remove from heat; stir in spinach, onions and a few grinds of fresh black pepper.
8. Toss until spinach is coated with dressing; serve immediately.

Macaroni Slaw

Serves 10

2 cups elbow macaroni (8 ounces)
1 cup real mayonnaise
3 tablespoons lemon juice
1½ teaspoons sugar
1½ teaspoons dry mustard

1 teaspoon salt
dash garlic powder
3 cups finely shredded cabbage
1 cup coarsely shredded carrots
½ cup minced green pepper

¼ cup minced onion

1. Cook macaroni according to package directions; rinse in cold water and drain.
2. Stir together mayonnaise, lemon juice, sugar, mustard, salt and garlic powder in large bowl.
3. Add macaroni, cabbage, carrots, green pepper and onion; toss to coat well.
4. Cover and refrigerate at least 2 hours.

Waldorf Macaroni Salad

Serves 8 to 10

1½ cups elbow macaroni
   (6 ounces)
1 cup real mayonnaise
2 tablespoons milk
2 tablespoons lemon juice
1 tablespoon sugar
½ teaspoon salt

1 can (11 ounces) mandarin orange
   sections, well drained
1 medium red apple, cored and
   diced
1 cup sliced celery
crisp lettuce leaves (optional)
sliced almonds (optional garnish)

1. Cook macaroni according to package instructions; rinse in cold water and drain.
2. Stir together mayonnaise, milk, lemon juice, sugar and salt in large bowl.
3. Add macaroni, orange sections, apple and celery; toss to coat well.
4. Cover and refrigerate at least 2 hours.
5. If desired, arrange on lettuce-lined platter and garnish with sliced almonds.

Summer Garden Salad

Serves 4

2 Granny Smith apples, cored
   and diced
½ pound small, red potatoes,
   cooked and sliced ¼-inch thick
1 cup frozen peas, thawed and
   drained

1 cup plain yogurt
2 teaspoons prepared horseradish
1 teaspoon chopped fresh mint
   or 1 teaspoon dried mint leaves
¼ teaspoon salt
crisp lettuce leaves

1. Combine apples, potatoes and peas in medium-size bowl.
2. Combine yogurt, horseradish, mint and salt in small bowl; mix well.
3. Pour dressing over apple mixture; toss.
4. Cover and chill several hours. Serve on lettuce.

Florida Fiesta Salad

Serves 4 to 6

3 Florida oranges, peeled and
   sectioned (1½ cups sections)
1 Florida grapefruit, peeled and
   sectioned (1 cup sections)
1 can (1 pound) red kidney
   beans, drained
1 cup very thinly sliced celery
3 tablespoons chopped pimiento
3 tablespoons chopped parsley

¼ cup corn oil
3 tablespoons Florida orange
   juice
3 tablespoons minced onion
½ teaspoon salt
½ teaspoon dried leaf oregano,
   crumbled
¼ teaspoon dried leaf thyme,
   crumbled

crisp lettuce leaves

1. Combine orange and grapefruit sections, kidney beans, celery, pimiento and parsley in large bowl.
2. Combine oil, orange juice, onion, salt, oregano and thyme in small jar or bowl; mix well and pour over salad.
3. Cover salad and refrigerate 2 hours.
4. To serve, spoon into lettuce-lined bowl.

Fresh Supper Salad
with Tangy Lemon Dressing

Serves 4

1½ cups shredded zucchini
1 cup shredded carrots
1 cup bean sprouts
3 slices American cheese,
   slivered

Tangy Lemon Dressing
crisp lettuce
4 hard-cooked eggs, halved
2 tomatoes, cut in wedges

1. Combine zucchini, carrots, bean sprouts and cheese in mixing bowl.
2. Pour ¼ cup Tangy Lemon Dressing over vegetables; toss lightly.
3. Line serving plate with lettuce; spoon vegetable mixture over lettuce.
4. Place egg halves and tomato wedges alternately around edge of plate; spoon remaining dressing over salad.

Tangy Lemon Dressing

Makes ½ cup

6 tablespoons corn oil
2 tablespoons freshly squeezed
   lemon juice
1 teaspoon chopped scallion
   or onion

1 teaspoon dried leaf oregano,
   crushed
1 clove garlic, crushed
½ teaspoon salt
dash pepper

Combine all ingredients in small bowl; mix well.

Tossed Orange Salad

Serves 4 to 6

1 teaspoon grated orange rind
⅓ cup orange juice
¼ cup corn oil
1½ teaspoons red wine vinegar
¼ teaspoon salt

6 cups torn romaine leaves
1 small zucchini, sliced (1 cup)
2 navel oranges, peeled and
  sectioned (1 cup)
1 small red onion, sliced (½ cup)

1. Place orange rind, juice, corn oil, vinegar and salt in small jar with tight-fitting lid; cover and shake well.
2. Refrigerate dressing several hours.
3. Toss together romaine, zucchini, oranges and onion in large bowl.
4. Just before serving, pour dressing over salad and toss to coat evenly.

Winter Haven Salad

Serves 4 to 6

2 Florida grapefruits, peeled
  and sectioned (2 cups sections)
2 small red onions, thinly sliced
  and separated into rings
1 can (1 pound) cut green beans,
  drained
1 can (1 pound) artichoke hearts,
  drained and cut in halves

⅓ cup stuffed green olives,
  sliced
¾ cup corn oil
⅓ cup tarragon wine vinegar
1 clove garlic, minced
½ teaspoon salt
¼ teaspoon pepper

1. Combine grapefruit, onions, green beans, artichoke hearts and olives in large bowl.
2. Combine oil, vinegar, garlic, salt and pepper in small bowl or small jar; mix well.
3. Pour dressing over salad; cover and refrigerate 2 hours before serving.

Fresh Citrus Pasta Salad

Serves 8

3 tablespoons corn oil
grated peel of ½ fresh lemon
juice of ½ fresh lemon
1 tablespoon Dijon-style
  mustard
½ teaspoon sugar (optional)
½ teaspoon garlic salt
½ teaspoon dried tarragon
  leaves, crushed

2 California-Arizona oranges,
  peeled and cut in quarter-
  cartwheels
2 cups Brussels sprouts, cut in
  half, cooked, and drained
¼ pound (4 ounces) spaghetti,
  broken in half, cooked,
  and drained
¼ cup sliced celery

¼ cup chopped green onion

1. Combine corn oil, lemon peel and juice, mustard, sugar, garlic salt and tarragon in large bowl.
2. Add remaining ingredients; toss gently.
3. Chill before serving.

NOTE: Two cups cooked broccoli can be substituted for Brussels sprouts.

Thanksgiving Cranberry Salad
with Sour Cream Dressing

Serves 6 to 8

2 cups sugar
½ cup water
1 pound cranberries, washed and cleaned
2 tablespoons unflavored gelatin
2 tablespoons cold water

1 tablespoon fresh lemon juice
1 cup chopped nuts
1 cup chopped celery
Sour Cream Dressing (optional)

1. Bring sugar and water to boil.
2. Add cranberries; boil until berries pop and can be mashed with a spoon.
3. Dissolve gelatin in cold water; add to hot berries.
4. Cool. Add lemon juice, nuts and celery.
5. Serve alone, or with Sour Cream Salad Dressing.

Sour Cream Dressing

¾ cup dairy sour cream
¼ cup cottage cheese
½ cup mayonnaise

Combine ingredients.

Dilled Clam & Tomato Aspic

Serves 6

2 bottles (8 ounces each) clam juice
2 teaspoons dill seed
2 packages unflavored gelatin
1 can (1 pint 2 ounces) tomato juice

¾ teaspoon instant onion powder
1 package (10 ounces) frozen mixed
  vegetables or peas, cooked and chilled
lettuce leaves (optional)

1. Combine 1 bottle clam juice and dill seed in small saucepan.
2. Bring to a boil; reduce heat and simmer 10 minutes.
3. Soften gelatin in ½ cup tomato juice.
4. Strain dill seeds from hot clam juice.
5. Add hot clam juice to gelatin; stir until dissolved.
6. Add remaining clam juice, tomato juice and onion powder to gelatin mixture.
7. Chill until consistency resembles unbeaten egg white.
8. Fold in mixed vegetables.
9. Spoon into 1½-quart mold. Chill until firm.
10. Unmold and serve on lettuce leaves, if desired.

NOTE: *Great for buffet table!*

Molded Cranberry Waldorf Salad

Serves 8 to 10

2 envelopes unflavored gelatin
½ cup cold water
2 cups boiling water
1 can (6 ounces) frozen concentrated
  cranberry or cranberry-apple juice
  cocktail, thawed and undiluted

1 cup apples, chopped
½ cup celery, chopped
½ cup walnuts, chopped
1 package (3 ounces) cream cheese,
  cut into ½-inch cubes

1. Soften gelatin in ½ cup cold water.
2. Pour 2 cups boiling water over softened gelatin; stir until dissolved.
3. Stir in cranberry juice cocktail concentrate.
4. Refrigerate, stirring often, until mixture mounds slightly when dropped from spoon.
5. Fold in remaining ingredients.
6. Turn into 6-cup mold. Refrigerate until set.

Cottage Cheese-Pecan Ball Salad

Serves 4 to 6

½ tablespoon gelatin
2 tablespoons cold water
1 cup cottage cheese
¾ teaspoon salt

½ teaspoon paprika
¾ cup cream
¼ cup Roquefort cheese, crumbled
pecan halves

1. Soak gelatin in cold water. Dissolve it by placing it over hot water. Let cool.
2. Combine cottage cheese, salt, paprika, cream and Roquefort cheese; beat until smooth.
3. Add cooled gelatin mixture.
4. Pour into round molds or custard cups; chill until almost set.
5. Remove and roll into more perfect balls; stud with pecans.

Corn Relish Salad Mold

Serves 4 to 6

1 package (3 ounces) lemon-
  flavored gelatin
1 cup boiling water
½ cup cold water

¼ cup mayonnaise
2 tablespoons prepared yellow mustard
1 can (12 ounces) whole kernel corn,
  drained

1. Dissolve gelatin in boiling water.
2. Stir in cold water; chill until partially set.
3. Beat in mayonnaise and mustard; stir in corn.
4. Pour into greased 1½-quart mold. Chill until set.

Chicken Mousse

Serves 6

1 envelope unflavored gelatin
1½ cups cold chicken stock
1 tablespoon fresh lemon juice
⅛ teaspoon Tabasco sauce

1½ cups cooked chicken, diced
½ cup celery, diced
1 cup heavy cream, whipped
salad greens

1. Sprinkle gelatin on ½ cup cold chicken stock in saucepan. Let soften.
2. Place pan over medium heat, stirring constantly, until gelatin is dissolved.
3. Remove from heat; add remaining stock, lemon juice and Tabasco.
4. Chill until mixture is the consistency of unbeaten egg white.
5. Mix in chicken and celery; fold in whipped cream.
6. Turn into a 4-cup mold or individual molds. Chill until firm.
7. Unmold on salad greens.

Salmon Luncheon Mold

Serves 6

2 envelopes unflavored gelatin
1 can (12½ ounces) chicken broth
1 tablespoon fresh lemon juice
¼ teaspoon salt
5 or 6 hard-cooked eggs
1 can (1 pound) red salmon ·
¼ cup salmon liquid
1 can (3 ounces) chopped mushrooms, drained

1 teaspoon instant minced onion
¼ cup water
¼ cup cider vinegar
2 teaspoons sugar
2 teaspoons ground marjoram
1 teaspoon parsley flakes
½ teaspoon celery salt
¼ teaspoon ground black pepper
½ cup heavy cream, whipped

marinated green beans

1. Sprinkle 1 envelope gelatin over ½ cup chicken broth in saucepan. Place over low heat and stir until gelatin is dissolved.
2. Remove from heat; stir in remaining broth, lemon juice and salt.
3. Pour into bottom of 6-cup ring mold. Chill until almost firm.
   Cut eggs in half lengthwise; arrange in gelatin, with yolks face down. Chill until gelatin is firm.
5. Drain salmon, reserving ¼ cup liquid. Remove bones from salmon; flake.
6. Add mushrooms and toss lightly.
7. Combine reserved salmon liquid and instant onion in saucepan. Add remaining gelatin, water, vinegar, sugar, marjoram, parsley, celery salt and black pepper.
8. Cook and stir over low heat until gelatin is dissolved.
9. Remove from heat; chill until consistency of unbeaten egg white.
10. Mix gelatin thoroughly with flaked salmon mixture; fold in whipped cream.
11. Spoon mixture lightly over eggs in ring mold; spread evenly with spatula. Chill until firm.
12. Unmold onto serving plate. Fill center with marinated green beans.

Easy Tomato Aspic

Serves 4

1 envelope unflavored gelatin
1¾ cups tomato juice
¼ teaspoon salt
½ teaspoon sugar
½ teaspoon original Worcestershire sauce

⅛ teaspoon Tabasco sauce
2 tablespoons fresh lemon or
  lime juice
salad greens
prepared salad dressing

1. Soften gelatin by sprinkling in ½ cup tomato juice in saucepan.
2. Heat over low heat, stirring constantly, until gelatin is dissolved.
3. Remove from heat. Add remaining tomato juice, salt, sugar, Worcestershire sauce, Tabasco sauce and lemon juice.
4. Pour into a 2-cup mold or individual molds. Chill until firm.
5. Unmold on salad greens and serve with salad dressing.

Chicken Perfection Salad

Serves 6

1 envelope unflavored gelatin
1 cup cold water
1 can (10½ ounces) chicken
  consommé, undiluted
¼ teaspoon salt
2 tablespoons fresh lemon juice
½ cup cabbage, finely shredded

¼ cup celery, chopped
2 tablespoons green pepper, chopped
2 tablespoons chopped pimiento
1 can (5 ounces) boned chicken or
  turkey, diced
lettuce
prepared salad dressing

1. Sprinkle gelatin on ½ cup cold water to soften.
2. Place over boiling water, stirring until gelatin is dissolved.
3. Blend remaining ½ cup cold water into soup.
4. Stir in dissolved gelatin, salt and lemon juice.
5. Chill until mixture is consistency of unbeaten egg white.
6. Fold in cabbage, celery, green pepper, pimiento, and chicken.
7. Turn into a 3-cup mold or individual molds. Chill until firm.
8. Unmold on lettuce and serve with salad dressing.

Dilled Halibut & Cucumber Salad

Serves 6

1 package (12 ounces) frozen halibut steaks
1 tablespoon instant minced onion
1 tablespoon dill seed
½ teaspoon salt

⅛ teaspoon ground white pepper
½ cup commercial sour cream
1 tablespoon fresh lemon juice
1 large cucumber, peeled and thinly sliced

1. Simmer fish in water to cover until done, 10 to 15 minutes.
2. Cool. Remove bones and skin.
3. Cut into small chunks; set aside.
4. Mix onion with 1 tablespoon water; let stand 10 minutes to soften.
5. Combine softened onion, dill seed, salt, white pepper, sour cream and lemon juice in salad bowl. Mix well.
6. Add fish and cucumber. Toss gently, coating with sour cream mixture.

Potato Salad Pie

Serves 6

1 envelope unflavored gelatin
¾ cup cold milk
1½ cups water
1 teaspoon salt
⅛ teaspoon freshly ground black pepper
1 package (7 ounces) instant potato

2 cups finely chopped celery
2 tablespoons minced onion
2 tablespoons minced fresh parsley
2 tablespoons chopped green pepper
⅓ cup mayonnaise
1 tablespoon vinegar
1 teaspoon prepared yellow mustard

radishes, green pepper strips and pimiento (for garnish)

1. Soften gelatin in ¼ cup milk.
2. Combine water, remaining milk, salt and pepper in saucepan. Bring to a boil.
3. Remove from heat; stir in softened gelatin and potato.
4. Cool. Add celery, onion, parsley, chopped green pepper, mayonnaise, vinegar and mustard to cool potato.
5. Press ⅔ potato mixture into 9-inch pie plate.
6. Using pastry tube or 2 spoons, decorate around edges with remaining potato mixture.
7. Chill several hours.
8. Before serving, garnish with radishes, green pepper strips and pimiento.

Molded Seafood Salad

Serves 6

1 envelope unflavored gelatin
¾ cup cold water
½ teaspoon salt
2 tablespoons fresh lemon juice
¼ teaspoon Tabasco sauce
¾ cup mayonnaise or salad dressing

1 cup celery, finely diced
¼ cup green pepper, finely diced
¼ cup chopped pimiento
1 cup flaked or finely cut seafood:
    tuna, salmon, crab meat, lobster or
    shrimp
salad greens

1. Sprinkle gelatin on cold water in saucepan to soften.
2. Place over low heat, stirring constantly, until dissolved.
3. Remove from heat; stir in salt, lemon juice and Tabasco.
4. Cool. Gradually stir into mayonnaise until blended.
5. Mix in remaining ingredients.
6. Turn into a 3-cup mold or individual molds. Chill until firm.
7. Unmold on salad greens.

NOTE: 1 cup of diced, cooked chicken, turkey or eggs (4 hard-cooked eggs) may b
substituted for the seafood.

Turkey Salad Mold

Serves 8 to 10

1 package (6 ounces) lemon-flavored gelatin
1½ cups hot water
2 cups dairy sour cream
1 teaspoon salt
½ teaspoon dry mustard
½ teaspoon paprika
¼ teaspoon onion salt

2 teaspoons prepared horseradish
1½ cups cooked turkey, diced
⅓ cup celery, diced
⅓ cup unpeeled cucumber, diced
2 tablespoons chopped pimiento
2 tablespoons green pepper, chopped
lettuce leaves

tomato wedges (optional)

1. Dissolve gelatin in hot water.
2. Cool slightly; set aside.
3. Combine sour cream with salt, mustard, paprika, onion salt and horseradish; blen
    well.
4. Blend sour cream mixture into cooled gelatin; chill until mixture begins to set.
5. Fold turkey, celery, cucumber, pimiento and green pepper into gelatin.
6. Spoon into individual molds and chill until firm.
7. Unmold on lettuce cups and garnish with tomato wedges, if desired.

Grape & Asparagus Aspic

Serves 10

1 can (15 ounces) asparagus tips
1 tablespoon unflavored gelatin
1 chicken bouillon cube
salt

paprika
2 cups imported winter
  seedless grapes
1 cup chopped celery

mayonnaise

1. Drain asparagus, reserving the liquid. (The tips may be cut in two or they may be used whole as a garnish around the edge of the mold.)
2. Soak gelatin in 3 tablespoons asparagus liquid.
3. Heat remaining asparagus liquid; dissolve gelatin in it.
4. Add enough chicken bouillon to make 2 cups liquid in all.
5. Season with salt and paprika. Chill.
6. When nearly set, add grapes, celery and asparagus tips. Chill until firm.
7. Unmold and serve with mayonnaise.

Tuna-Tomato Mousse

Serves 4

Tomato Layer

1 envelope unflavored gelatin
¼ cup cold water

1½ cups tomato juice
1 tablespoon lemon juice

1. Mix gelatin with cold water in bowl; let stand 1 minute.
2. Bring tomato juice to a boil; add to gelatin liquid, stirring until gelatin is completely dissolved.
3. Stir in lemon juice.
4. Pour into 5-cup mold; chill until firm.

Tuna Layer

2 cans (6½ or 7 ounces) tuna
  packed in water, drained
¾ cup mayonnaise
1 tablespoon lemon juice
1 teaspoon dried tarragon,
  crumbled

⅓ cup minced celery
⅓ cup finely chopped almonds
1 envelope unflavored gelatin
¼ cup cold water
½ cup heavy cream, whipped

1. In large bowl of electric mixer, beat together tuna, mayonnaise, lemon juice and tarragon until fairly smooth; stir in celery and nuts.
2. Mix gelatin with cold water in small saucepan; let stand 1 minute.
3. Stir gelatin over medium heat until completely dissolved, about 1 minute.
4. Stir gelatin mixture into tuna mixture; fold in whipped cream.
5. Spoon tuna layer onto tomato layer in mold; chill until firm.
6. Unmold to serve.

Buffet Jellied Cantaloupe Salad

Serves 12 to 14

3 envelopes unflavored gelatin
1 cup dry sherry
1 quart stewed tomatoes
2 tablespoons onion, grated
½ cup celery leaves, finely chopped
1 large bay leaf

1 teaspoon salt
pinch cayenne pepper
2 tablespoons tarragon vinegar
1 teaspoon confectioners' sugar
cantaloupe balls
crisp lettuce leaves

mayonnaise

1. Soften gelatin in sherry 10 minutes.
2. Combine in pan tomatoes, onion, celery leaves, bay leaf, salt and cayenne; simmer 1! minutes.
3. Remove from heat. Add gelatin, vinegar and confectioners' sugar; stir until gelatin i thoroughly dissolved and mixture well blended.
4. Strain through a fine wire sieve into lightly oiled individual molds, each containing 5 o 6 small cantaloupe balls.
5. Chill thoroughly and serve on lettuce leaves with mayonnaise.

NOTE: *Terrific for covered-dish supper or buffet table.*

Molded Fruit Medley

Serves 6

1 envelope unflavored gelatin
¼ cup sugar
⅛ teaspoon salt
1½ cups very hot water

¼ cup fresh lemon or lime juice
2 cups mixed cut-up fruit, fresh, canned, or frozen
whipped cream (optional)

1. Mix together gelatin, sugar and salt.
2. Add hot water, stirring until gelatin is dissolved.
3. Stir in lemon juice.
4. Chill until mixture is the consistency of unbeaten egg white.
5. Fold in fruit.
6. Turn into a 3-cup mold or individual molds and chill until firm.
7. Unmold and serve plain or with whipped cream.

Frosty Citrus Mold

Serves 6

2 packages (3 ounces each) lime-
  flavored gelatin
½ teaspoon salt
2 cups boiling water

1½ cups mayonnaise
½ cup dairy sour cream
1 jar (16 ounces) chilled fruit salad
crisp lettuce

1. Dissolve lime gelatin and salt in boiling water; cool.
2. Combine mayonnaise and sour cream; mix well.
3. Gradually stir in gelatin; chill until partially set.
4. Fold in fruit and pour into 1½-quart mold. Chill until firm.
5. Unmold on serving platter; surround with lettuce.

Lei Day Salad

Serves 8 to 10

1 can (1 pound 4 ounces) sliced pineapple
  in juice
½ cup pineapple-flavored yogurt
1 tablespoon chopped chutney
1 teaspoon fresh lime juice
⅛ teaspoon ground ginger
salad greens
1 papaya, sliced
1 cup strawberries, halved
2 cups honeydew balls
1 large banana, sliced

1. Drain pineapple, reserving 2 tablespoons juice.
2. Blend together pineapple juice, yogurt, chutney, lime juice and ground ginger.
3. Arrange salad greens on a large serving platter.
4. Arrange sliced pineapple, papaya, strawberry halves, honeydew balls and sliced banana in sections on greens.
5. Serve with dressing.

Supreme Molded Fruit Salad

Serves 12

1 large box (6 ounces) cherry gelatin
1 large bowl low-calorie whipped topping
1 small bag walnuts
1 regular-size bag miniature
  marshmallows

2 large or 3 small bananas
1 apple, cleaned, skinned, seeded
  and chopped
1 small bag coconut
1 large can fruit cocktail, drained

1. Prepare cherry gelatin according to box directions; chill.
2. Add whipped topping, walnuts, marshmallows, bananas, apple and coconut after gelatin starts to set; add fruit cocktail.
3. Stir and refrigerate until set.

Creamy Peach Salad Mold

Serves 6

1 package peach-flavored gelatin	½ cup peach syrup
1 cup boiling water	1 cup plain yogurt
1 cup canned peach chunks	

1. Dissolve gelatin in boiling water.
2. Stir in peach syrup.
3. Slowly blend into yogurt.
4. Chill mixture until slightly thickened.
5. Fold in canned peach chunks.
6. Pour mixture into a fancy-shaped 3-cup mold; chill until firm.

Pineapple Glow Salad

Serves 10

2 cans (8 ounces each) crushed pineapple in juice	2 cups boiling water
1 package (6 ounces) orange, lemon or lime-flavored gelatin	2 tablespoons lemon juice
	1 cup carrot, finely grated
½ teaspoon salt	crisp salad greens (optional)
	mayonnaise (optional)

1. Drain pineapple, measuring juice. Add water to make 1½ cups liquid.
2. Dissolve gelatin and salt in boiling water.
3. Add measured liquid and lemon juice; chill until thickened.
4. Fold in pineapple and carrot.
5. Spoon into 6-cup mold or individual molds and chill until firm, about 6 hours.
6. Unmold. Serve with crisp salad greens and mayonnaise, if desired.

Sparkling Cherry Fruit Mold

Serves 10

2 packages (3 ounces each) cherry or raspberry-flavored gelatin	1 can (16 ounces) sliced peaches
	2 tablespoons Worcestershire sauce
2 cups boiling water	2 cups diced celery
crisp lettuce leaves	

1. Dissolve gelatin in boiling water.
2. Drain peaches, reserving syrup. Add enough cold water to syrup to make 2 cups.
3. Stir syrup into gelatin with Worcestershire sauce; chill until partially thickened.
4. Fold in peaches and celery.
5. Pour into oiled 2-quart mold; chill until set.
6. Unmold on bed of lettuce. Fine for salad or dessert offering.

Fresh Pear-Mint Salad

Serves 4 to 6

1 envelope plain gelatin
½ cup pineapple juice
2 tablespoons water
1 tablespoon sugar
½ teaspoon salt
2 tablespoons fresh lemon or lime juice
3 tablespoons chopped fresh mint

2 tablespoons onion, finely chopped
1 package (3 ounces) cream cheese
1 cup dairy sour cream
½ cup mayonnaise
3 fresh California Bartlett pears
½ cup celery, thinly sliced
lettuce leaves

6 to 8 mint sprigs (for garnish)

1. Combine gelatin, pineapple juice and water in saucepan; heat gently, stirring until gelatin is dissolved.
2. Remove from heat and stir in sugar, salt, lemon juice, mint and onion.
3. Beat cream cheese with sour cream and mayonnaise until smooth.
4. Beat in gelatin mixture, then chill until it begins to thicken.
5. Meanwhile, halve and core 2 pears; dice to get 1½ to 2 cups; fold into softly-set gelatin along with celery.
6. Mound mixture into individual salad bowls lined with lettuce. (Try to get a fluffy mounded look.)
7. Chill until ready to serve.
8. Garnish each salad with a mint sprig and freshly cut slices from 1 pear.

Lemony Walnut-Vegetable Mold

Serves 4 to 6

1 package (3 ounces) lemon-flavored gelatin
1 cup boiling water
¾ cup cold water
2 teaspoons fresh lemon juice
¼ teaspoon salt
½ cup carrots, thinly sliced
½ cup cauliflower, thinly sliced

2 tablespoons green pepper, diced, or stuffed olives
⅓ cup chopped California walnuts
½ cup dairy sour cream
½ teaspoon horseradish
½ teaspoon prepared mustard
1 green onion, sliced

1 tablespoon parsley, finely chopped

. Dissolve gelatin in boiling water.
. Stir in cold water, lemon juice and salt.
. Set aside ¾ cup gelatin mixture; chill remainder until syrupy.
. Stir carrots, cauliflower, green pepper and walnuts into chilled gelatin.
. Pour into 1-quart mold. Chill until firm.
. Stir sour cream until smooth; blend in rest of ingredients and reserved gelatin.
. Pour over vegetables in mold. Chill.

Fresh Strawberry Mold

Serves 8

2 envelopes unflavored gelatin
½ cup cold water
1 cup sugar
1¾ cups fresh orange juice

1 cup strawberry purée
1 tablespoon fresh lemon juice
1 cup sliced strawberries
whipped cream

1. Sprinkle gelatin over water in medium saucepan. Place over low heat, stirring constantly until gelatin dissolves.
2. Remove from heat. Add sugar, stirring until dissolved.
3. Stir in orange juice, strawberry purée and lemon juice. Chill, stirring occasionally, until mixture mounds slightly when dropped from a spoon.
4. Fold in sliced strawberries.
5. Turn into 4-cup mold and chill until firm.
6. To serve, unmold and garnish with whipped cream.

NOTE: *Serve on salad or as dessert.*

In-the-Pink Strawberry Salad Mold

Serves 8

2 packages frozen strawberries
2 small packages strawberry gelatin
2 cups hot water
1 can (12 ounces) crushed pineapple

2 bananas, chopped
pinch salt
juice of 1 lemon
1 pint container dairy sour cream

1. Combine all ingredients, except sour cream.
2. Divide mixture in half. Place one half of mixture in refrigerator and chill until firmly congealed.
3. Place second half of mixture in dish in warm water to prevent it from setting in meantime.
4. When first half has firmly gelled, spread sour cream over top.
5. Pour second half of gelatin mixture over sour cream. Refrigerate until set.
6. Cut into squares and serve.

Ginger Pear Salad Mold

Serves 6 to 8

1 can (16 ounces) pear halves
1 package (3 ounces) apricot, orange or lemon-flavored gelatin
1 package (3 ounces) cream cheese

½ teaspoon ground ginger
1 small can (5.33 ounces) evaporated milk
1 cup ginger ale
lettuce leaves

1. Drain liquid from pear halves, saving ¾ cup liquid.
2. Heat liquid to boiling. Remove from heat and stir in gelatin until dissolved.
3. Beat cream cheese and ginger in small bowl; gradually beat in hot gelatin mixture.
4. Stir in milk and ginger ale. Chill until mixture holds its shape.
5. Beat chilled mixture until it doubles in volume.
6. Arrange drained pear halves, cut-side down, in round 8¼ x 1¾-inch-deep baking pan or 8-inch square baking pan.
7. Pour beaten gelatin mixture over pears. Chill until set.
8. Unmold and serve on lettuce leaves.

Fruit Fluff Dessert Salad, Microwaved

Serves 4 to 6

½ cup sugar
¼ cup light corn syrup
3 tablespoons water
1 teaspoon finely grated orange peel
1 egg white, stiffly beaten
1 cup orange yogurt

1 pint fresh strawberries, cleaned and halved
2 bananas, sliced
2 oranges, peeled and sliced
1 cup seedless green grapes
1 cup seedless red grapes
1 cup blueberries

1. Combine sugar, syrup, water and orange peel in 1-quart glass measuring cup; microcook on HIGH 2 minutes, or until sugar has dissolved.
2. Stir; microcook on HIGH until mixture reaches 236° F., or soft ball stage, 3 to 4 minutes.
3. Very slowly add hot syrup into stiffly beaten egg white.
4. Fold in yogurt; chill.
5. Combine fruits in serving dish, reserving a few strawberry halves for garnish.
6. Spoon dressing over top; garnish with strawberry halves.

NOTE: Feel free to add any fresh fruits in season. A tasty and delightful finale to any meal!

Basic French Dressing

Makes 2½ cups

2 teaspoons salt
1 teaspoon sugar
½ teaspoon dry mustard
½ teaspoon pepper

¼ cup water
2 cups peanut oil
⅔ cup white vinegar or
  lemon juice

1. Combine salt, sugar, dry mustard, pepper and water in a large jar.
2. Cover tightly and shake until well mixed.
3. Add peanut oil and vinegar. Cover and shake vigorously until thoroughly blended.

Basic Mayonnaise Plus Variations

Makes about 1¼ cups

1 egg yolk
½ teaspoon salt
½ teaspoon sugar
½ teaspoon dry mustard

dash cayenne
2 tablespoons fresh lemon juice
  or vinegar
1 cup salad oil

1. Blend egg, salt, sugar, mustard and cayenne in deep bowl.
2. Mix in lemon juice.
3. Add ¼ cup oil, a few drops at a time, and beat well with rotary beater or electric mi
   (at medium speed) after each addition; add remaining oil, about 2 tablespoons a
   time.

Green Goddess

1¼ cups Basic Mayonnaise
2 tablespoons minced parsley
2 tablespoons minced chives

1 tablespoon tarragon vinegar
1 tablespoon fresh lemon juice
½ clove garlic, pressed

2 tablespoons chopped anchovy fillets

Combine all ingredients.

Thousand Island

1¼ cups Basic Mayonnaise
¼ cup chili sauce

2 tablespoons chopped pimiento
1 tablespoon grated onion

2 tablespoons chopped green pepper

Combine all ingredients.

Spicy French Dressing

Makes 1 cup

1 cup Basic French Dressing
 (page 252)
2 tablespoons catsup

1 tablespoon onion, grated
1 teaspoon prepared mustard
½ teaspoon chili powder
¼ teaspoon Tabasco sauce

1. Combine Basic French Dressing, catsup, onion, mustard, chili powder and Tabasco in a jar.
2. Cover tightly and shake vigorously until thoroughly mixed.
3. Chill before serving.

Slender Blender Dressing Plus Variations

Makes about 1½ cups

1 cup cottage cheese, creamed or
 dry curd

½ cup buttermilk
2 tablespoons vinegar

Whirl all ingredients together in blender until smooth.

Blue Cheese (Variation)

½ cup Slender Blender Dressing

2 tablespoons blue cheese dry salad
 dressing mix

Whirl all ingredients together in blender until smooth.

Onion (Variation)

½ cup Slender Blender Dressing
2 tablespoons minced onion

few drops non-caloric sweetener
salt to taste
pepper to taste

Whirl all ingredients together in blender until smooth.

Thousand Island (Variation)

½ cup Slender Blender Dressing
2 tablespoons catsup
1 tablespoon sweet pickle relish

1 teaspoon minced onion
salt to taste
pepper to taste

Whirl all ingredients together in blender until smooth.

Garlic Mayonnaise Dressing

Makes ½ cup

3 tablespoons real mayonnaise
3 tablespoons salad oil
2 tablespoons cider vinegar
1 teaspoon instant minced onion

⅛ teaspoon instant garlic powder
½ teaspoon salt
dash of cayenne
1 hard-cooked egg, minced

1. Combine mayonnaise, salad oil, vinegar, minced onion, garlic powder, salt, cayenne and egg.
2. Add to salad. Toss lightly.

Tarragon Salad Dressing

Makes ½ cup

¼ cup dairy sour cream
¼ cup real mayonnaise
¾ teaspoon tarragon leaves, crumbled
1 teaspoon fresh lemon juice

⅛ teaspoon instant onion powder
⅛ teaspoon salt
1/16 teaspoon ground black pepper

1. Blend all ingredients; mix well.
2. Chill 1 hour before serving.
3. Serve with one of the following combinations:

   Sliced bananas and pineapple chunks
   Apples, celery and chopped walnuts
   Chicken or tuna chunks, celery and seedless grapes
   Shredded cabbage and crushed pineapple
   Grated carrots, seedless raisins and chopped nuts

Ripe Olive French Dressing

Makes about 1⅓ cups

⅔ cup corn oil
¼ cup dry sherry
3 tablespoons lemon juice
1 tablespoon bottled salad dressing

2 tablespoons frozen or freeze-dried chopped chives
½ teaspoon sugar
½ cup ripe olives, chopped

1. Combine all ingredients in a jar.
2. Cover tightly and shake thoroughly to blend.
3. Shake again just before using.
4. Pour over salad and toss lightly.

NOTE: *Great tossed with bite-size chunks of western iceberg lettuce, combined with any of the following: radish and cucumber slices, red onion rings, green pepper chunks, tomato wedges, fresh mushroom slices, or avocado rings.*

Garlic Vinaigrette

Makes about 1½ cups

2 teaspoons Dijon mustard
2 tablespoons wine vinegar
3 to 5 cloves fresh garlic,
    crushed or finely chopped

1 egg yolk
salt to taste
pepper to taste
1½ cups olive oil

1. Mix together mustard, vinegar, egg yolk, garlic, salt and pepper together with a wire whisk.
2. Slowly begin adding the olive oil, in a thin stream, whisking all the while.
3. When about half the oil has been added, pour it in more rapidly while whisking.
4. Store the vinaigrette in the refrigerator. It will keep about 3 days.

Golden Nugget Dressing

Makes 1⅓ cups

1 package (3 ounces) cream cheese
⅓ cup finely chopped California walnuts,
    plain or toasted
⅓ cup real mayonnaise

⅓ cup fresh orange juice
1 tablespoon fresh lemon juice
1 tablespoon sugar
¼ teaspoon salt

1. Soften cream cheese; add walnuts and remaining ingredients.
2. Beat with rotary beater until well blended.
3. Store in covered container in refrigerator.

NOTE: For variation, add ¼ cup Roquefort cheese.

South of the Border Salad Dressing

Makes about 1½ cups

1 cup corn oil
⅓ cup white vinegar
¼ cup orange juice
1 tablespoon minced onion
1 small clove garlic, crushed

2 teaspoons sugar
1½ teaspoons salt
1 teaspoon ground cumin
1 teaspoon dried oregano leaves
¼ teaspoon crushed dried red pepper

1. In 1-pint jar with tight-fitting lid, place corn oil, vinegar, orange juice, onion, garlic, sugar, salt, cumin, oregano and red pepper.
2. Cover and shake well.
3. Refrigerate at least 1 hour.
4. Remove garlic.
5. Shake thoroughly before serving. Serve on assorted salad greens, using 2 teaspoons of dressing for each 1 cup of loosely measured greens.

LOW CALORIE VERSION: Follow recipe for South of the Border Salad Dressing. Decrease corn oil to ¾ cup; add ¼ cup water. Omit sugar and cumin. Decrease salt to 1 teaspoon. Add ½ teaspoon chili powder. Makes about 1½ cups.

San Francisco Dressing

Makes about 1⅓ cups

1 cup real mayonnaise
3 tablespoons catsup
2 tablespoons lemon juice
½ teaspoon salt

1 tablespoon frozen or freeze-dried
  chopped chives
¼ cup grated Parmesan cheese
½ teaspoon lemon peel, grated

1. Blend all ingredients together.
2. If desired, chill before serving on salad.

NOTE: For a whole-meal salad on that hot summer night, toss chunks of crisp western ice
berg lettuce with tomato wedges, hard-cooked egg slices, and cooked shrimp or crab legs
Top with zippy San Francisco Dressing.

Wonderful Ranch Salad Dressing

Makes about 1 cup

½ cup real mayonnaise
½ cup buttermilk
1½ teaspoons dried parsley flakes

1 teaspoon instant minced onion
¼ teaspoon salt
⅛ teaspoon celery salt

big pinch garlic powder

1. Put mayonnaise and buttermilk in mixing bowl; stir until mayonnaise and buttermilk ar
   well blended.
2. Add parsley, onion, salt, celery salt and garlic powder. Stir until ingredients are we
   mixed.
3. Put dressing in covered jar in refrigerator until ready to use.

Summer Salad Dressing

Makes about 1½ cups

1 cup corn oil
½ cup fresh lime juice
2 teaspoons dried dill weed, or
  1 tablespoon finely chopped
  fresh dill

1½ teaspoons salt
1 teaspoon sugar
1 teaspoon minced onion
½ teaspoon celery seed

1. In 1-pint jar with tight-fitting lid, place corn oil, lime juice, dill weed, salt, sugar, onio
   and celery seed.
2. Cover and shake well.
3. Refrigerate at least 1 hour.
4. Shake thoroughly before serving. Serve on assorted salad greens using 2 teaspoons
   dressing for each 1 cup of loosely measured greens.

LOW-CALORIE VERSION: Follow recipe for Summer Salad Dressing. Decrease oil to
cup; add ¼ cup water. Omit sugar and decrease salt to 1 teaspoon. Makes about 1½ cups

NOTE: An interesting salad dressing to use on mixed fruits or cabbage.

HL-IMY 3206-1/